JOURNEYS OF A PURE NATURALIST

Joe "B" Billings

Praise for Journeys of a Pure Naturalist

Journeys of a Pure Naturalist provides both inspiration and guidance for anyone who loves the mountains and the deserts of Arizona and the rugged coast surrounding the Gulf of California. Joe Billings' stories will make you long for the isolation and beauty of these few remaining wild places.

—Howard Hall, Director, *Shadows of a Desert Sea*, Howard Hall Productions.

Great work! A well-written, well-researched, fun-to-read package of writing.

—Rick Brusca, Executive Director Emeritus, Arizona-Sonora Desert Museum

Billings' *Journeys* exemplifies the dedication of a talented naturalist over many years to the life of the most beloved invertebrate being in America. His tagging of monarchs in the Desert Southwest has literally rewritten what we know of their migration patterns. No one in our region has contributed more to their cause.

Gary Nabhan, coauthor of *The Forgotten Pollinators* and editor of *Migratory Pollinators and Their Corridors in Western North America*.

Journeys of a Pure Naturalist

Joe "JB" Billings

MonarchQuestAZ
Vail, Arizona

ISBN: 979-8-9898649-0-4 (print)
ISBN: 979-8-9898649-1-1 (e-book)

MonarchQuestAZ logo by Joe "JB" Billings.

Interior and cover design, map creation, and photo editing by Sharon K. Miller, www.buckskinbooks.com. All photographs, illustrations, and maps are the property of the author unless otherwise credited.

This book tells the true story of the author's adventures in the wilderness areas of the Southwest and Mexico. The narrative runs parallel with a strong conservation ethic that occasionally emerges in the form of site restoration/clean-up projects, tracking down historic journals, and exposés associated with threatened wildlife species. This goes hand in hand with the author's more recent field research and wildlands restoration plantings towards the conservation of the monarch butterfly. The incidents described here are for informational purposes and should not be considered advice or recommendations for others to follow as they explore wilderness areas. Neither the author nor the publisher shall be held liable for any injury or damages experienced by a reader who attempts similar activities. Readers are advised not to participate in wilderness experiences or activities in remote areas for which they have neither appropriate skills nor knowledge.

For my parents:

Carl Emery Billings, MD

Virginia Troup Billings

Something hidden. Go and find it.
Go and look behind the ranges—Something lost behind the ranges.
Lost and waiting for you.
Go!

Rudyard Kipling

Contents

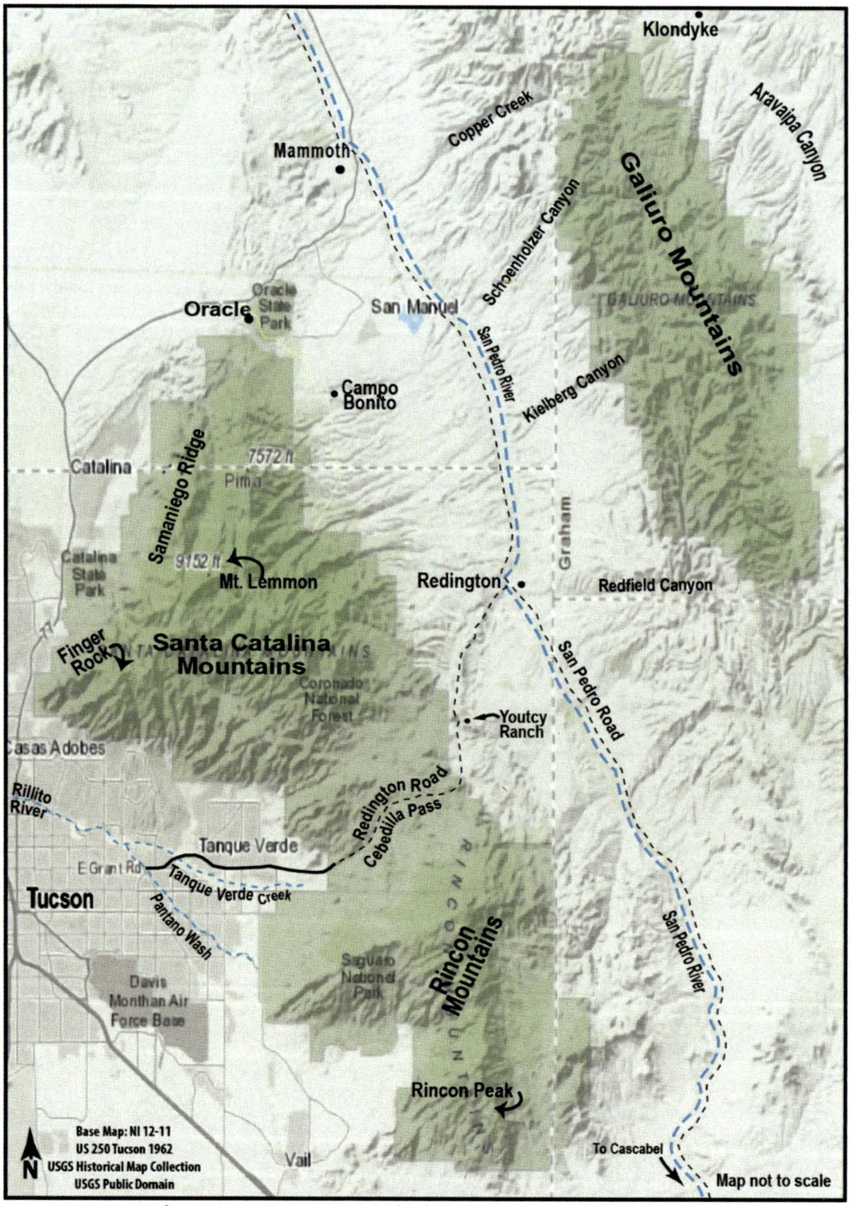

Southern Arizona and the Greater Tucson Area

Part 1

naturalist—Explorer—Artist

The author, JB, displaying huge andesite spall in stone quarry. (Photo by Elton Kerr)

Hard to imagine looking back on so many adventures across the vastness of Arizona, Sonora, Mexico, and Baja, California Sur and then return to and retrace my steps through each one. Most of these expeditions—or study projects—took place in the 1970's and 1980's, though I began wandering off into remote wildlands long before then. I've tried to bring the best and most meaningful ones to the forefront, while I want my readers to know there was a lot left on the "cutting room floor."

Such as the questionable bicycle ride on impulse up Sonoita Highway 83 one time in February in the late 1970s. I ran out of water and got resupplied after knocking on the door of the Thurber Ranch halfway to Sonoita. Once I turned off on Greaterville Road, I got caught in a snowstorm and was taken in by a local family overnight. Shouldering my bike the next morning, I bushwhack-hiked in the snow over Melendrez Pass of the Santa Rita Mountains down to the Old Nogales Highway and back to Tucson.

With some experiences, the deciding factor for selection was the lack of photos taken. An exceptional first-time exploration of the isolated Eagletail

Mountains of western Arizona in the late 1980s is a case in point. Several days of roaming the interior revealed a wild and fascinating place where I woke up to the reverberating sounds of hooves atop the overhang I had been sleeping beneath. Using stealth, I was able to creep up to a spot where I literally sat motionless next to a female desert bighorn trotting back and forth so closely I could have touched her! But lacking a camera, I returned with no pictures; just a nice biface I chipped out of a chunk of variegated pink-red silicified sandstone.

A number of my earliest "bike/hikes" were concentrated around the west-facing slopes of the Santa Catalina Mountains. From this side of the range I bushwhacked up into Cargodera Canyon, Walnut Spring, and Samaniego Peak. Along the way—biking and hiking—I had friendly encounters with the legendary rancher Bill Raftery at his Anvil Ranch and the knowledgeable Arizona Game and Fish field officer and naturalist, John Stair, along the mountain trails. One day I met John leading a group of boy scouts on the way to do restorative work at Walnut Spring.

I grew up in the shadow of my home range, the Santa Catalina Mountains, north of Tucson, Arizona. Picture a small boy staring upward in awe, listening to the wind whistling through the spines of a colossal foothill stand of majestic saguaros upslope from the Tanque Verde Wash, far above the desert plain, miles to the south from where the family homestead sat. I trekked further and further beyond these foothill ramparts, ascending into all the canyons and peaks above them of the Catalina front range. My bedroom dresser drawers were filled with treasured collections of leaves and pinecones brought down from the upper elevation pine-oak-juniper zones and lower canyon riparian tree galleries. These were remote places seldom visited, long before the bulldozers and construction enterprises forever altered the landscape.

The "bike/hike" thing actually got started when I was a sophomore in high school. I had a beat-up, fat tire, one-speed bicycle I

Pink-red silicified sandstone core from Eagletail Mountains and biface made on location (Late 1980s trip)

used to ride north to the southern edge of the Catalinas. There, I would stash it under a bush and hike all over the greater Sabino Canyon area. One day on a whim, I took off, venturing far out to the southeast to explore the distant, unknown Rincon Valley and the adjacent Rincon Mountains. Route-finding, I made my way upslope to a large, remote hillside water tank which actually had a faucet, providing crystal-clear cold water, where I quenched my searing thirst and re-filled my one canteen.

From there, I bushwhack-hiked over a long, arduous route upward through thick brush and steep, rocky terrain until I finally emerged atop the summit of Rincon Peak (8,482') just before sunset. So, with darkness enveloping the peak and February temperatures dropping below freezing, I was in for a very long and difficult night. But by a fortunate stroke of luck, someone had left matches in the ammo box containing the summit registry. So, I built a small, glowing fire and spent a night of fitful, intermittent sleep upon that lofty perch, semi-blanketed by green juniper boughs. In retrospect, had I not found the matches, my only other option would have been to work my way downslope, keeping myself moving in order to generate body heat to fend off the cold.

Of course, I hadn't anticipated staying overnight, so I made haste back down the mountain slopes early the next morning and resumed the long ride back along Spanish Trail. Once I rounded the bend—going west-to-north beyond the Rincon Creek crossing—my attention was alerted to a green pick-up truck suddenly swerving around in a U-turn and heading in my direction. It pulled off alongside, and a uniformed official stepped out. It was Les Gunzel, Superintendent of Saguaro National Monument. We loaded the bike in the back and drove back towards town. Of course, since my worried parents had contacted him, I got scolded, but not too harshly. In fact, he was a really nice man. It turns out I knew his son, Steve, from Palo Verde High School. A big, strong multisport athlete, gentle-natured, and a great guy! Unfortunately, after that adventure, I returned from my next all day-long Sabino Canyon hike to discover that my trusty bike had been stolen!

Eventually I joined the working world and got settled into a compatible rental in a rural area to the west along Fort Lowell Road—still within striking distance of my sacred Santa Catalinas. I began doing annual two-day treks up through the front range, all the way to the summit in the heart of the range atop Mount Lemmon (9,152'). This meant walking, hitchhiking–or both–to get to the end of Craycroft Road in the foothills, then bushwhacking across the desert and dropping into Ventana Canyon. This was a favorite secluded refuge of rocky cataracts, sandy seepwillow-scented streambeds, and deep rock pools, amidst lush, dense thickets of native shrubbery. Magnificent towering saguaros were showcased against spectacular rock walls and trailed down from even higher escarpments above. Frequently, the canyon trail was so overgrown that it wasn't easy to follow. It led to the *Ventana* or Window Rock formation upon a distant skyline ridge.

From the outset of my naturalistic ramblings into remote, wild places, those experiences were all-consuming at the time, and prior to my making note of them in written form. But eventually, I began to develop the habit of dutifully recording most of these outings. While my memory is keen and reliable for many of the unrecorded expeditions, these notebook and journal entries have provided a treasure trove of substantive detail that I'm able to share with you, my readers. I would strongly encourage all others with a penchant for wandering into the outdoors to carry a "Marble Memo" in their pocket for this purpose. Truth be told, I wish I could have written up all the hundreds of day hikes and bushwhacks—however seemingly insignificant at the time—since, in some way, through expending extreme physical exertion to surmount some unique challenge or exposure to something unknown, they contributed something meaningful to my overall experience and knowledge.

Throughout this book you will see quoted content from journals, field notebooks, and literary sources framed as an indented text block, such as this Mt. Lemmon, "Desert—to—the Pines" backpacking adventure from my 1970s home base along Ft. Lowell Road in Tucson, Arizona:

> MAY 12-13, 1979; HIKE: (About 25 miles)
>
> HOUSE → WINDOW ROCK → CATHEDRAL ROCK (7,952') → MT. LEMMON (9,150') SANTA CATALINA MOUNTAINS
>
> Left house 8:30 a.m., still good flow of water in Ventana Cañon. 1 blacktail rattler (3 and ½') encountered. From "D12" Saddle, going was quite easier than anticipated to base of Cathedral Rock. Turned back on 1st attempt but returned with rope at sunset and was successful in making first ascent. Descended after dark and bivouacked up high. Took a quick, refreshing dip in pool of W. Fork—Sabino, before making it on up to Mt. Lemmon, reaching top at 2:00 p.m. Sunday.
>
> JB Training/Expedition Logbook, 2/01/1978—8/29/1981

With respect to this account: A remarkable happenstance occurred up there when I turned over a flat rock near the base and found a coiled rope! Following my climb, I returned it to the exact same spot. I have no idea if I made a summit registry entry, or what I wrote, if I did. Chances are, I left a brief one since it was getting dark. Perhaps some future intrepid adventurer might yet discover it at the bottom of the ammo box typically found atop summits. Another thing necessary to mention in response to an anticipated question: YES, once the summit of

Mt. Lemmon was attained, my only real option was hitchhiking from Summerhaven, down the Catalina Highway and back home to Tucson.

Another of my rare scrambling/climbing adventures occurred during the late summer of the following year: After a long, rigorous, and extremely steep bushwhack above Finger Rock Canyon, I somehow managed to free solo climb Finger Rock and made my way safely back down on August 3rd, 1980. Surmounting some of the steep and sheer escarpments below the Finger in my ascent to reach the base were nearly as difficult as the climb itself.

This book resonates with the power of connections: those re-established after thirty-five to forty-plus years from long-ago personal encounters in distant, remote parts of the Galiuro Mountains Wilderness, Mexico, *Baja California Sur*, and elsewhere. Remarkably, more recent connections have been made with a host of dedicated, passionate Sea of Cortez scientists making a difference in bringing about a stronger conservation ethic, educationally, and in direct practice through intensive fieldwork and studies.

Readers of this book will be positively affected by its contents. That is my written guarantee at the outset: The only thing that's required is simply following along, seeing and experiencing through the eyes and mind of the pure naturalist: A naturalist who followed his instincts and passion for the wildlands from day one. Who found himself in all the right places at all the right times, however they happened. Purity is the key. I took full advantage of all the wide-open natural spaces around me as a child and never faltered from that path. Following this path as it is laid out here is akin to an extended celebration of some of the most magnificent and alluring—as well as dangerous—places in this region of Planet Earth.

You might be asking, "JB, why are there monarch butterflies on the cover?" That's a fair question: the book covers much of my earliest developmental experiences, usually over wild, remote terrain and ocean water which served as my primary training grounds. All the skills and knowledge I took from those experiences was applied to more recent, purposeful pursuits involving extensive wildlands exploration, monarch butterfly field research and restoration plantings. These great adventures will arise in a future manifestation of "The Pure Naturalist."

Until that time, I thank you from my heart and soul—so glad you are along for the journeys!

JB / *El Fuerte de las Mariposas* / Vail, Arizona

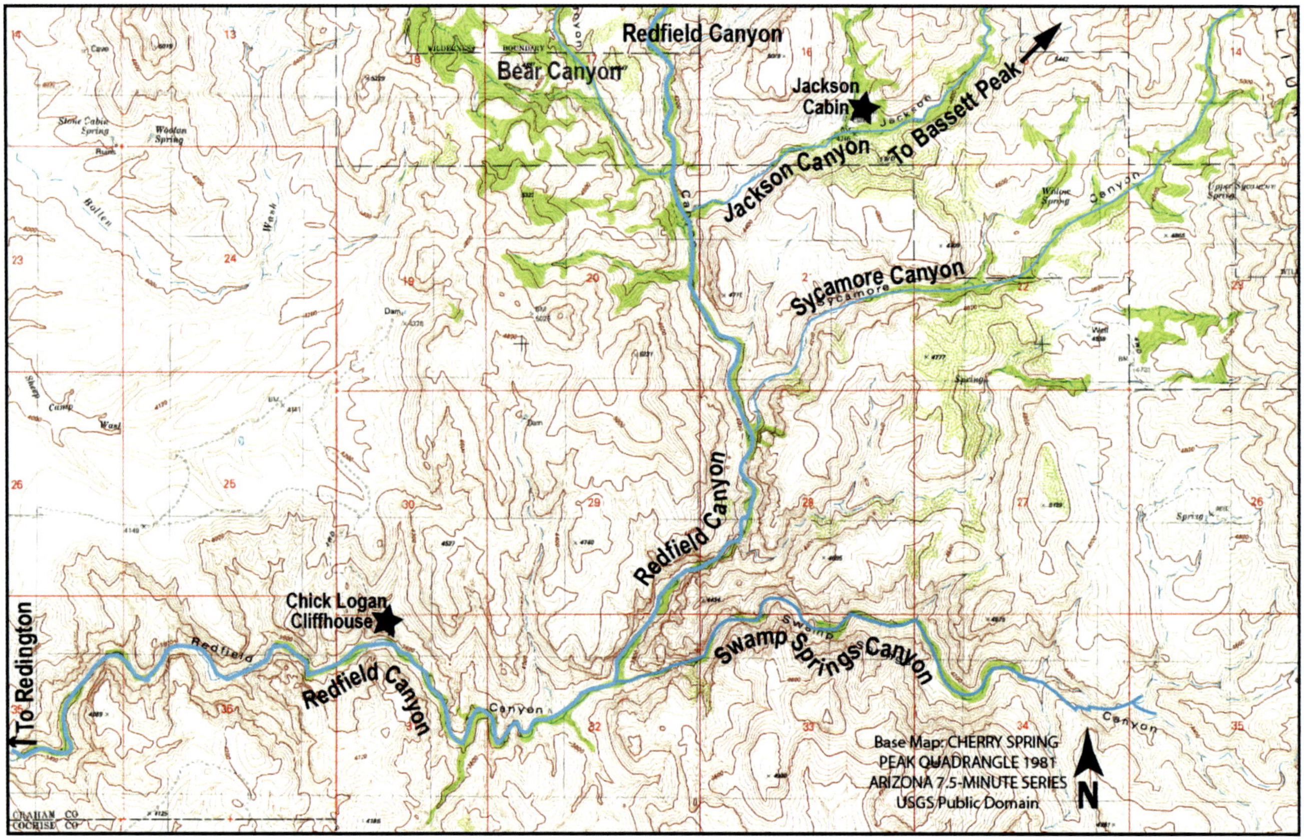

Southern area of the Galiuro Mountains

Chapter One

The Galiuro Mountains Wilderness: Redfield Canyon

Back in the early 1970s the sheer walls and intriguing terrain of Redfield Canyon in the Galiuro Mountains just literally jumped off the topographic maps at me. While it wasn't that great a distance from Tucson, it was in a pretty inaccessible spot for a guy who depended on a bicycle to get around. Nevertheless, I set out on my first backpacking expeditions to explore the magical canyon and adjoining wilderness.

Sheer wall vulture roost, lower Redfield Canyon (Early 1970s)

I arranged to be dropped off at the end of the pavement on east Redington Road as the starting point for each backpacking expedition. Then, from there, it was usually a long walk over Cebadilla Pass (4,300'), known today as Redington Pass, since at that time there was almost no traffic. And if there were, it was more often a miner or two from distant San Manuel heading in the wrong direction towards Tucson—unless I got really lucky!

It was always with great anticipation (and relief) reaching Redington, after twenty-three miles of rambling washboard-rutted road over the top of the pass down to where it meets the San Pedro Road. Another half mile east through the narrow lane past the rustic Carlink Ranch was required before reaching a broad expanse of sandy wash bed that stretched eastward towards the far horizon. The magnificent cliff walls of Redfield Canyon were at least six miles from the canyon's confluence with the San Pedro River. I remember on one of the earliest treks waking up while camped out along this stretch to the very loud agonized, hoarse calls of a bobcat in heat. The reverberation of back-and-forth distant coyote choruses across the valley were ever present, too, during those night encampments.

At the mouth of the canyon where volcanic rock walls met blue sky, a running stream gurgled along near a gallery of massive, tall cottonwoods. A small stone house was set back on a low terrace amongst these trees. Further upstream through a winding corridor of precipitous cliffs, roosting vultures were perched high above on rounded ledges of tan-to-pinkish rhyolite. (See photo on previous page.) Fish of all different sizes were abundant in the canyon pools. When I waded into the pools along the streambed, my bare feet were pleasantly nibbled on by swarms of small fishes.

Approaching rising walls of lower Redfield Canyon (Early 1970s)

*Illustration of roundtail chub (*Gila robusta*) by Joe Tomelleri*

On one of my earliest ventures into Redfield, the amount of hiking over the pass led to a very late afternoon approach to the canyon. By the time I reached the towering fortress-like entrance it was dark and a group of campers was huddled around a campfire above the streambed. Only they weren't campers: they were Arizona Game and Fish personnel conducting a native fish survey of the canyon. They explained that they were using electronic devices that stunned the fish temporarily, allowing them to sample and examine the existing population. At that time, there were at least four species in this area of the canyon: Longfin dace, speckled dace, roundtail chub and the Sonoran sucker. (Griffith and Tiersch, 1989) One of the group was a personable, friendly wildlife manager named John Holcomb whom I encountered years later after he'd been transferred to the Safford area. I was sitting on a bucket in the remote Whitlock Mountains badlands chipping a chunk of fine-grained basalt when John came walking up and we had another great conversation. When I re-established contact with John some forty-five years later, he recalled our meetings:

> Yes, I remember meeting you two times as you describe! As I remember our Redfield meeting was after dark when you surprised us by appearing at our campfire from out of nowhere as you had hiked in from the main road. Our Whitlock conversation included Indian arrowheads and how you had found a few over the years and that I had never found one. Nothing has changed, I still haven't found one! ...
>
> Email message, September 24, 2020

"Sleeping Cowboy," lower Redfield Canyon (8/17/76)

Tracks of bobcat, fox, raccoon, javelina, mule deer, coatimundi, mountain lion, and skunk were preserved in the mudbanks. (Murie, 1974) The high-pitched wailing cry could be heard of a disturbed black hawk soaring above. I climbed high up into a tall Arizona alder in order to snap a photo of a nest at close to eye level.Nests of these reclusive large raptors were in the crotches of tall sycamores farther ahead into the canyon.

Rounding a bend in the middle portion of this lower stretch, I witnessed a scrambling of furry shapes into nearby trees. A large troop of around thirty coatimundi had been surprised by my sudden appearance and were hastily climbing trees and rock faces to escape. Several of the smaller juveniles stared down from low hanging perches while I tried to focus my puny Sedic pocket camera from beneath. I could imagine how much they resembled monkeys in a tropical jungle. A large adult coati with a beautiful orangish coat growled and scolded men-

Black hawk soaring near rock pinnacle, lower Redfield Canyon (early 1970s)

Black hawk nest in crotch of tall sycamore (early-mid 1970s)

Adult coatimundi on ledge

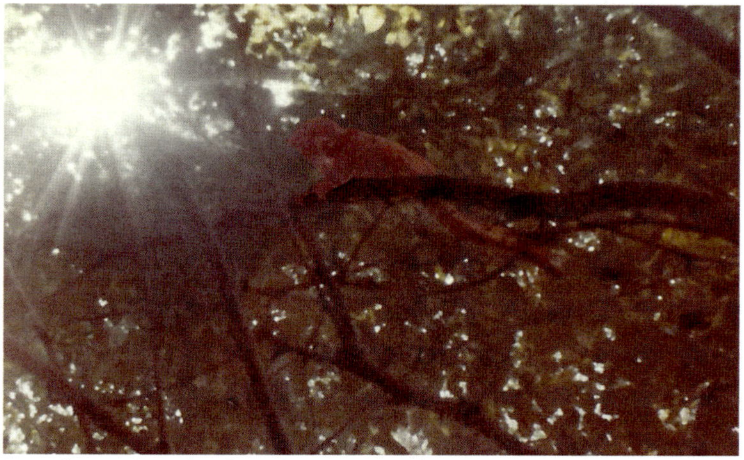

Juvenile coatimundi in branches overhead (early-mid 1970s)

Mid-Canyon floor, grassy park-like terrace below the cliff house

Redfield Canyon Cliff House (also known as Chick Logan or Hope Jones Cabin), mid-Canyon (8/17/76)

acingly from an adjacent rock perch. Coatimundis are long-snouted mammals of the raccoon family (*Procyonidae*) and adults are at least as large or larger than a full-sized raccoon. They forage in large groups, frequently with their long, banded tails held erect. (Jaeger, 1961) One morning in the lower canyon I looked up to see a long, single file line of them trailing upward across a huge rock slab way up high below the rim. Clearly, I had found my way into a wonderland of wildlife unlike any place I'd been before.

Not far from this encounter, another surprise of a different sort awaited me along an open stretch of canyon that had a park-like feel to it. Lush, green grass patches encircled by river rock cobbles covered the terraces between stands of tall Arizona alder and sycamore. I caught a glimpse—in a double take—of something up above that appeared very out of place and looked again. Against the north wall, underneath an overhang was the most immaculate and impressive cliff dwelling I had ever seen! Only it was not truly of aboriginal origin.

I was astounded to ascend steps through a patio and into this masterpiece of precision-laid stone and mortar construction, complete with wood floors and hardwood paneling. In one corner stood a kerosene-powered refrigerator, and adjoining rooms contained bedsprings with mattresses which had been damaged by rodents. Who had been possessed to create this dream house in such a wild, remote, and spectacular setting? A true labor of love and a work of art. Only much later would I learn the story of Chick Logan, the cowboy who built it and briefly lived here with his wife, Harriet, back in the 1930's. (Cowgill, 1975a)

Canyon wall above streambed, lower-mid canyon

Streambed, pools, and thick Arizona alder stands in mid-canyon

An accomplished writer/photographer named Sam Negri interviewed a number of local residents who provided rich details of the Cliff house and its history. Chick Logan, who was born in 1909, and Harriet began building the house in 1936, finishing it in 1939. He had become settled in the area earlier and rounded up wild horses in Redfield Canyon. Through later research, I discovered some additional historical anecdotes: Logan had been living in Prescott, Arizona, before moving to Queensland where he worked with Australian saddlemaker Robin Yates in Sydney. Logan became a very gifted saddlemaker later in his life, while living outside of Brisbane, in the state of Queensland, Australia. He died of leukemia in 1971, just shy of his 63rd birthday. (Negri, 2001)

Logan crossed paths with a well-known American couple, Lyman and Alaire Tenney from Willcox, Arizona. These two managed large outback cattle stations, founded the Paint Horse Association of Australia and put on horsemanship clinics all over the country. (Tenney, 2020)

Canyon view from cliff wall perch, lower-mid canyon

Subsequent expeditions would allow me to explore much further upstream into more remote sections of Redfield just before and after the canyon made a gradual northward bend. Some interesting trips explored Swamp Springs, Sycamore, Jackson, Bear, and Walnut Spring Canyons. On one occasion, in the early 1980s I was exploring Swamp Springs Canyon when I came upon the scattered remains of a desert bighorn sheep. I brought the pair of horns home and later received a note from Ron Olding of the Arizona Game and Fish Department in answer to my inquiry:

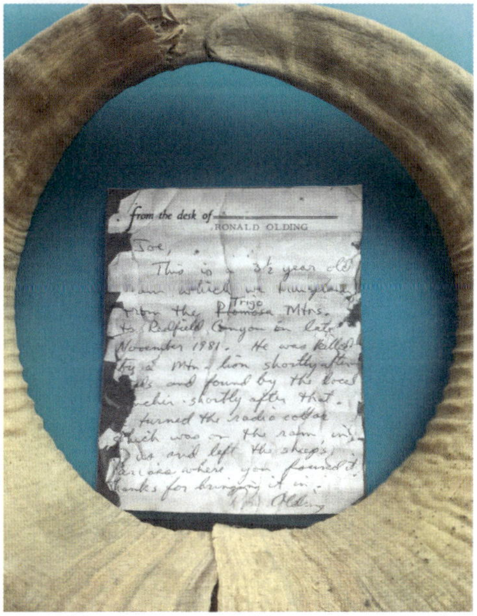

Ron Olding's note, ringed by ram horns (Early 1980s)

From the desk of Ronald Olding:

Joe,

This is a 3½ year old ram which we transplanted from the Trigo Mountains to Redfield Canyon in late November 1981. He was killed by a mountain lion shortly afterwards and found by the local rancher shortly after that. He turned the radio collar, which was on the ram, in to us, and left the sheep's carcass where you found it. Thanks for bringing it in.

Ron Olding

Redfield Canyon and its tributaries, such as Swamp Springs, with towering, precipitous walls, and monumental rock fortifications, would seem the ideal domain for bighorn sheep. I was aware of the Game and Fish release pen, located above the rim of the canyon. On later excursions into the Galiuros, I ventured much deeper into the heart of the range. This often meant descending into the Rattlesnake Creek Basin, far to the north. A guy could likely spend a lifetime along this corridor, exploring all the tributaries radiating outward from it, visiting Powers Garden, numerous side canyons, and all the peaks, ridgetops, and routes along the East and West Divides.

However, I was most often drawn back to the deep, timeless, haunting recesses of Redfield Canyon, and eventually found a more accessible route to reach it through the C-Spear Ranch, southeast of Redington. This occurred through a happenstance of attempting to ride my beat-up Peugeot PR-10 bicycle all the way up Interstate 10 to Benson, turning onto the San Pedro Road in Pomerene and following it out as far as I could to the northwest. Somewhere close to my destination, I suddenly needed to stop and examine my front tire. Horrified, I watched as a bulging portion of the tubing continued to expand through a split in the tire wall like a balloon, until it exploded with a BANG! Amplified by the heat and stillness, the gunshot-like reverberation rang back and forth from the surrounding desert hills and mountain slopes. Dumbstruck, I felt a sense of utter futility. What the hell was I going to do NOW without a spare tire or tube?

Well, good fortune arrived not long after in a Jeep coming down the nearly deserted dirt road, as I walked along the shoulder. It was Federico Valdez Gamez of the nearby C-Spear Ranch. "Freddie" could not have been more friendly and helpful as we loaded the bike and roared back to the ranch. Digging through an assortment of tools, patches, and sealants in the ranch tool shed brought forth the necessary ingredients to effectively patch and seal tire and tube, however unconventionally. From that fortuitous meeting, I was welcome there and soon gained access to the rough eight-mile jeep trail to the south rim overlooking Redfield Canyon.

Freddie Gamez was not the first descendant of one of Redington's pioneer families with whom I had crossed paths. On earlier expeditions, I had met Cayetano "Tano" S. Ronquillo, foreman of the Carlink Ranch, while on my way into the Galiuros. On one occasion, returning from a week spent in the heart of the range, I was welcomed into the beautiful home of Tano and his wife, Alicia Valdez Ronquillo. They were a quiet, dignified couple who hardly said a word. There were several pots simmering on the wood-burning stove from which Señora Ronquillo scooped generous portions onto tortillas, making burros for my journey back over the pass. I was famished coming out of the mountains and relished this wonderful hot meal while sitting under a mesquite tree along the San Pedro Road.

On January 2, 1981, I was slowly motoring along the rugged two-track from the C-Spear Ranch towards the south rim of Redfield Canyon in my recently acquired 1968 Jeepster Commando. I was on a mission of sorts: to clean-up, make small repairs, and put the canyon cliff

JB and Jeepster Commando at El Fuerte *(Photo by Suzi Mendoza)*

house back in good order. The house was known either by the name of the original builder as the Chick Logan House, or, as it was later called, the Hope Jones Cabin, after the legendary horsewoman who came out west and purchased the C-Spear in either 1939 or 1940. (Negri, 2001) Unfortunately, the rock house had fallen into serious disrepair over the years with graffiti and tons of trash left by an increasing number of the wrong kind of visitors.

The late, legendary Pete Cowgill, who wrote a weekly outdoor column for the *Arizona Daily Star* for over thirty years, had first visited the site back in the spring of 1966. He penned a piece initially focused on the large water tank mounted at the rear portion of the cliff house:

> The 500-gallon water tank is in a cave at the bottom of a deep canyon on the western side of the Galiuro Mountains. No road goes to the cave, or even close to it.
>
> The water tank, the kerosene refrigerator, the porcelain kitchen sink, wash basin and commode, the sofa and chairs, beds and mattresses, wood paneling for the four-room house, glass for the windows, cement and paint, and all other supplies and equipment needed to set up housekeeping were brought in on the back of a mule or sledded down from the mesa above the canyon. (Cowgill, 1966)

Nine years later, in a March 1975 article, Pete reflected upon his two visits—nine years apart:

> With considerable misgivings, I ran a story and two pictures of the place nine years ago. At that time the windows were out and most doors and screens were useless. Some gun-crazy nut had shot holes in the refrigerator and the upholstery of the sofa was exposed in many places. Mattresses for the two metal twin beds had been chewed by rodents. But the main structure of the four-room house was intact.
>
> Last Monday I hiked in to the house again. I had visions of an almost complete demolition as more and more people heard of the house and the ways to get there. The ridge I followed to the canyon bottom had a followable trail which to me meant

> the foot traffic was increasingly heavy. Down at the bottom I saw several sets of recent footprints. I almost turned around and went back out.
>
> Like Tom Caid [of Hearn and Caid in Tucson] who fabricated the 500-gallon tank, I also was amazed at what I saw, but for an entirely different reason. The place looked exactly as it had nearly 10 years before. There were no [additional] bullet holes in the refrigerator and some of the screens and doors were akimbo. The mattresses were still serviceable. All of the hardwood paneling in the west wing of the house was still intact as were all the rounded rock which made up the outside walls. But what impressed me the most was the water tank stuck in an alcove adjacent to the kitchen. There was not one bullet hole in it. (Cowgill, 1975a)

Unfortunately, the accumulative abuse I observed there, nearly five years later, was directly the opposite of Pete Cowgill's experience in 1975. Something HAD to be done; somebody HAD to do it; and that somebody was ME!

Every time I enter the canyon domain alone in this isolated and deeply mystical refuge, I am so overwhelmed with emotions welling up internally, it is almost unbearable. Of course, for the most part, the mission I was driven to accomplish precluded that. Once I arrived at the house from my encampment on the rim, I immediately went to work. I found a way to make a sturdy, serviceable broom out of bundles of thick grass stems tightly lashed in place. Then, picking up the immense volume of trash, inside, outside, and all over the surrounding vicinity became the main priority. Because of the massive amount collected, I had to store a portion of it in a large basement firewood bin. I was able to burn much of the rest, and later pack out some in very large bags. I attended to whatever I could clean, remove, or fix up, as well as graffiti and other tasks. I swept everywhere except west adjoining rooms since I was running out of time! Before leaving the house at twilight on Sunday the 4th, I provided a thick loose-leaf notebook for visitors' entries. This was intended to encourage greater care, respect, and help in packing out some of the stored trash, while discouraging cutting down trees for firewood! Reaching the slope and trail ascending to the canyon rim, I hiked back in darkness hauling up my heavy burden of refuse before returning to the glow of civilization.

Later that summer, I would return to the canyon for a couple days of remote hiking and exploring. I revisited the Chick Logan Cliff House and to my surprise the place was shipshape and in good order. Apparently, my efforts and the journal seemed to have changed the culture. Even more intriguing was a recent entry left by a woman who had lived there as a child, six or seven years old at the time. Her father was a cowboy who worked for Hope Jones on the C-Spear Ranch. Writer Sam Negri's fine *Arizona Highways* article provides much more through his research and visits to the Chick Logan Cliff House, including this revelation: The spiral-bound journal I established there during my three-day project still existed twenty years later in 2001. The whereabouts of it currently is unknown.

Following my visit to the cliff house I roamed freely around my favorite subterranean refuge—the canyon of infinite possibilities—where a tempting rocky "stairwell" to the rim or a mysterious hidden alcove might yet be found around the next bend or side canyon. My wanderings one morning resulted in a truly extraordinary experience: I came face-to-face with a phenomenon I had only read about in a favorite poem about a flash flood in Edward Abbey's classic book, *Desert Solitaire.* (1968)

HIKE: REDFIELD CANYON

Fed tomatoes to horses at Youtcy Camp. Breathtaking sky revealed above San Pedro coming down to crossing—had to go to bridge N of Redington, River running bank to bank and strong! Fed cats at C-Spear. Lost road due to prior flash flooding but made it up to good campsite on ridge. Next day provided experience of a lifetime—was down in Redfield Canyon a short distance from trail-point when I stopped for breakfast and got under an overhang and out of rain and did it rain—HARD—for 20-30 min. Suddenly, without warning, a thundering, frothy wall of water, roared around the bend, gradually inundating my abandoned spot with 4 feet of water and transforming a quiet canyon stream into a deafeningly loud torrent of debris-laden, tomato soup-colored water!!

JB Training/Expedition Logbook, July 11-12, 1981

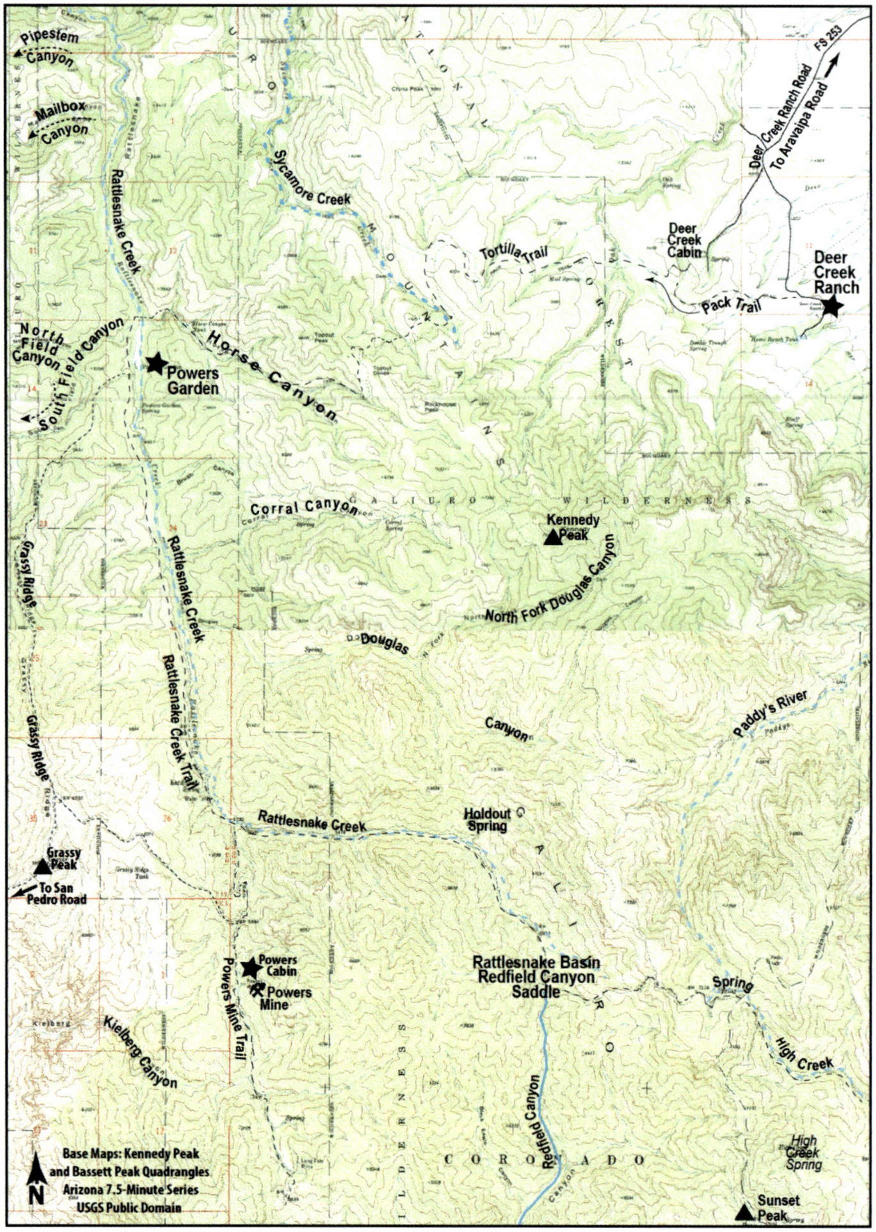

The heart of the range and Powers Garden area in the central Galiuros

Chapter Two

The Galiuro Mountains Wilderness: Into the Heart of the Range and Beyond

Angel Wings formation along the southern skyline ridge of the Galiuros

No matter what kind of circumstances or decisions preceded each adventure, it always felt right to get lost inside the most remote and spectacular wildlands in every instance. There has never been another mountain range I'd ever explored that could fulfill that feeling as much as being deep into the heart of the Galiuros. There were many options from different sides of the range to begin such journeys, but most often I chose the long, winding sometimes precipitous corridor of Redfield Canyon.

From the San Pedro Riverbed at Redington, it's roughly a twelve-mile stretch of winding canyon bends of ever-increasingly sheer walls before you reach the confluence with Swamp Springs Canyon, the first major side tributary entering from the east. (See map on page 6.) If you were to roam into Swamp Springs Canyon blind-folded for a mile or so, you could still imagine yourself inside Redfield. This side canyon oasis of high cliff walls usually has ample ephemeral stream flows, pools, and similar lush riparian vegetation. Meandering southeastward, it eventually intersects the two-track trail coming up from the Muleshoe Ranch after around five miles.

Beginning in 1973, my first explorations venturing wide-eyed into this wild, unknown domain were focused with great fascination and wonder upon all the elements and levels of the lower canyon, high along the rim and in the streambed below. Then, progressively, I explored beyond Swamp Springs Canyon where Redfield gradually bends away from the east before following a meandering northward corridor for the remainder of its length. Continuing on this path, each tempting side canyon—named or unnamed—offered to lure me upward into its mystical heights among the rocks above. Occasionally, I've given in to this temptation and ventured into these forbidden cataracts.

One day while climbing high above the bedrock of one such ravine I wound up at the opening of a small rockshelter, or shallow cave, hidden among steep rocky escarpments. There was barely enough room to squeeze into it, and before me lay a few scattered artifactual leavings of the ancient occupants. I did not linger and left the shelter as I had found it. Just to gaze out through the opening across that magnificent vista, imagining a primitive existence so long ago was more than ample reward for my climbing efforts. Continuing up Redfield beyond the Swamp Springs confluence, one enters a most precipitous section. Here the canyon narrows, becoming a deep abyss of ever higher sheer cliff faces above.

Welcome to "Boulder Choke I" and upstream, after a short respite, "Boulder Choke II!" This is where all the fitness training leading up to every expedition gets put to the test. It is as if earthquakes shattered the rocky rims above and brought huge house-sized boulders and debris down to fill in the canyon passageway. Frequently, I had to unshoulder my backpack and raise and lower it, with a cord attached, while descending or climbing over obstructions, or through narrow passages. It was tediously slow climbing upward, and around gigantic boulders, rock debris formations, and other obstacles in order to proceed upstream.

Once that first section is passed, the canyon opens up but somewhere around the Sycamore Canyon confluence, it abruptly closes again. Ahead is another narrow, treacherous, and brutally difficult defile to navigate. While trying to traverse the steep-banked slopes above the canyon floor, I found out the hard way that the high rock walls prevented much progress. Sooner or later one reaches a dead end where further progress is impeded by impossibly steep, sheer cliffs! In that event you have no choice other than to turn around and backtrack all the way down. This will cost you dearly in loss of momentum and precious energy expended.

High cliff walls and saguaros, north Redfield Canyon (August 2013)

In these types of what seem to be impossibly difficult situations, I was always self-aware of one of two attitudes I could adopt: often there's a tendency to be overly aggressive, as if you're fighting against the obstacles you're trying to overcome. This approach is fundamentally grounded in resistance. I preferred to ascend to a higher power—if you will—adopting the more effective attitude of fully embracing the challenge, rather than the former. Fighting and resistance results in greater fatigue and eventual exhaustion. By embracing the challenge, I tended to be less concerned with the slow pace. I paid closer attention to my movements and how I was applying my skills to the situation. Also, the necessity of breathing more deeply and rhythmically is important, and I believe it really helps keep the mind more alert, focused, and less vulnerable to stress. And dealing with the high degree of stress IS the key. Of course, it takes a lot of conscious effort to sustain this optimal level of mindfulness, although in the end, it conserves energy, and I'll feel a LOT better once I persevere through the difficulty at hand and reach my destination.

Once you've managed to grind through the second boulder choke, over roughly a mile or so, it's a huge relief to finally emerge from the grueling tunnel of pain into the bright sunshine. Whew! Walking over a relatively level sandy streambed of an open canyon again is a joy never more fully appreciated! Up ahead lay the next intersection of a major tributary with Redfield Canyon. A high, thin, sheer pinnacle of rock along the west bank of the canyon serves as a landmark preceding the upstream confluence of Jackson Canyon, entering Redfield from the opposite side. A clearly distinguishable man's shoulder, head and extended arm atop the pinnacle seem to point the way, as if to say, "Go north, young man!"

Just upstream from "The Pointer" is an ephemeral seep where fresh water emerges from the sandy streambed and slowly trickles downstream. This was one of the spots in Redfield Canyon I had discovered and where I regularly refilled my canteens. Locating sources of fresh, potable water becomes a critical factor in planning routes, on- and off-trail throughout the Galiuro Mountains Wilderness, especially in the summer months. I admit to being a primitive: I have always trusted my senses and instincts in determining if water is potable or not. Somehow, perhaps given a certain amount of luck, I've never experienced any ill effects of water contamination that I'm aware of. I've maintained this approach for a long time over a wide range of wild places. I'm happy to assume my own personal risk—as with everything else—and am not going out of my way to promote it; to each their own.

"The Pointer," in August 2013 (left) and August 1976 (right) in north Redfield Canyon near Jackson Canyon confluence

The shadows sway and seem to say
Tonight, we pray for water, cool, water
And way up there,
He'll hear our prayer.
And show us where there's water, cool, clear water. (Nolan, 1936)

In August of 1976, I had ventured from my usual starting point all the way up Redfield Canyon to reach "The Pointer" near the entrance to Jackson Canyon. On a previous expedition, I had explored the bone-dry lower portion of Bear Canyon, just upstream from Jackson. This time I turned into Bear to find the most magnificent summer rain-filled pool and swimming hole I had ever seen!

Bear Canyon pool, off North Redfield near Jackson Confluence

Bear Canyon pool, view from rim above (8/19/76)

This idyllic oasis even had a waterfall cascading over the rock rim above. It was the perfect reward and refreshing, invigorating dip after another long arduous ascent through the boulder choke sections downstream. No human architect could ever come close to creating such a natural masterpiece.

Jackson Canyon is one of the more well-known side canyons of Redfield. Historically, it was a main hub of cattle roundups with a well-built, sturdy bunkhouse a half mile or so upstream from its confluence with Redfield Canyon. (Browning, 1999) I knew about the presence of Jackson Cabin from my topo maps, but strategically I was focused mainly on this side canyon as a bushwhack-hiking route for my first ascent of Bassett Peak, the highest point in the Galiuros (7,663'). Of course, I seem to excel at doing things the hard way, and probably couldn't have chosen a more difficult route. Very long—very steep and rocky—very brushy and frequently disorienting, as I was out of the line of sight of the summit much of the time, direction-wise. But finally, after a rough climb, I eventually reached the summit. Here, I was amply rewarded with stunning views of both the East and West Divides tapering northward, and the intermontane corridor between them.

"Peak-bagging," that is, climbing a mountain just to add to a list, was never an overriding interest, but it's essential to explore all areas of mountain terrain from the highest peaks to the lowermost canyons that comprise the major drainages. These mountaintops are also the uppermost reaches of the watersheds for those same drainage systems.

Jackson Cabin, close-up of rockwork, from rear (August 2013)

Jackson Cabin site—stone outbuilding (August 2013)

View of Bassett Peak from East Divide Trail (mid-1970s)

Plane wreckage below the peak (Same mid-1970s. RIP)

Coming off the summit, I stopped momentarily to shoot a few photos along the East Divide Trail back toward the peak. One of my photos revealed a large, long, whitish-toned fuselage of a plane down in the timber below. This turned out to be the wreckage of a vintage WWII bomber—a B-24 Liberator—that had flown from Davis-Monthan AFB in Tucson on a night training run in January 1943. The impact upon the mountain completely destroyed the aircraft and took the lives of eleven airmen. This plane crash testifies to the remote isolation of the Galiuros: remarkably, the crash site wasn't discovered until early March—over a month and a half later. (Forton, 2021) It has been designated as an historic site by the Coronado National Forest Heritage Program. When I asked Cayetano "Tano" Ronquillo about it in a brief conversation while passing through the Carlink Ranch in Redington, he told of taking pack strings of horses to the site at that time.

Now that I had ventured this far into the range and into unknown territory, I decided to head down from the East Divide Trail into Ash Creek, below the northeast slope of Bassett Peak. Once past the tall stand of quaking aspens around Ash Spring, the trail seemed to resemble a tunnel along the lower stretches, through bigtooth maples and surrounding dense vegetation. This is very likely the only presence of *Populus tremuloides* in the Galiuros. The good news was that I had found a water source, so I sustained my momentum, hiking clear

Aspens at Ash Spring, above Ash Creek (Mid 1970s)

Trail forming a tunnel along Ash Creek (Mid 1970s)

down into the valley. As I walked along Ash Creek Road, a friendly rancher in a pickup pulled up alongside and asked me if I needed a ride. I thought for a moment, and said, "Sure—thank you!" and hopped in. Preston Larson of the nearby Larson Ranch was about as nice a guy as you could meet. We drove a ways northeast, then turned off onto High Creek Road back towards the mountains until we came close to where the road turns into a rough two-track. He wished me well on my journey as I retrieved my pack from the truck bed, thanking him in return.

Not long afterward I found the perfect spot to set up camp amongst the open oak stands of lower High Creek. I unfolded my nylon rain poncho that served as a ground cover. On top of it I unrolled the ensulite ground pad that was strapped to the bottom of the backpack frame. Next, I loosened the straps that fastened a ruck sack containing my sleeping bag, also strapped to the frame. Once I had my bed made, I prepared and ate my evening meal, while enjoying the solitude and diminishing sounds of birds ringing through the forest in the fading twilight. When it was time to go to sleep, I simply tucked my shoes (running shoes, not hiking boots) and clothes underneath my sleeping bag to make a pillow. (Sometimes camped in a washbed, I would make a mound of sand to achieve the same purpose.) Blissfully reposed and reflecting on all the rigorous moments of the day, up Redfield and Jackson Canyons and the steep route up Bassett and beyond, I slept like a rock!

I had made the previous day's decision in the spur of the moment, and it felt good waking up early the next day in the crisp, chilly morning air of lower High Creek. A skunk was still busily going about its nightly foraging, rustling through the leaves nearby. While I gradually worked my way upward along the trail, I gazed at two very impressive rocky peaks above the canyon, one shaped like a pyramid. Continuing through *terra incognita*, I crossed over to the West Divide, after first refilling canteens at Holdout Spring. Following an uneven, sometimes barely recognizable trail marked with cairns, I traversed the broad expanse of Grassy Peak, back downslope to the San Pedro Road and hitchhiked back to Tucson.

A couple of years later, in the fall, I undertook a more ambitious expedition, retracing my usual route up Redfield Canyon. Here are the brief notes for the first half of that adventure:

> **GALIURO MTNS. EXPEDITION V (9/16/78-9/23/78)**
> 9/16: Walked to within 2 mi. of Youtcy Camp and stopped for the night in canyon wash.
> 9/17: After a few mi., got ride to Redington Bridge. Camped 3-4 mi. beyond mouth of [Redfield] Canyon.

Holdout Spring in upper Rattlesnake Basin

Peaks above High Creek (Mid 1970s)

9/18: Ate breakfast at Logan [Cliff] House. Camped 2-3 mi. beyond Walnut Spring Canyon.
9/19: Went up Cedar Spr. Canyon and over ridge to locate trail. Decided to return to Redfield. Camped below spring.

JB Expedition/Training Logbook,
2/01/1978—8/29/1981

On this expedition, I was excited to explore the upper reaches of Redfield Canyon and whatever side canyons drew me into their mysterious, hidden labyrinths. On Day Three (9/18) I covered around ten miles from the Redfield Canyon Cliff House, hiking around the 90° angle east-to-north bend past Swamp Springs Canyon and beyond Jackson, Walnut Spring, and Mitchell Canyons to where I finally made camp. Not a bad day's trek, considering another grueling passage climbing through the notorious boulder chokes. From my encampment roughly a mile upstream from where Muleshoe Canyon enters from the northwest, I resumed my path northward, continuing further up Redfield the next morning.

I can probably anticipate the question: "Hey JB, how come you couldn't find a way to circumvent the boulder chokes? There's a quick and easy answer to that: because it's virtually impossible, given the rugged nature of this country with numerous steep-sided ravines, cliffs, and rocky escarpments that can make progress excruciatingly difficult. So, I guess you have to "pick your poison." Attempting to circumvent this stretch of Redfield Canyon by going overland is likely to cost you far more in terms of energy expenditure, time, stress, and water supplies. I'm open to the possibility of a route, but chances are it will take you far out of your way and might be disadvantageous to the nature of your expedition in the long run. I think with repetitive exposure, I became better at navigating through it, too. Sometimes the straight path—full of difficult obstacles—is the BEST path.

Over the first mile of Day Four, the canyon floor opened up, expanding across a wide flat, unlike any stretch I had encountered. Then as I roamed through the very widest portion, it abruptly became narrow again and a discernible track in the sand indicated something interesting lay ahead. After a little more than a quarter mile around a bend, I came upon Hooker Cabin. This solidly-built, small wood structure was a line shack that served the needs of working cowboys over this part of the range. While having a more conventional appearance than Jackson Cabin, a big sycamore towered over the cabin on the right-hand side, blending it into the surrounding tree gallery. I had no need to linger, other than a quick look-see, although the door was locked. At Jackson Cabin, on a previous trip, I had walked a short ways in, taken a look around, and walked out. The place was well-kept, neat and orderly, with beds made and everything set for the next round-up crew.

Hooker Cabin, north Redfield Canyon

From the cabin, I continued upcanyon around meandering bends for another mile or so, while anticipating the confluence of a major canyon tributary from the east. When a suitably wide inlet appeared along the east bank, I turned into it and went a couple of hundred yards, maybe more, until I clearly recognized where Negro (Black) Canyon joined South Negro Canyon, as I had visualized from the topo

View of Bassett Peak from Cedar Flat (September 1978)

map. South Negro Canyon looked to be a favorable off-trail/bushwhack hiking route to Bassett Peak—for a future expedition—over a relatively level streambed before the ascent up to the East Divide Trail. Now that I had established my bearings, I had about another mile and a half before the bottom of the trail northwest into Cedar Flat would appear on the opposite bank.

My plan on this trip, was to circumvent all the rugged bushwhacking I knew lay ahead working up the headwall of the upper Redfield watershed if I could locate and follow the trail through Cedar Flat. Then, I could follow a more direct route past a couple of the historic mine sites and the head of Kielberg Canyon to a point where I could drop into the Rattlesnake drainage corridor and continue northward. The Galiuro Range features an interesting, unique symmetry: the major drainage corridors—Redfield on the south and Rattlesnake to the north—and the adjoining East and West summit skyline ridges on either flank—are all aligned south-to-north.

My plan didn't work out. The more sloping country on either side of Cedar Flat was a pleasant change from steep-walled Redfield. But beyond a couple miles in, the trail became impossibly difficult to follow, requiring constant backtracking. There comes a point where the route becomes sorely questioned, knowing the trail lying farther ahead may likely be even less discernible. Of course, on the far north end, close to Rattlesnake Basin, I'm sure it was followable, but NOT here. So, I decided to return to Redfield. I hiked upstream in the canyon until I found the perfect overnight spot to camp, beneath a spring flowing out of a rocky ravine along the east bank.

I'm glad I slept well that night, for Day Five promised to be a formidable challenge, navigating upward through the innumerable side tributaries of the uppermost reaches of Redfield until the main channel itself became indistinguishable. There is a profound difference in degree of difficulty between following a side tributary to reach a major drainage channel downstream as opposed to following a major drainage channel upstream to its source. Everything converges moving downstream while going upstream everything spreads outward. The difficulty level increases as you get closer to the summit of the watershed. There are no signs to guide you nor trails, and even the topo map is of very limited use at this point. Forget about the map and concentrate on generating some good forward momentum instead. Your best guide is your own instincts and route-finding abilities. But no matter what, prepare for a long, steep, brushy grind into real *terra incognita*, for endless hours and hours. This is where the "Embrace the Challenge" mantra comes into play once again, just as it did going through the interminable boulder chokes. Sure glad I was able to top off those canteens the night before!

Day Five was indeed a long steep grind, once well beyond the comfort of the familiar main canyon. I got disoriented several times—par for the course—but kept my momentum going forward. I wound up traversing the juniper and oak-studded terrain northeastward until I eventually came out atop the East Divide ridge two to three miles northwest of Sunset Peak. All things considered, I was not terribly far off-course and now I could just follow a familiar trail along the ridge and down to Holdout Spring near the headwaters of Rattlesnake Creek. By the time I finally reached the spring, I was about as parched, thirsty, and dehydrated as I've ever been. Hard-core bushwhacking really consumes water supplies. It's more than the fact you're grinding hard and sweating buckets but also the stress involved. Once settled, it is so nice to make camp near a reliable water source where you can drink ample amounts with meals and top off your canteens for the next day.

In light of Day Five, I hear another question arising: "OK JB, what the hell were you doing in the middle of the wilderness without a compass?" My answer: Compass? What compass? I acknowledge that it is a fair question but the truth is it never occurred to me to carry one. It harkens back to my "Purity is the key" theme. Keeping it as simple as possible with an emphasis on using my God-given instincts and developing my route-finding skills without any tools, devices, or other aids. I did not even carry a flashlight! I voluntarily put myself in wilderness situations where I had to overcome fear, stress, disorientation, extreme thirst/hunger, darkness, and fatigue under the pressure of a high degree of difficulty. I suppose there was an underlying sense of pride in rambling over the mountains and through canyons in much the same way as the historic Apache warriors and earlier aboriginal Native American hunters. So, another disclaimer is warranted: please do NOT go into the wilderness without

Early morning start, upper Redfield Canyon

Whitetail buck along Rattlesnake Creek trail

a compass! It's a good thing to learn to use a compass, and for certain it's essential on the ocean.

Starting out on the morning of Day Six (9/21/78), it felt strange to have the luxury of hiking on a well-established trail. It was a perfect bright, sunny day, and I had around seven miles across the floor of Rattlesnake Creek to cover before reaching the Powers Garden cabin and assorted outbuildings. My first visit to the cabin had occurred under much different circumstances during the winter of 1977. This was another "Bike/Hike" adventure as I had ridden my Peugeot PR-10 over Cebadilla Pass, occasionally walking up the steepest hills, to reach Redington. From there I rode north up the San Pedro Road to the mouth of Kielberg Canyon. I ditched the bike and bushwhack-hiked up to the head of the canyon, reaching the Powers Mine Trail in late afternoon, under gathering storm clouds. The first-time bushwhack up Kielberg had burned a lot of daylight, so I wound up hiking most of the way up the Rattlesnake Trail in the dark. Light snow flurries were increasing, and it became bitterly cold as I kept up a good pace—maintaining body heat— towards Powers Garden. I was never so glad to come upon such a welcome sight in my life as I approached the cabin under a full-on snowstorm! Having had that experience made me appreciate this unique and wonderful wilderness refuge that much more. After enjoying what, to me, were luxury accommodations overnight, I headed back the next morning towards the West Divide Trail, returning by way of Grassy Peak back down to the San Pedro Road. I chose not to take the washboard-rutted Cebadilla Pass route but rode the long way back up through San Manuel, Oracle, and back around to Tucson.

Powers Garden: meadow scene along southern edge (Sept. 1978)

Powers Garden: meadow scene with distant log (Sept. 1978)

Now, it was a welcome sight to once again enter the broad pastures of Powers Garden with its collection of rustic buildings along the west floodplain of Rattlesnake Creek. This would be my first opportunity to "chill out" and enjoy the surroundings of this place and its stunning natural beauty. I roamed up and down the adjacent meadows, taking a few photos to best capture the scene. Then I went over on the east side of the central pasture to walk the rocky Creekbed—not much water pres-

Powers Garden: View of pond from inside cabin

Powers Garden: View of cabin, approaching from south

View of San Pedro River and Valley from the West Divide/Rhodes Peak

ent except a few small intermittent pools. There was water in the pond out back, that you had a view of through a rear window of the cabin. I did a short-distance recon of a couple tributaries to the west and north—Field and Horse Canyons—before returning to fix my supper, read through the "Cow Camp Guest Book" and prepare for the next day's adventure heading out westward.

9/22: Day Seven

After breakfast, etc., did chores and headed up towards <u>Field Canyon</u> trail. Remained on new trail which goes along ridge and meets Field Canyon trail further north. Continued along W Divide trail to head of <u>Schoenholzer Canyon</u>. Proceeded down Canyon after sunset to <u>Rhodes Ranch</u>.

JB Expedition/
Training Logbook,
2/01/78—8/29/81

I enjoyed hiking over the Field Canyon trail for the first time and made steady progress towards the West Divide trail. After about six miles or so, I finally stood atop Rhodes Peak (7,116'), taking in the magnificent views of the distant San Pedro Valley. Of course, all the trail hiking up until now was merely a warm-up for "The Main Event." That would await me just beyond another couple of miles farther up the trail when I would be looking down the precariously steep headwall of Schoenholzer Canyon.

When you transition from trail-hiking to off-trail hard core bushwhack-hiking and climbing, it helps to ease into it slowly, becoming focused on adapting your muscles and skill set gradually to the much more difficult, steep terrain and frequently thick, thorny stands of brush. One of the things you often encounter descending steep, headwall canyons is suddenly winding up above impossibly sheer drop-offs and then having to hike a long, circuitous route to get around. As the sun was sinking below the western horizon, I approached the lowermost section of the canyon, which was considerably steeper.

In the gathering darkness, I lost my footing momentarily and tumbled and slid down the steep chute, grabbing onto a bush I crashed into. I was also very fortunate to quickly avert a close encounter with a rattlesnake in the dark, while semi-sliding and climbing down over the drainage's thick accumulation of leaves. Of course, I'm sure that rattlesnake was just as shocked as I was! Once I arrived at a more level stretch, I took stock of all my numerous cuts and scratches—par for the course. ("If you're not bleedin', you're not tryin'.") I hiked out of the bottom of the canyon, following a trail towards the Rhodes Ranch, not knowing what to expect.

One of the most memorable takeaways from these expeditions are the rare but high quality and interesting people you meet. This night was no exception as I neared Rhodes Ranch. A stocky, mid-40-ish gentleman opened the door, examined this 'sight for sore eyes' and immediately welcomed me inside. Dr. Tom Hendrickson was the proprietor of the ranch and a dentist with a practice in Oracle. As I related my harrowing descent down Schoenholzer Canyon, he could not have been more gracious and hospitable. I turned down his offer of putting me up for the night as politely as I could, saying, "I'm used to sleeping outside, and the weather's nice." In the morning he said he would be heading out, so he could drop me off at the San Pedro River. The next morning I sloshed across the San Pedro and continued, barefoot, until I reached the main road. From there I managed to catch a ride all the way back to Tucson.

9/23: Day Eight

Caught ride to <u>S</u> <u>Pedro</u> <u>River</u>, cross channel and walk barefoot to main rd., then hitchhike back to Tucson.

JB Expedition/Training Logbook, 2/01/78—8/29/81

In the early 1980s I set out to explore the northern end of the range. This turned out to be a misadventure for reasons I'll explain. My plan was to enter from the far northwest through Copper Creek. I drove up the San Pedro Road, turning off at Kielberg Canyon into a familiar area. I motored a short ways into the canyon up the rough two track where I parked the Jeepster Commando in a secure spot. Then I strapped on my backpack and walked up the San Pedro Road at the beginning of what I envisioned would be a wide circular loop route from far northwest-to-northeast, then southward into the Rattlesnake Creek corridor, then across to the West Divide, and back down through Kielberg Canyon. Somewhere below the town of Mammoth, I headed east from the main road into the unknown terrain of Copper Creek Canyon.

I encamped at several locations along and above the creek and roamed through the ruins of the historic mining district. All that remained were the foundations of an enterprise begun early in the nineteenth century when the Copper Creek Post Office was established in 1907. The company went bankrupt in 1914 and the town and buildings were eventually abandoned. (Wilson, 1977) (Gillespie et. al., 1995)

I continued for several days, across to the east side of the range, dropping down into Four Mile Creek. That is where, examining the hard, cold facts of my situation, I had an epiphany!

Throughout the course of all of my backpacking expeditions, there is always a push—pull, tug-of-war going on when loading up food supplies. I insist on traveling as light as possible, allowing me to cover maximum ground, on-trail or off-trail in all types of terrain. So, I think you know where I'm going with this: sometimes—as in this case—the trade-offs for weight reduction can be too extreme. What I absolutely knew then, taking inventory, was that in a few short days, I was going to run completely out of food! So, given this stark reality, what were my choices? A) Return in the direction I came in from, along a mostly followable trail? Or B) Immediately head southward to complete my circular loop route through Rattlesnake Creek, then westward along the Divide and back down Kielberg Canyon?

Instead of A or B, I chose C: hike down Four Mile Creek to the store in Klondyke, load up on extra provisions, and return to the mountains. Fortunately, I had a stash of emergency cash tucked away in my pack. Judging by the topo, I was looking at between eight and ten miles. So, off I went, setting a good pace along the mostly downhill route. It was interesting because there was a guy in a pickup truck from a nearby ranch who came up beside me and warned me—now walking along a dirt road to Klondyke—that I was trespassing on private property. Several miles farther, the same guy came alongside again. Unfazed, I continued without breaking stride towards the store. A very unpleasant surprise awaited me when I finally arrived there.

STORE CLOSED. Yep, that's what the sign said. It turns out that the Post Office was still open but the store had closed six months prior to my arrival. I went down and talked to the one guy in the BLM Ranger Station. He said there had been a recent flood event and no one was currently in Aravaipa Canyon. If I wanted he would issue me a permit on the spot to explore THAT whole place all by myself. But, of course, my only real option was to make tracks back to the Galiuros, and it would have been a very long route back to the Jeepster from the opposite end of the canyon. I was essentially in the first stages of starvation, though I wasn't thinking much about it in those terms. I made it back up into Four Mile Creek fortunately without any rude interruptions.

I suppose given all I've experienced and learned since then, I'm confident I would now be much more resourceful and a better problem-solver in that situation in terms of finding food. But back then, I was in "Galiuro Kid" mode, taking and adapting to whatever comes and just toughing it out. I knew a few things from my affinity for and studies of native plants. So, I munched on manzanita berries whenever I could. Someone familiar with the Powers Garden Cabin might raise the question, "Hey JB, you could have found food in the cabinets at the cabin!" Honestly, that never occurred to me. Yes, I had left a few items there in past visits—as a good guest would—but the thought of removing food supplies never entered my mind. That was also in step with the "Kid's" code. More on Powers Garden later on.

Hunger is an interesting sensation. It's like a cramp in your stomach that never goes away. I still enjoyed covering the lengthy terrain that I did, though in a profanely irritable mood. Once I got down from the headwall of Kielberg to a more level streambed, I began finding scattered clumps of miner's lettuce (*Claytonia perfoliata*—back then listed as *Montia*). I suppose I got some energy from consuming these lush green leaves but they did little to abate my hunger. Since it was February, most of the flora was in a dormant

Closeup of miner's lettuce (Photo courtesy of Satinflower Nurseries)

stage with precious few resources available. I'm glad to say that my energy level remained constant, over a very long grind back to my semi-hidden Jeepster. Yes, hard lessons have to be learned the HARD way (in accordance with "The Kid's" code).

Sometime during the same period, I finally retraced the entire length of Redfield Canyon from the very apex of the watershed, between it and the other side which drops down into Rattlesnake Basin. So, harking back to the September 1978 Expedition, I got to experience the opposite of tracing a major drainage to the top of a watershed where it vanishes into myriad rivulets going everywhere across the slope. So, by following this method, I took a much different and direct path bushwhacking down to the main canyon than I did then on Day Five (September 20, 1978, as described on page 30). Now I could just follow any and all of the deepening rills as they all coalesced into more substantial tributaries downslope. One of the benefits of this route was stumbling upon a large log cabin ruin in a very remote spot. I have no idea who built it, but they put a LOT of work into it (using handtools)! Once I got down to the open, broad, sandy washbed of Redfield, the sun had set and I was soon walking in darkness. But the canyon was very amenable and I wanted to continue over this stretch as far as I could.

Log cabin ruin, upper Redfield watershed area.

In the pitch-black darkness, there was something in the distance that looked eerie, strange, and out of place. A halo of bright light rose up from the canyon floor. The closer I got, the more the light flickered. Sure enough, I'd chanced upon a bunch of cowboys on a round-up sitting around a huge campfire. As I approached, I called out from a ways off, thinking I would be less likely to startle them than just walking right in. After all, who would ever expect someone to come walking up in the middle of the night through the remotest area of the Galiuro Mountains Wilderness? Wow! It's kind of a shock to meet people after traversing in solitude for so long. But here, I was more than welcome, and the cowboys were laughing and super friendly. While I described the route of my current adventure, one called out, "SORE FEET!" Thankfully, I didn't suffer from that, but I was feeling the effects of a long day and began looking for a spot nearby to bed down.

I awoke the next morning to loud munching sounds of horses chewing off the outer canopy branches of the huge hackberry tree I had been sleeping beneath. Once I was up and around, a lean, hard-looking but very friendly cowboy strolled up to have a chat. It was the foreman of the outfit, the legendary Alvin Browning, who'd probably covered more miles on horseback in the Galiuros than any living or passed soul. He pointed up to the horizon at a distant ridge above the canyon, "See that window in the rock?" Yup, there it was, plain as day! He began talking about cattle and what it takes to care for and protect them. Which meant occasionally hunting down mountain lions. I listened intently as a lover of cats big and small, trying to see things from his perspective. I could never kill a mountain lion—except, perhaps, in highly unlikely self-defense—but even if I did, there are many more out there to take its place.

Alvin Browning was the ultimate "Mountain Cowboy," which is the fitting title of his autobiography. The book was published in 1999, the same year that he was inducted into the Willcox Cowboy Hall of Fame. Here's his job description:

> To be a good cowboy you have to build fence, pack all kinds of things on pack mules, ride a bucking horse, put shoes on horses, work on windmills, break and train young horses, diagnose and treat sick animals, handle big or small herds of cattle, rope in all kinds of situations, trap stock killing lions, wolves and coyotes, cook for yourself or a crew, haul hay, feed horses and cattle, tell the age and weight of cattle only by looking at them. All this really isn't an easy chore. (Browning, 1999)

During Alvin Browning's time working cattle in the Galiuro Mountains, he constructed at least five cement dams across bedrock ravines. These dams created rain-filled water impoundments benefitting both cattle and wildlife. One of these dams, bearing his name on the topo maps, is in a side ravine of Muleshoe Canyon about a mile upstream from its confluence with Redfield.

I wish I could have talked longer with him, but you know, sometimes work interrupts a good conversation. I also needed to sustain my own momentum with a lot of miles ahead down Redfield. Soon enough, I would be passing Jackson Canyon which led to the cowboys' bunkhouse. What could be better than living and working in the magnificent Galiuro Mountains Wilderness? The more I learned about Alvin's life later on, the more I felt privileged to have met him there so long ago at that round-up campfire.

"Sky Castle" above Rattlesnake Basin, north of Powers Garden (12/11/2020)

Chapter Three

The Galiuro Mountains Wilderness: Powers Garden

On December 11th of 2020 I was driving back to one of the most unique places on Planet Earth tucked away inside the impregnable wilderness corridor of the Galiuro Mountains. Nearly forty-four years had passed since I first entered the Powers Garden cabin in the dark, shivering with cold, during a February snowstorm. Now I was traveling back in time as my truck got closer to the Aravaipa Valley, and the turnoff to Deer Creek Ranch. In retracing my past steps as the Galiuro Kid through that wilderness corridor, I had reached out and become friends with Mr. Mike Isley, former owner of the Deer Creek Ranch, through our phone conversations between Idaho and Arizona.

Motoring slowly through the dense fog that blanketed the muddy, slick Aravaipa Road, I was headed into the Galiuro Mountains Wilderness on a mission of a different kind than the backpacking expeditions of the past. My plan was simple: to revisit the Powers Garden cabin and confirm whether any of the old "Cow Camp Chronicles" or "Cow Camp Guest Book" journals of the mid-1970s and early 1980s were still there. The journals were established by Mike and Nornie Isley, who ran their cattle operation into the Rattlesnake Creek corridor and adjacent areas of the Galiuro Mountains from Deer Creek Ranch.

These original journals provide numerous detailed entries of the ranching workday in this primitive wilderness area from the late 20th Century. Entries were left primarily by Mike, Nornie, their daughters and son, and later by members of the Von Trapp family after they became the new owners of Deer Creek Ranch in the early 1980s. In between, Forest Service personnel left notes on their activities during visits, as did occasional hikers, horseback riders—and every now and then—a trapper, bear, or lion hunter. The entries described a wide range of daily chores and places such as the many corridor side canyons where people worked, rode, or walked to, weather-related events, trails blazed or "brushed" (cleared of debris and overgrowth), water sources improved, personal ruminations and sometimes humorous anecdotes. They present a colorful, detailed picture of a past era of ranching history within the Galiuro Mountains Wilderness that has significant historical value.

Once I reached Deer Creek Ranch Road, I was relieved to be on a more stable surface. I had barely avoided swerving across slippery clay slicks on the Aravaipa Road into the ditch along the shoulder. Now, I had finally emerged through the dense fog and was heading south over an upper grassland plain, with just over eight miles ahead to the Deer Creek Trailhead. At a point high above along the trail, the view of the fogged-in Aravaipa Valley and snow-capped Mt. Graham of the Pinaleños to the north were astounding! I was following the Tortilla Trail (#254) that Mike Isley and a small crew began building in 1976-1977 as a more direct, efficient route for driving cattle into the wilderness corridor and back from ranch headquarters.

The road into Deer Creek Ranch on the northeast flank of the Galiuros.

Tortilla Trail sign at Rattlesnake Creek Trail junction.

According to Mike, the work lasted several months and involved extensive use of rock drills and dynamite. These were critical in clearing a route between seven and eight miles long, before it intersected the main Rattlesnake Creek Trail. The trail diverted from Sycamore Can-

View overlooking fog-blanketed Aravaipa Valley

Looking out over Galiuro Mountain Wilderness from the Tortilla Trail.

yon Trail (#278) at Mud Spring, cutting across a wide area westward between Sycamore and Horse Canyons. Truth be told, the trail was not authorized by the Forest Service at that time, but it was allowed to remain and has since become a regular route into the Rattlesnake Creek corridor with its many side canyons and Powers Garden. (Duncan, personal communication, 2023)

According to historical records, the closest any of the Spanish explorers or European missionaries came to the Galiuro mountains occurred in 1697. An Italian Jesuit priest, Father Eusebio Francisco Kino, ventured down the San Pedro River and visited a Sobaipuri Indian village near the present town of Mammoth, Arizona, where he stayed overnight on the fourteenth of November. (Wilson, 1977) Since Father Kino became renowned for establishing cattle ranching in Mexico and the southwest, I wonder what he would have thought of the pastoral surroundings of

Powers Garden. Here among the lush floodplain at least twenty acres or more of pastures extended north and south of the cabin and outbuildings.

In the early 1900s an Angora goat ranching operation was established in this verdant paradise run by a man named Pete Spence. At that time it was known as Rattlesnake Springs in reference to the springs found roughly a quarter mile south of the cabin. Later on, around 1911, Spence's Goat Ranch was purchased by the Power family who settled in the Rattlesnake Creek corridor after emigrating west from Texas by way of New Mexico. Jeff Power, his daughter, and three sons built corrals, raised horses and cattle, expanded the main cabin and outbuildings, and planted a garden. (Wilson, 1977, 1995) It's a peculiar quirk of fate that their name—synonymous with Powers Garden—has become an accepted misnomer: Powers rather than Power.

By 1917 the Power family had left their headquarters at Rattlesnake Springs and moved southwest to the mine they'd established near the head of Kielberg Canyon where they settled into a sturdy one-room log cabin. In February 1918, a posse of lawmen set out towards Rattlesnake Springs to serve arrest warrants on two of Power's sons, Tom and John, age 24 and 26 respectively, for draft evasion. When they failed to find them at their former homestead, they moved on to the cabin by the mine. What followed resulted in one of the deadliest shootouts in western history, one which became extensively written and speculated about. The family patriarch, Jeff Power, was shot in the doorway and later died from his wounds. When the smoke cleared, three lawmen, Graham County Sheriff Frank McBride, and his two deputies, Martin Kempton and Kane Wootan, lay dead outside the cabin. The sole survivor of the posse, U.S. Marshal Frank Haynes, bolted from the scene and arrived in Klondyke later in the day, his horse completely spent. (Wilson, 1977, Power and Whitlach, 1981, Trejo, 2015, Osselaer, 2018)

Powers Garden cabin and front yard (View from south).

Powers Garden: view from north of wagon and old pickup.

One of the largest, most exhaustive manhunts in Arizona history ensued with hundreds of men and posses combing the landscape throughout the region. Remarkably, despite serious injuries from the gunfight, the two brothers and their hired hand, Tom Sisson, remained on the loose for nearly a month. The fugitives rode the horses of the deceased members of the posse through Redfield Canyon to the San Pedro River, into the Dragoon Mountains, until finally reaching the Chiricahua Mountains near the New Mexico border where their horses gave out. They continued southeastward on foot through the bitter winter cold into New Mexico and ultimately surrendered to authorities just inside the Mexican border. Once they were brought back to stand trial, they received life prison sentences which kept them incarcerated for over forty years until they were paroled in 1960. Tom Sisson had passed away in prison earlier in 1957. (Kreutz, 2006) In 2006, *Arizona Daily Star* columnist, Doug Kreutz previewed Pete Cowgill's forthcoming presentation, "The Great Shootout at Power Cabin," in which Cowgill would share the story of that historic tragedy. Kreutz quoted Cowgill's account of a chance meeting with John Power in the Galiuro Mountains in 1964:

> It was in Kielberg Canyon (in the vicinity of the cabin site). I was backpacking in there when I met him. He had a pack on his back and a big old .45 on his hip. He was short and stocky and looked as hard as nails—but he was very pleasant. He said he had some mining claims up there. (Kreutz, 2006).

The rugged character of the Power clan and the rigorous existence they forged out of this remote wilderness setting is synonymous with the rugged nature of the mountains that surrounded them. As the author Thomas Cobb—who in 2012 wrote an award-winning novel, *With Blood in Their Eyes*, on the historic event—related in an outtake from the documentary film, *Power's War*:

> They were really 19th Century people.... They were born in the 19th Century, they understood the 19th Century.... I think it was the 20th Century that just bewildered them and they just could not deal with it. (Trejo, 2015)

On April 2nd of 1980, the Galiuro Kid returned to the Galiuro Mountains Wilderness for the second time through High Creek. For this adventure, I was joined by my compatible hiking companion, Trica, a savvy naturalist in her own right as well as a University of Arizona student in the Renewable Natural Resources program. Our plan was to follow the usual route into Rattlesnake Basin, past Holdout Spring towards Powers Garden and then return by way of a different trail from the main Rattlesnake Creek corridor back to High Creek.

GALIURO EXPEDITION VI

Note: There were more expeditions than the ones recorded in the JB Logbook; some were officially recorded; others were not.

4/2: We begin hiking up High Creek Rd after dark until campsite reached just below trail junction; where there is a tributary on S. side of Creek (High Cr. Spring?)

4/3: Leisurely morning. Dusk finds us atop Redfield/Rattlesnake Saddle before we finally decide to bed down near Holdout Spring after dark. Heard whiskered owl and poorwill.

4/4: Big day. Interesting stops along Rattlesnake Trail. We explore mine tunnel; examine long-eared bats at close range. At Powers Mine Tr. junction, there is entry by Robert McBride, 66-yr. old son of sheriff of same name, who was one of the victims of the Powers brothers during the 1918 shootout. Finally reached Powers Garden in late afternoon. Headed north into Horse Canyon where we discovered and named Madrone Arch. [That is, we named it—on the spot—for the beautiful Arizona madrone tree underneath] This is an intriguing canyon.

4/5: Bathe in icy creek. Return to Garden and linger for a while. Trica prepares a delicious meal w/eggs, chives etc. We make entries in journal and say farewell to the Garden, heading south to Corral Canyon. As the sky darkens and stars brighten we make our way to a suitable campsite.

JB Training/Expedition Logbook, 02/01/1978—8/29/1981

The Powers Garden cabin had certain amenities such as a wood-burning stove that allowed for cooking meals. I believe at that time there was also a butane-powered refrigerator. Of course, we brought our own food with us. Up until now I haven't addressed the lingering question, "JB, what were you packing food-wise into the wilderness?" I never kept notes on my expedition food items nor did I retain any grocery lists prior to a trip. But simplicity was always the rule, and mobility was the far higher priority than mealtime ambience. I did not carry a stove (too much weight—ultra compact models did not exist) nor a tent, for that matter. One of my big mainstays was a granola called Oat Crunch that came in three-pound, clear plastic bags. To go with that, I had mixed nuts, sesame sticks, and lots of those little red boxes of Sunmaid Raisins—remember them?—and packets of Carnation instant non-fat dry milk. (I stirred a heaping tablespoon of powdered nutritional yeast into my milk.) I stocked cans of tuna and sardines, and probably had a small pot stowed with some rice or ramen in case I made a small fire somewhere. I also took along perishable items for the early portion of the trip like a few boiled eggs, avocados, beef-chile-bean burros, and so on. But as far as camp sustenance goes, that's about it—pretty "bare bones" trail cuisine!

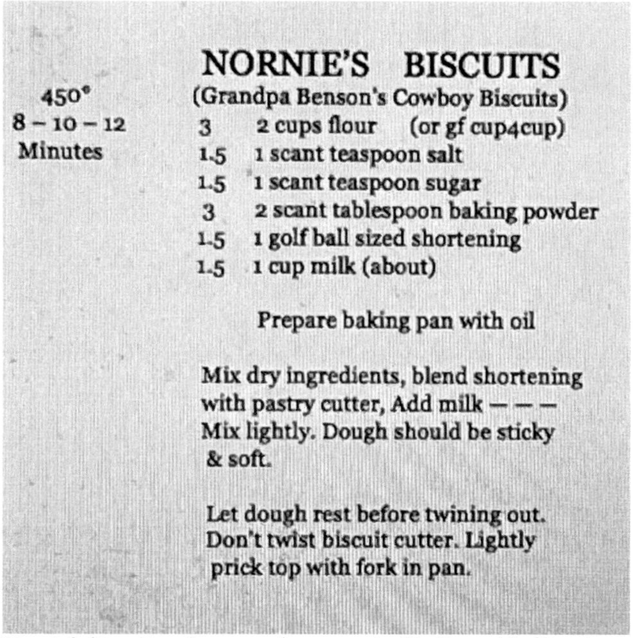
NORNIE'S BISCUITS
(Grandpa Benson's Cowboy Biscuits)

450°
8 – 10 – 12
Minutes

3	2 cups flour (or gf cup4cup)	
1.5	1 scant teaspoon salt	
1.5	1 scant teaspoon sugar	
3	2 scant tablespoon baking powder	
1.5	1 golf ball sized shortening	
1.5	1 cup milk (about)	

Prepare baking pan with oil

Mix dry ingredients, blend shortening with pastry cutter, Add milk — — — Mix lightly. Dough should be sticky & soft.

Let dough rest before twining out. Don't twist biscuit cutter. Lightly prick top with fork in pan.

Nornie's biscuit recipe was always posted in the cabin (Courtesy of Mike and Bettina Isley)

Trica, on the other hand, was far more resourceful. Besides eggs and chives, she served up cucumber slices, herring, cheese, granola mixed with peanut butter and honey, and lots of other goodies. On an earlier adventure, a couple months prior, we had hiked in from a point about midway up the Redfield Wash to the Chick Logan Cliff House in the steep-walled mid-canyon realm. During our night spent there, the ghostlike sounds coming from the basement below turned out to be the nocturnally active, resident ring-tailed cat! This is a unique, small mammal in the racoon family (*Procyonidae*) with a distinctive white and black-banded tail that inhabits rocky desert canyons. One time when we were sitting on the outer retaining wall, this long, fluffy-tailed little beast slithered right underneath us. From Powers Garden on April 6th, we headed back to High Creek via a different route through Corral Canyon:

> 4/6: Day Five: I am anxious to explore Corral Canyon for the first time. Splendid views and ragged weather-eroded rock outcrops along almost constantly flowing stream. Some confusion, until we recognize trail going up N. side of Canyon and proceed along switchbacks, pausing occasionally to sample pinyon nuts (doesn't seem worth the effort). Eventually Kennedy Saddle is attained and shortly thereafter we are rewarded for our efforts with some fine views atop Kennedy Peak (7540'). Trica speaks "fluent Raven" I discover and we lunch heartily on herring, cheese, cucumber slices, granola mixed w/ peanut butter and honey etc. Our best "mileage day," we sustain a good pace until the trail becomes somewhat hazy between Paddy's River Tr. junction and High Creek Trail. Relying on the map, we follow the ridge further where we encounter a greater degree of difficulty and are forced to stop—our momentum lost! Gradually, thru persistent efforts, I am delighted to gain sight of the trail sign which marks our return to the original main trail. Tired but happy, we push on towards High Creek and stumble upon a desirable campsite at last!
>
> 4/7: Day Six: Upon awakening, we enjoy sights and sounds of the birdlife as usual, gather our gear and return to our 1st campsite where Trica retrieves her stashed camera. Taking last drinks of the cold refreshing waters out of several clear pools along an intermittent but lively stream; we head down to the waiting Kharman Ghia and home.
>
> Notes: Weather: 1st 2 nights cold—below freezing, some cloudiness in morn giving way to clear sky and very pleasant temperatures. Spring just getting underway oaks and maples (Gambel oak) still leafless and not many wildflowers blooming.
>
> JB Training/Expedition Logbook, 2/01/1978—8/29/1981

Fast forward from the 20th century to December 11, 2020, when I set out to revisit the Powers Garden cabin to confirm whether any of the old "Cow Camp Chronicles" or "Cow Camp Guest Book" journals of the mid-1970's and early 1980s were still there: once I arrived at the cabin in the late afternoon there wasn't any trace of the original journals. In fact, the earliest date I could find among the existing spiral-bound notebooks was 1998. Of course, I truly did not expect to find them still present in the cabin, after over forty years and all the changes that have taken place: beginning back in 1979 with something called the RARE II

Initiative (Roadless Area Review and Evaluation). This legislative action brought changes to the Galiuro Mountains Wilderness corridor when it was enacted in 1984. While there were some allowances for continuing grazing leases, the corridor was re-designated as a roadless area, effectively closing off the rough dirt access road over Rattlesnake Mesa and Powers Hill to all motorized vehicles. Thus, just as in the early 20th Century, the only means of travel into the Galiuro Mountains Wilderness were now either by hiking or on horseback. In addition, there were plans to remove some of the manmade structures along the corridor such as mining cabins, equipment, and a reduction of the buildings at Powers Garden. (Wilson, 1995)

The outdoor writer Pete Cowgill related the history of the access road into the Rattlesnake Creek corridor and its condition before it was eventually closed off by the Forest Service:

> About 60 years ago three men by the name of Power (Tom Sr. and Jr. and John) [Pete mistakenly referred to the father, Jeff Power, as Tom] built a wagon road from their mine in Kielberg Canyon out to the "main" road near Klondyke, a distance of more than 20 miles through the heart of the Galiuro Mountains. The toughest part of the road was coming out of Rattlesnake Canyon to get on a mesa above. Being practical men, the Powers built this part straight up, no switchbacks or frills. It climbs more than 400 feet in a quarter mile. Over the years the road has weathered. Although at one time it might have been fairly smooth, today much dirt and loose rock has washed away leaving many high rock "steps" and each additional rain loosens more rock and soil. It was "designed" as a wagon road although at least two old pickup trucks were driven down the hill and left at the bottom, one near the hill and the other at Powers Garden. In 1932 most of the Galiuro Mountains, located east of the San Pedro River about 35 miles northwest of Willcox, was made a primitive area. And in 1964 the range was designated a wilderness. Excluded

Meadow scene looking north

> from the wilderness area was the corridor extending from near Powers Hill down Rattlesnake Canyon by Powers Garden and over into Kielberg Canyon. (Cowgill, 1975b)

Cowgill continued in his "On the Trail" column, objecting strongly to the loud, disruptive, and physical impacts of four-wheel drive vehicles that periodically entered the pristine wilderness corridor over this one-time wagon road all the way to Powers Garden:

> Modern self-propelled, wheeled vehicles have no business in the Galiuro Corridor. In the first place the corridor is a ten-mile-long finger bordered by the Galiuro Wilderness Area. Any intrusion by motor vehicles will certainly destroy the wilderness characteristics of the corridor with such by-products as muffler noise and tire tracks. And, secondly, the U. S. Forest Service has tried to close off the road leading into the corridor but has met with little cooperation. (Cowgill, 1975c)

When I first walked down the spectacular half-mile long meadow at Powers Garden in September of 1978 I was astonished at what I saw. Tall pines rose up from thick tree stands above a scene that resembled a higher elevation alpine meadow than the one I was standing on at 4,900 feet. Tree galleries farther back, along both sides of the floodplain, displayed rich multi-colored foliage, including tall, white-barked sycamores and evergreens such as large Arizona cypress and Utah junipers. You could also hear the creek running from some distance away.

Back in April of 1980 when Trica and I visited, I read Mike Isley's response to the journal entry left by the Galiuro Kid on September 22, 1978. More than three weeks after that entry, Mike had replied, "Thanks Joe: Sounds like you had a dandy walk and got to look at some new country."

Of course, I had never met Mike and Nornie in person, I had missed them by four days as evidenced by their journal entry of September 18th:

Concrete horse trough at Powers Garden

> On our way out—branded 2 big heifer calves and one eighteen-month-old maverick heifer this AM. Put 44 head in Kielberg [Canyon] and ten in N. Field [Canyon] (1 steer in Kielberg)—Water is turned off here to force water to run into the Horse Trough—Please turn water off when not in use until water is more plentiful—Be in again soon with more dry cows—
>
> Mike and Nornie Isley, Powers Garden Journals, Part 4: August 6, 1978—March 23, 1979

"So, okay JB, what about these Powers Garden Journals?" I drafted a proposal titled, THE POWERS GARDEN JOURNAL ASSOCIATION (PGJA) PROJECT:

> Prospectus/Mission Statement: I, Joe Billings, as a longtime naturalist who has extensively explored and become familiar with much of the Galiuro Mountains and surrounding area—beginning in the early 1970s—have taken it upon myself to reach out to as many persons who have longstanding working experience and a deep connection to this range; especially within the Powers Garden area along the Rattlesnake Creek corridor. My primary mission is to track down the original journals kept at the Powers Garden cabin during the 1970s through the 1980s, and perhaps earlier. These original journals provide numerous detailed entries of the ranching workday in this primitive wilderness area, as well as those left by visiting horseback riders or hikers such as myself. I vividly remember reading through these journals: they present a colorful, detailed picture of a past era of a rugged style of ranching in this locality that has significant historical value.

New journal binder with historic photos left in cabin by JB

My objective was to reach out to former ranchers, cowboys and cowgirls, ranch owners, former hunting/wilderness guides, current and retired U. S. Forest Service personnel, current and retired Arizona Game and Fish Department managers, local historians and others.

At the same time, thanks to the kindness of Jim Tenney of Willcox, Arizona, Peta-Anne Tenney, and Kathy Klump of the Sulphur Springs Valley Historical Society in Willcox, I gained access to historical volumes of the early pioneers, homesteaders, ranchers, and cowboys in the periphery of the Galiuro Mountains and vicinity of Willcox, Arizona. I was also welcome to visit and peruse the resources of the Sulphur Springs Valley Historical Society in Willcox. So, where did all this lead?

I was most fortunate to have conversations with Mike Isley from his home in Idaho, who was very helpful in suggesting a number of people to contact. I worked up a list of fifteen people from varied walks of life from Mike's suggestions and through my own research. I mailed out my two-page PGJA-Project forms, ornamented with historic photos, to all fifteen on the list. In addition, I contacted just over half directly by phone.

Mural near the Rex Allen "Arizona Cowboy" Museum and Willcox Cowboy Hall of Fame, Willcox, Arizona

Ultimately, David Mehalic, a U.S. Forest Service archaeologist, was instrumental in locating the original journals and provided them in digital format. They were in six spiral binders and ranged over about three-and-a-half years between August 28, 1977 through February 14, 1981. My plan was to provide them in both digital and printed form in a large binder to the Sulphur Springs Valley Historical Society where they could be archived and made available to the public.

The Powers Garden Journals open a window into historic cattle ranching in a mountain wilderness by a close-knit family that all pulled together in the same direction to get each day's work done. Except on rare occasions to deliver hay bales or mattresses to the cabin—in one instance—all supplies were brought in from Deer Creek Ranch over the nine or ten miles of trail by pack strings of two-five horses; occasionally with a mule in the mix. The trip took about three hours each way and items packed in included salt blocks, horse feed (grain-oats), food items for the cabin, hardware for fixing gates and water lines, etc., and butane for the refrigerator.

Both Mike and Nornie Isley were born and raised in Lemhi County, Idaho, near the town of Salmon. Nornie grew up in a rural setting without television and radio where reading and storytelling became a big part of family life. She attended the University of Idaho, majoring in English. Mike grew up loving the cowboy life, and those aspirations led to him qualifying for the High School Rodeo finals at Hattetsville, Texas, where he won 3rd place in the saddle bronc riding event. He joined the Idaho Cowboys Association in 1955; a group that later inducted him into the Idaho Cowboy Hall of Fame in 2008. In 1957 he became a member of the national Rodeo Cowboys Association (before it changed to the PRCA). In both 1961 and 1963 he qualified for the National Finals Rodeo in bareback bronc riding.

Nornie, who was born into a pioneer ranching family, joined another one when she and Mike were married in Salmon, Idaho, in 1956. In the mid-1970's the Isley family left their ranching operation in Lemhi County, relocating to Deer Creek Ranch in a remote part of Graham County, Arizona. Over the next eight years, they would make their new home next door to the Galiuro Mountains Wilderness. The nearest towns were Willcox, fifty-five miles to the southeast and Safford, fifty-eight miles to the northeast. In this isolated area, there was no TV reception and limited signals from radio stations. The ranch consisted of 160 deeded acres with 2,000 acres of state leased land. Hereford cattle were the predominant breed. (Stark, 2011)

I did not grow up on a ranch but had exposure to horses and cattle through early camping experiences and many years of hiking across rangelands. Throwing a rope, or lariat, either

Mike upside down, flipped off saddle bronc; both airborne (Photo by John DeVere Helfrich and courtesy of Mike Isley.)

Mike Isley on Slick leading a pack string back to Deer Creek Ranch from Powers Garden (Photo by Nornie Isley).

houlihan or western style, came naturally to me. On occasion, I met and got to know individual ranchers. As I began to read through the journals, I wasn't sure how I could interpret them to a wide audience of readers. But I kept at it, reading over them continuously while selecting certain ones that were good descriptions of the seasonal stocking of cattle into the winter range, or taking them out during the spring and summer round-up periods. Gradually, I began to perceive a regular pattern in the way all these activities were linked over the course of a full year.

There were essentially five primary activities integrated into this pattern of fall/winter and spring/summer seasons and the preliminary preparation periods for each season.

1) Scouting resources over winter range areas, usually within favored canyons and removing overgrowth and clearing trails was a major preliminary task. Forest Service personnel, cooperatively, engaged in much of this trail-clearing work, sometimes referred to as "brushing," on a regular basis. Affirming the presence of available water resources beforehand in canyon streambeds and at springs was critical.

2) Packing in salt blocks to distribute around these same areas was done in advance and sometimes additional blocks were brought in later. According to Mike Isley, the main reasons for putting out salt blocks for cattle are the minerals contained in them, and since cattle are drawn to them, the blocks also help to concentrate cattle in areas where they can be more effectively rounded up later on.

3) Packing in supplies for sustained work periods during winter range-stocking and spring/summer round-up periods: this was also something done in advance and on occasion pack strings were ridden out to supply camps set up further out into the range where much open country was being scouted for cattle, such as in the Holdout Spring country, at Sycamore Canyon and other parts.

Tortilla Trail: View from interior of the range

4) Now the stage was set for the main function of the ranching op-

eration: concentrating cattle in areas of the mountains with prime forage and sufficient water resources from late fall, winter and spring. Cattle would remain on these grounds between three and a half to seven or eight months.

5) Then, beginning in late spring, advance scouting across the range for these same foraging cattle would serve as preparation for the other principal function of the ranching operation: rounding up cattle across all the prime forage areas and herding them back towards headquarters. This sometimes required several stages during which cattle were temporarily penned in a holding pasture before being moved further down the Tortilla Trail towards the Deer Creek Ranch.

The journal entries also describe cattle driven far enough "over the top" along the Tortilla Trail, where the trail descends steeply towards Sycamore Creek. From this point, most of the cattle continued gradually to Mud Springs—a major watering hole—before eventually winding up at the ranch. Of course, stragglers remaining along the trail were later moved along upon the Isleys' return to headquarters.

Both the fall/winter range-stocking season and spring/summer round-up periods often required staying out in field camps on the range or at the Powers Garden cabin, for up to two to three weeks in order to fully accomplish the work mission.

From late August 1977 through mid-February of 1981, which covers all six binders of the Powers Garden Journals, there were 204 entries written. Those who lived at the Deer Creek Ranch Headquarters accounted for 102 of these: 93 from the Isley family and 9 from the Von Trapp family who succeeded the Isleys as owners later in the early 1980's. U.S. Forest Service personnel left 46 entries, with the remaining 56 from mostly visitors hiking in or riding in on horseback, along with a few occasional 4-wheelers. The six members of the Isley family had distinctive writing styles that could be recognized in the absence of the name at the top or bottom of each entry.

Rustic barn at Powers Garden

The simplified chart below reflects my best and most accurate interpretations of all the movements of cattle between the Ranch and the Galiuro Mountains Wilderness over a two-year period. Individual chart dates for entries selected as representative journal entries associated with the chart are marked with ♦:

INVENTORY OF CATTLE MOVED BETWEEN DEER CREEK RANCH HEADQUARTERS AND THE RATTLESNAKE CREEK CORRIDOR/GALIURO WILDERNESS DURING 1977, 1978, and 1979

DATE	CATTLE FROM HQ >	CORRIDOR	/ CATTLE TO HQ >
	WINTER STOCKING THE RANGE		
♦10/23/77	117 head >	Pipestem Canyon	
12/03/77	37 + 5 (Sycamore C.) >	Lower Mailbox Canyon	
1/15/78	59 (heifers) >	Holdout Spring Country	
	SPRING THROUGH SUMMER ROUND-UP		
♦4/20/78		From Rattlesnake Corr >	20 head
♦5/02/78		From Holdout Spring >	50 head
5/09/78		From Little Horse C. >	15 head
5/10/78		From Little Horse C. >	13 head
5/15/78		From Pipestem Canyon >	17 head
♦5/22/78		From Pipestem Canyon >	15 head
5/23/78		From Pipestem Canyon >	18 head
5/27/78		From Pipestem Canyon >	23 head
7/04/78		From Rattlesnake Corr >	8 head
	WINTER STOCKING THE RANGE		
9/16/78	50 head (dry cows) >	Kielberg C. (40), N. Field C. (10)	

11/07/78	175 head >	Pipestem, Field C. and other areas
3/22/79	20 cows + 6 bulls* >	Douglas and N. Field Canyons
3/31/79	15 head (+ calves) >	Douglas Canyon

SPRING THROUGH SUMMER ROUND-UP

5/24/79	From P-stem > Horse >	40-50 head
5/30/79	From Mailbox > L. Horse >	14 head
6/01/79	From Rattlesnake Corr >	5 head
6/09/79	From Lower Mailbox C. >	3 head
6/13/70	From P-stem > "a good sized bunch"	
6/15/79	From Sonora Basin** >	22 head
6/26/79	From ? > Holding Pasture >	10 head
8/14/79	From Rattlesnake Corr >	10 head

*St. Gertrudis Bulls

** Area between Horse and Sycamore Canyons, within 1 mile E of Rattlesnake Creek Trail.

October 10, 1977

Wife, Nornie and I in from Deer Creek, 2 saddle horses, 1 pack mule, and 1 pack horse. Going to muck trail out up Pipestem [Canyon] and put out salt in same canyon. Should be in with some cattle in about a wk or 10 days.

Powers Garden Journals, Part 1

♦October 23, 1977 (Sunday)

The "cow crew" made it in at around 6:30 pm. Bettina and Lola came in earlier to start supper, etc. We left H.Q. at 6:30 am. That's 12 hours of hard work and riding! We brought in all (we think) 117 head. That is quite a deal getting' um in! But they're all here so .... Whoose complaining? Nornie will come in today to help get the cattle to Pipestem. Bettina and Lola will go out today cuz I have to go to school tomorrow. (Sigh!) —

Bettina Isley, Powers Garden Journals, Part 1

January 5, 1978

Mick Isley came from Headquarters via Sycamore Canyon, went up Pipestem and came down Mailbox. Next day went up to Holdout to check the water after the rain. Leaving today Jan. 5. Place was very tidy.

Mick Isley, Powers Garden Journals: Part 2

April 16, 1978 (Sunday)

Mike and Nornie Isley arrived P.M. yesterday with a 2 head pack string—(mostly oats)—we'll be here till Thursday to make ready for spring work back here—Rattlesnake really ran big again both water gaps out again —

N. I., Powers Garden Journals, Part 3

♦April 20, 1978 (Thursday)

Leaving: Taking about 20 head of cows, 1 bull—and at last count 4 calves out with us for a start to the front—Will be in again very soon to round up and take out heifers from Holdout [Spring pasture]—

Mike and Nornie Isley, Powers Garden Journals, Part 3

♦May 2, 1978 (Tuesday)

We got in with about 50 head of cattle Saturday evening just before dark—Camped three nites just below mine at Gold Mountain—mine entrance makes a lovely refrigerator—Rode Holdout country—Went over into Redfield and checked out Kielberg. We are still out a few head but have most of them—Paul and Sandra Wallace [friends from Safford, AZ] left Sunday AM. and later that morning we we took our cattle and moved them into the stock driveway up Little Horse Canyon—Most of them will drift to Headquarters on their own—the stragglers we'll have to push—Yesterday we worked up Little Horse all day and when we arrived home in the rain were welcomed by Walt and Chuck from the U.S.F.S. district office in Safford—In to take some pictures and analyze the fire situation. Rained 30/100 during the night but early this morning they left on a long trip up to Kielberg Saddle, Grassy Peak, Grassy Ridge and along the High Trail to Pipestem and down—Started raining about 8AM but they will surely persevere in defense of our nation's resources—!—We have been graining our horses twice a day and letting them run on the mountain—This morning for the first time, they refused to come down when Mike called them. — We certainly appreciate the intelligence of our horses—they knew it was going to be a soaker and that we had no business out in it. — So—We'll watch it rain from the comfort of the cabin while we bake and clean a little and rest a lot —

Mike and Nornie Isley, Powers Garden Journals, Part 3

♦May 22, 1978 (Monday)

Arrived in from upper Pipestem yesterday afternoon — met a trail crew of YACC men [Young Adult Conservation Corps] — So happy they are going to clear the High Trail to Grassy Ridge — Cotton Gatlin [USFS trail maintenance foreman, YACC Co-ordinator and mule packer] is packing for them — and will be here at the Gardens till the end of the week. — I am going out today for a few supplies and to check in at headquarters — Will bring in Bettina and be back Wednesday — Mike will stay and finish shaking cattle out of Pipestem — We have been in here two weeks — Fun — Work! —

Mike and Nornie Isley, Powers Garden Journals: Part 3

August 7, 1978

Forest Service crew leaving this morning by way of Sycamore Trail. Spent week brushing Mailbox to Pipestem and part of Douglas Trails. We worked on pasture gates but ran out of wire so did what we could with what we had. Hope to be back in two weeks to brush up to Crooked Dam.

Rick Shirley (USFS), Powers Garden Journal: Part 4

December 19, 1978

Three rain-soaked hikers arrived here yesterday (same as those of Dec. 15) and fully appreciated having a dry, warm cabin to stay in. We were camped right below Rhodes Peak on the west ridge trail when the storm came with rain and high winds. Stayed there two nights but left yesterday morning in the pouring rain to seek more protection. Hiked down South Field Trail to Powers Garden; the creek along the trail was flooding and we repeatedly had to cross the creek in fast and deep water. Huge waterfalls, tumbling rocks, mud, very exciting but very wet. Arrived at the cabin finally, drenched and cold, and saw that Rattlesnake Creek was flooding. The creek was a raging torrent and came a third of the way up the corral below the cabin — The tall Ponderosa pines in the field were in the middle of the creek. The pond was overflowing and water was just pouring down the mountains. Rain finally stopped last night and the creek went down considerably but is still very high— too high to cross safely. So we hiked around today, chopped wood, dried out and hope to leave early tomorrow if it doesn't rain again tonight. Looks threatening, though. Thanks for the open cabin.

Susan Georgette (Santa Cruz, CA), Powers Garden Journals: Part 4

February 3, 1980 (Sunday)

Ground Hog sure saw his shadow yesterday — Weather last two days beautiful — Shirt sleeve — When Mike got in Wednesday evening, he had two cats top packed on that big blue horse. They made the trip quite nicely — a black and white pussy named Beauty and a yellow striped tom named Chester (had a bad gimp in his younger days). We have a feeder for them in the back room and they have the run of the place — Please treat them kindly — They're working — Mice and rats take notice. We packed salt yesterday — Mike in Field (N and S) and Mailbox — and I went up Corral and Douglas — No sign of cattle above Corral — Will go out tomorrow — — Be in again soon to work on water system and see about cats.

Nornie Isley, Powers Garden Journals: Part 5

Saturday, April 5, 1980

Hello all -

I'm ½ of the young couple from Tucson that Brent mentioned. We met those nice gentlemen here yesterday and decided to sleep elsewhere: at the mouth of Horse Canyon. H was quite nice indeed. We came back here this morning to a very clean house; those guys sure did well. We will also do our part for this special place, thank you all. I was brought here by "the Galiuro Kid" himself, a respectable young man who knows these mountains quite well. I'm honored. Perhaps someday everyone could meet everyone; there would be a lot to talk about. Sounds like you guys are quite busy in here. That's a good thought.

The cats are doing well — lots of food left for them. They were given steak bones by the men here last night — FAT CATS! Doing their job well! There's about 4 cows hanging around here, one with a fiesty young calf. Looking good — Take care, sure appreciate the sweet afternoon spent here.

Sincerely, Trica, Powers Garden Journals, Part 6

April 5, 1980

Howdy Folks, Well, it's been a while since my last trip thru here back in September of 1978 when I went from Redington to the Garden and out Schoenholzer Canyon to the west. I'm pleased to see everything in good shape; with the exception of vehicle tracks all the way down to the beginning of the jeep road beyond Holdout Spring: Vehicles do not belong in here! This time came in from High Creek accompanied by a little blonde wildcat named Trica who shares the same feelings I have for these unique mountains — may they always remain as they are now — wild and remote with their own special beauty! Going out through some new country for "The Kid," up Corral Canyon to Kennedy Pk and back to High Creek Road. As usual, enjoyed stay (Horse Canyon) and use of cabin. Will return, regards, Your friend,

Joe "Galiuro Kid" Billings, Powers Garden Journals, Part 6

Tortilla Trail: View of northeast side of the range

Flintknapping tools

Chapter Four

Self-Taught Flintknapper

During an early period, an all-consuming passion found me spending long hours out under the hot sun roaming over the landscape, seeking to make sense of all the scattered flaked stone remnants left by ancient hunter craftsmen. My personal study of flaked stone tool technology and interpretation of lithic materials began through the "hands-on" method of learning and developing skills, with only the most rudimentary notion of the Hertzian cone principle. The simple physics of this are best demonstrated by a drive-by shooting into a plate glass window: The perpendicular force of the bullet striking the glass creates a cone-shaped hole by the 130° angle of force radiating outward from the point of impact and measuring 100° on the inside. This is the most fundamental guiding principle of the craft and applying it soon becomes second nature. (Callahan, 1979, Waldorf, 1984)

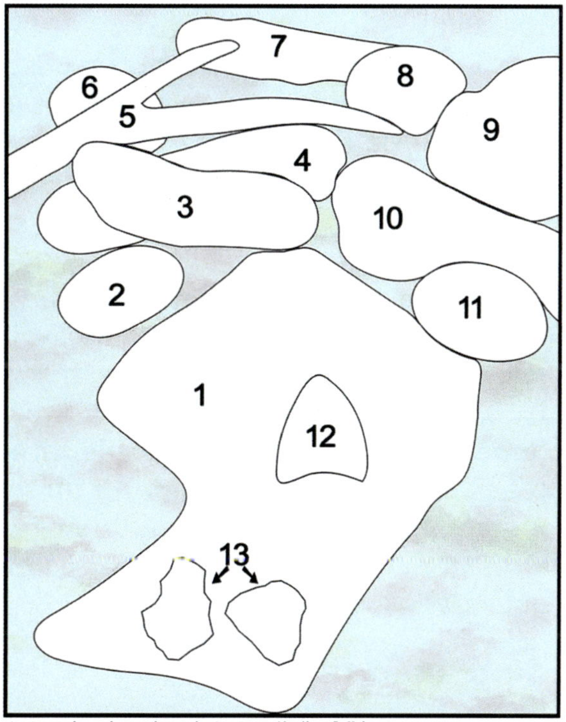

1: Leather hand pad, 2: Small, "soft" hammerstone, 3: Deer antler billet, 4: Stone billet, 5: Double tine deer antler flaker, 6: Hammerstone, 7: Billet, 8: Ball of modeling clay, 9: Pumice grinding stone, 10: Elk antler billet, 11: Small quartzite hammerstone, 12: Fluted spearpoint, 13: Channel flakes

Acquiring a feel for working various native rock types through constant practice over a long period of time was essential for attaining progressively higher skill levels. One of my first raw material procurement/working sites was within the vast acreage of the old Irvington Landfill site of Pima County, on Tucson's southeast side. Here I spent hours sitting on an overturned five-gallon bucket under the blazing summer sun and questionable shade of a Palo Verde tree, chipping out some of my first crude bifaces and points from locally gathered surface rock.

Fine-grained basalt arrowpoint made from Whitlock quarry location

My approach focused on using the same tool kit available to the aboriginal craftsman: an assortment of different sized hammerstones and antler billets were the primary instruments for initial reduction and percussion flaking. Later, finishing-stage pressure flaking to sharpen the edges was accomplished using stone-ground, sharpened antler tines while holding the point with a protective leather pad. Concurrent with knapping practice, developing a trained eye for recognizing and finding suitable raw materials was gained with continuous trial and error sampling, and many miles of prospecting over the desert landscape. If the ancient flintknappers were the first geologists, then I too, was taking a crude, caveman back door route into this field of science! (Billings, 2016)

Along this path, I developed a good basic working knowledge of paleontology and archaeology that led to becoming a crew member with an archaeological excavation and survey firm, Cultural and Environmental Systems, Inc., based in Tucson, Arizona. My own "hands-on" approach towards acquiring knowledge seemed to be perfectly compatible with the Company's "learn by doing" philosophy! From spring through fall of 1989, I had a unique opportunity to get paid doing archaeological excavation work, drawing maps, screening/recording artifacts and doing field surveys.

Green metasediment arrowpoint made at old Irvington Landfill location

Cienega Man

At the same time, there was continuing independent exploration to add to my base of knowledge discovering or verifying remote prehistoric stone quarry sites. Many prospective sites were the result of intensively studying unique features and tantalizing areas found on topographic maps, or well-worn, ancient issues of *The Desert Magazine*. One such destination was in the area of the Whitlock Mountains, east of Safford, Arizona. Here amongst the most remote, desolate, but fascinating badlands along the east edge of the San Simon Valley, I found extensive outcroppings of a fine-grained black basaltic rock. Several raw chunks of this material were later worked into some of my earliest arrowheads. Exploration deeper into this area of outcroppings led to a core area where it was evident that much aboriginal quarrying had taken place here.

An extensive number of assorted flakes, shatter, cores and debris were visible throughout a wide expanse and radiating outward from the site. Occasionally, while exploring distant areas several miles from the site, flakes of this familiar basaltic rock would be re-sighted. On

View of hilltop quarry outcrop overlooking Rincon Valley (Photo by Elton Kerr)

one frigidly cold night in early January 1989, while wearing a headlamp, I discovered a scrub jay—one of my favorite birds—asleep tucked into a rock crevice. I carefully and gently removed it just long enough to examine it, before putting it back into the same exact spot. The bird did not awaken.

Another very different site in the Rincon Mountains, near Tucson, was discovered in the early 1990s. A distinctive blue-black rock stood out in sharp contrast to the surrounding geology, atop a rocky ridge. Here were outcroppings intensively worked, with abundant stacks of broken chunks of rock with some very large spalls. The outlying terrace around the outcrops was densely paved with smaller flaking debris, with some unusually large hammerstones embedded in the ground. A series of motifs, or petroglyphs, pecked into the brownish patina of large outcropping boulders were found in another locus of the site. (Simpson and Wells, 1984)

In July 1993, I returned to the quarry site, accompanied by good friend and photographer Elton Kerr. We covered the site systematically to fully document existing artifacts, such as the hammerstones, petroglyphs, the core outcrop area, surrounding flake debris field, and scenic views in all directions. Elton was intrigued with blooming barrel cacti *(Ferocactus sp.)* onsite, and his photos captured cactus flowers in the red—orange—yellow color spectrum. The different forms and sizes of hammerstones embedded in the desert pavement were truly impressive! Roughly softball-sized, or ellipsoid-shaped ones for one-handed usage were more common. Then, in the two-handed category, several very large, oblong hammerstones were found that weighed at least an es-

Close-up of petroglyph at hilltop quarry in the Rincons

timated thirty to forty pounds! All examined and photographed hammerstones were then replaced back in embedded *in situ* locations. Fortunately, this unique and precious ancient site became part of the newly expanded Saguaro National Park East unit later in 1993.

Large, oblong embedded hammerstone weighing twenty to twenty-five pounds

Once you've gained some proficiency with chipping out some decent spearpoints, it's a natural progression to start figuring out how to assemble the complete weaponry. At least this was true in my case. These pursuits began in the late 1980s but came to the greatest fruition in the early 1990s. Just as with the flintknapping toolkit, all of my projects employed only stone tools and the same natural materials that would have been available to the ancient hunter-craftsman. These activities were primarily centered in the areas surrounding Cienega Creek, east of Vail, Arizona; hence, the adoption of my paleo alter ego, "Cienega Man."

Running concurrently with projects and of critical importance, I conducted intensive research at the University of Arizona Main, Science, and Museum Libraries. This research produced detailed descriptions of atlatls (spear throwers) and their associated spears or more appropriately described "dart shafts" recovered from caves. (Guernsey and Kidder 1921, Guernsey 1931, Fenenga and Wheat 1940, Cosgrove 1947)

Blue-black biface made from Rincon quarry andesite

Side profile of biface

My first compound atlatl, or spear thrower project, began in February of 1990, after I discovered a fallen cottonwood sapling (*Populus fremontii*) while exploring along the Creek. Once I found a suitable branch, I cut it to an appropriate length, planed and shaped the surface, using sharp-edged stone flakes. Being a compound rather than a one-piece atlatl meant that instead of carving out a groove and spur into the wood of one end, as was customary with most aboriginal models, I needed an antler spur. I cut and shaped a whitetail deer antler spur, trimmed and worked it into the desired shape by scraping, planing, and grinding. The base resembled an elongated wedge with vertical scoring along the sides added for better adherence. I gouged a notch into the thickest end of the atlatl to receive the precision-made spur. During this process, my earlier research into ethnobotanical sources, Castetter and Underhill, 1935, Bell and Castetter, 1937, and Bell and Castetter, 1941, came in handy. I collected resin from local brittlebush shrubs (*Encelia farinosa*), heated it to a liquid state, and poured it into the antler spur slot, and set the spur firmly into place. (It works like Super Glue.)

Compound atlatl made using fresh-struck stone tools

For the next stage, I had to wait until March when daytime temperatures reached at least 82°F, allowing the dark sap of mesquite trees to begin running. In the meantime, I was fortunate to discover an exposed root section of a large catclaw bush *(Acacia greggii)*, due to recent excavation work along the railroad embankment above Cienega Creek. I used a length of this root for forming the finger loops near the handle into a pattern shaped like a pair of scissors. I scored the edge and undersides of the distal end of the atlatl shaft in preparation for binding the finger loops to it. Then I wrapped the portion

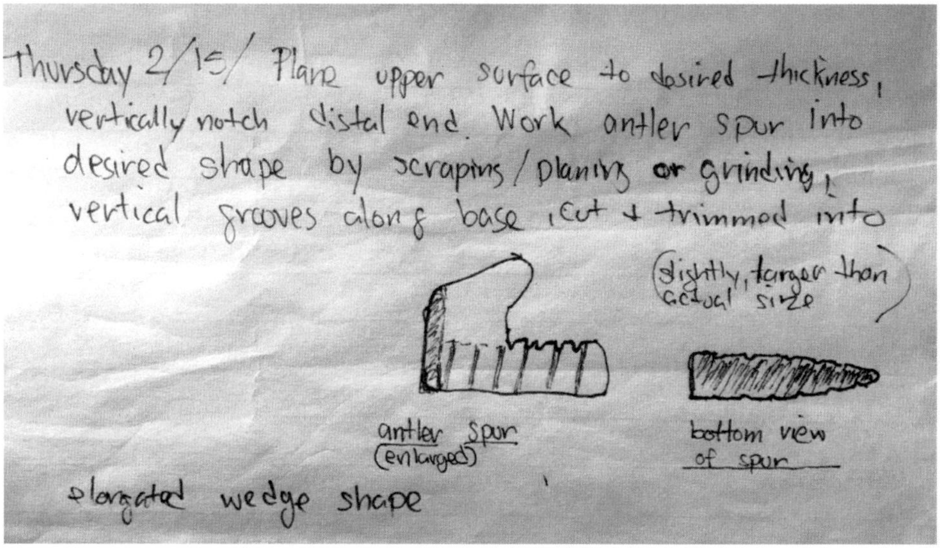

Illustration of antler spur; side and bottom profile

against the shaft with yucca fiber bindings (*Yucca baccata*).

On Sunday, March 5th, I found an ideal stand of trees above the north bank of Cienega Creek near Marsh Station Road, not far from where it intersects Interstate 10. One tree in particular was especially productive with furrows below seeps of sap acting like little "ink wells!" I went back four or five times to this tree. I applied this mesquite resin (*Prosopis velutina*) to the lower section of the handle—finger loops—to strengthen, seal, and protect the yucca fiber bindings. I used sections of yucca measuring one quarter of an inch by four inches as brushes, scraping fleshy skin off both sides and separating individual fibers. As soon as resin hardened while using one, I discarded it and put another one to use, or I simply used the opposite ends in similar fashion. Then the same binding and resin coat was applied to the antler spur end of the atlatl, and I set it aside to allow the resin to harden and cure satisfactorily. As a finishing touch, the ends were sanded down with a piece of sandstone.

My dart shafts were made from mostly vertical willow shoots (*Salix spp.*) which I detached along the creek bed at ground level with a sharp-edged stone flake knife. I also collected a small number of non-native salt cedar (*Tamarix spp.*) shoots, but I discarded these harder wood shafts due to a tendency to dry out and split apart.

Once gathered, the next stage for the five-to-six foot green dart shafts involved trimming and planing off irregularities with fresh-struck, sharp-edged flakes. A small campfire produced a circle of glowing embers which I used to heat points along the shafts that needed to be straightened. Then a gentle bending with just the right amount of force at each point, resulted in a truer alignment. A grooved pumice stone could also be heated in the embers and the shafts inserted within the groove, for more direct application of heat. I found the former technique satisfactory, however, and mainly used the grooved pumice stone for evenly smoothing the shafts down as a finishing task.

I opportunistically gathered feathers from road kills (roadrunners, usually) for fletching the shafts to improve flight stability or from local aviaries (turkeys, etc.). Three split tail feather sections were mounted on the proximal ends and wrapped with either sinew (also from occasional road kills) or fine-threaded yucca fiber. At the end of this shaft, I drilled a small cup-shaped hole—using a stone drill—to fit the spur of my first handmade compound atlatl!

Roaming across the desert landscape carrying a spear or stone tool, one becomes aware of the hand-brain connection and how that link stimulates thinking and one's perception of himself. I believe this same self-awareness and perception experienced by primitive hunter-craftsmen and myself—a 20th century caveman—are universal. Now that I—Cienega Man—possessed a functional compound atlatl, my weaponry kit was more or less complete! While I learned how to craft short fore shafts with hafted stone projectile points, I left most of my finished dart shafts with either blunt, or roughly pointed ends, especially since they were going to be subjected to severe usage with the extensive practice required for learning how to throw them with the atlatl.

The spear thrower, also referred to by the Aztec name *atl atl*, proliferated around the world prehistorically, is still suspected to be in recent use by Eskimos, Australian bushmen, and remote Mexican and South American Indians. (Stirling 1960, Gould 1970, Raymond 1970) In effect, it is a lever, or extension of the human arm that can throw a spear at least two or three times farther and with more penetrating power than with the arm alone. Both the atlatl and dart shaft can be viewed as springs loading and releasing energy. I did not attempt to do more extensive studies and testing beyond just getting a basic feel for the proper use of the weaponry with a limited amount of quantified field testing.

Fortunately, I had ample room in the adjacent cow pasture across from where I lived to set up several targets using anchored wire cages. Upon this structure I fastened 3½ by 3½ foot, 4-layered cardboard panels, with the top edge at four to five feet above the ground. One-half-inch plywood sections of similar dimensions were placed behind these cardboard panels. Initial distances were fifteen paces marked off, or from forty-five to fifty feet. When I established some consistency hitting the center of these targets, distances were extended out to twenty to twenty-five yards, or sixty to seventy-five feet.

From the outset, accuracy and control were difficult to master so I studied Anan Raymond's essay on the atlatl which includes description and illustrations of proper throwing motion, (Raymond, 1986) a helpful model of throwing technique. In the beginning of the motion, the index and middle fingers occupy the finger loops with the thumb and ring finger loosely clasping the dart shaft. As I see it, the motion is essentially a forward lunge with three parts: 1) With weight on back foot, spear is "cocked" or extended backward while being raised slightly, maintaining spear in a level plane. 2) With spear in cocked position, thrower steps toward target planting the opposite foot well enough forward to achieve bent knee at 90° or so. 3) With thrower in "cocked-lunge" position, thrower "fires" the dart in straight line toward the target with follow through as wrist rotates downward, flexing atlatl (like bow) before release.

The penetrating force and power of Cienega Man's first spear thrower were self-evident. The darts with unmodified, blunt ends repeatedly went through the half inch plywood backing on successive throws. Consistent accuracy at hitting small six inch by six inch, or slightly larger bullseyes proved to be elusive, though with extended practice and refinement of weaponry, this could be significantly improved. I did not consider using attached stone weights as were sometimes found on aboriginal models. (Fenenga and Wheat, 1940) An experienced experimental archaeologist in the El Paso, Texas area named George Bird (1985) claimed there was no noticeable difference in performance between weighted and unweighted atlatls. Overall, this was only a very rudimentary field test of limited depth, using a single atlatl model and a narrow size range of dart shafts. It raised questions regarding the relationship of atlatl length to dart length: Longer spears may well be better balanced and controlled with longer atlatls.

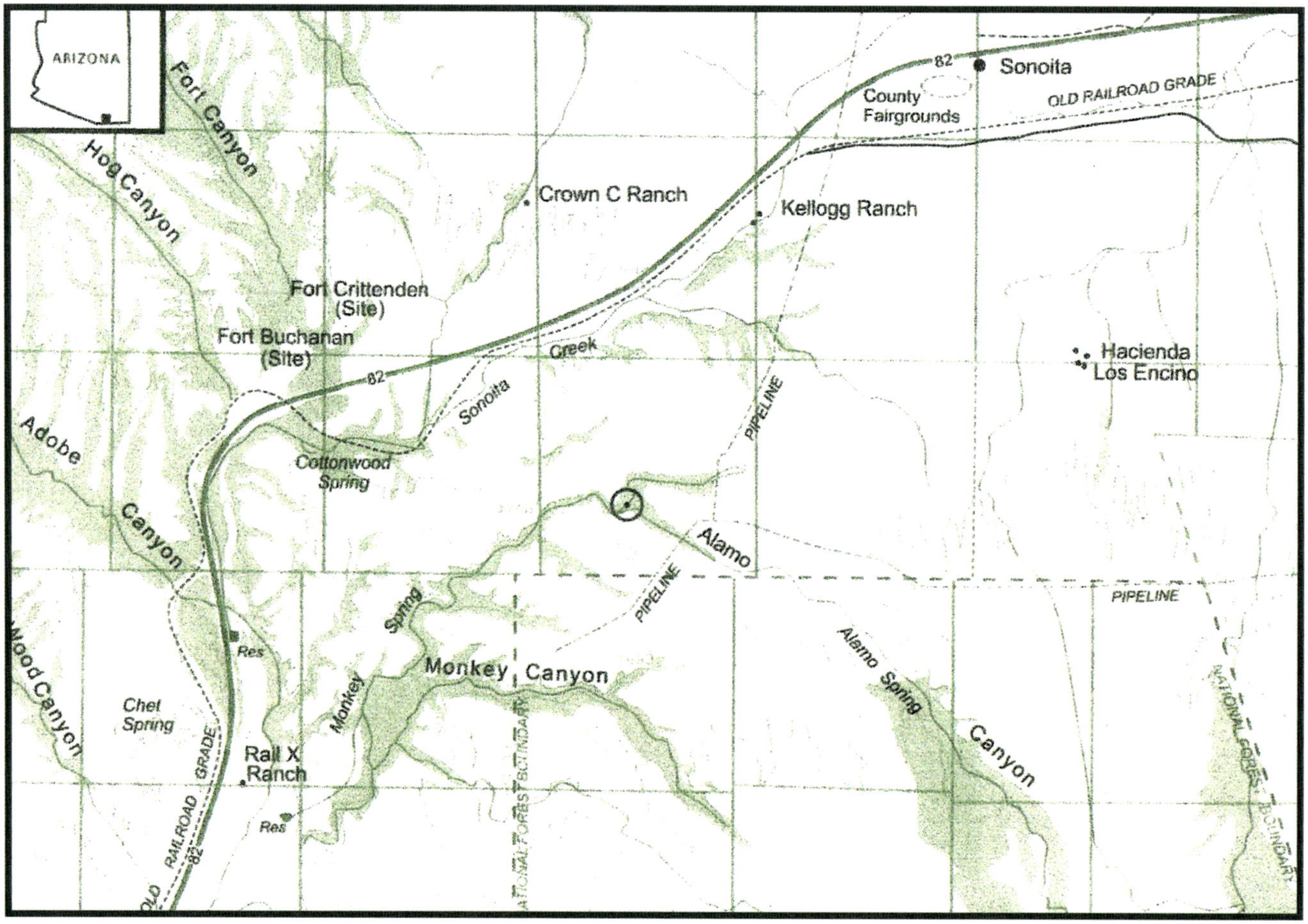

Map of the Alamo Canyon area of Southern Arizona showing the location of the Billings mastodon find. (Map courtesy of C. Vance Haynes, Jr.; image copied from USGS Elgin 15-minute quadrangle)

Chapter Five

The 11,000-Year-Old Mastodon

Arroyo bank with the Billings Mastodon skeletal remains (Photo by C. Vance Haynes, Jr.)

On a clear sunny day back in July of 1985, I was working solo on a landscaping project—setting railroad tie steps down a hillside property—for a client in the Tunnel Springs area south of Sonoita, Arizona. After work, I took off to roam and explore the surrounding countryside. Coming around a curving bend of Alamo Canyon, while closely scanning a steeply cut earthen bank, a cluster of small whitish flecks trailing down the embankment caught my attention. As I moved in for closer inspection, the whitish material did not resemble any rock I was familiar with—turning out instead to be small pieces of ivory! I gazed upward above the trail of this exotic material to the barely recognizable outline of something embedded in the steep bank above me.

Using a small sharp stick, I ever so carefully removed the soil around this object until it was fully exposed enough to gently loosen and lift out clear of the bank. This strange and amazing piece I held in my hand, was clearly some sort of tooth, but of what? (Indeed, there were visible green stains still encrusted upon it!)

What I didn't know then, but soon came to find out, was that I was now in possession of perhaps the most diagnostically distinct piece—a molar—with which to identify one particular large, extinct mammal of the late Pleistocene megafauna: *Mammut americanum*, or American mastodon—a Proboscidean of the family *Mammutidae.* While appearing similar in form to *Mammuthus*, of the elephant tribe, mastodons are actually distant relatives. Compared to the Colombian mammoths that also inhabited Arizona during the Pleistocene, mastodons were smaller, with flatter heads and shorter legs. They were primarily browsers, using their massive tusks gathering twigs, leaves and roots, in forested environments. In contrast, the great mammoths were grazers, consuming huge quantities of grass while roaming upon the open plains. (Amman, et al., 1998)

Mastodon molar extracted from arroyo bank. (Photo by C. Vance Haynes, Jr.)

So, when placed side-by-side, the flat grinding tooth plates of the mammoth and the cone-shaped ridges of the mastodon molar reveal a clear distinction between these two large beasts. (Stock, 1972)

I contacted the property owner and the University of Arizona Department of Geosciences, and from that discovery forward over the next several months, plans for an upcoming site excavation were coordinated. I took the molar specimen into the University of Arizona Laboratory of Paleontology (UALP). Here, Lab Curator Kevin Moody placed it in a vacuum chamber in a process that removed all existing moisture and effectively sealed the specimen, hardening it with a preservative and making it much less susceptible to deterioration.

Close-up of the arroyo bank showing channel (above trench shovel) containing mastodon bones between the large root and its shadow. (Photo by C. Vance Haynes, Jr.)

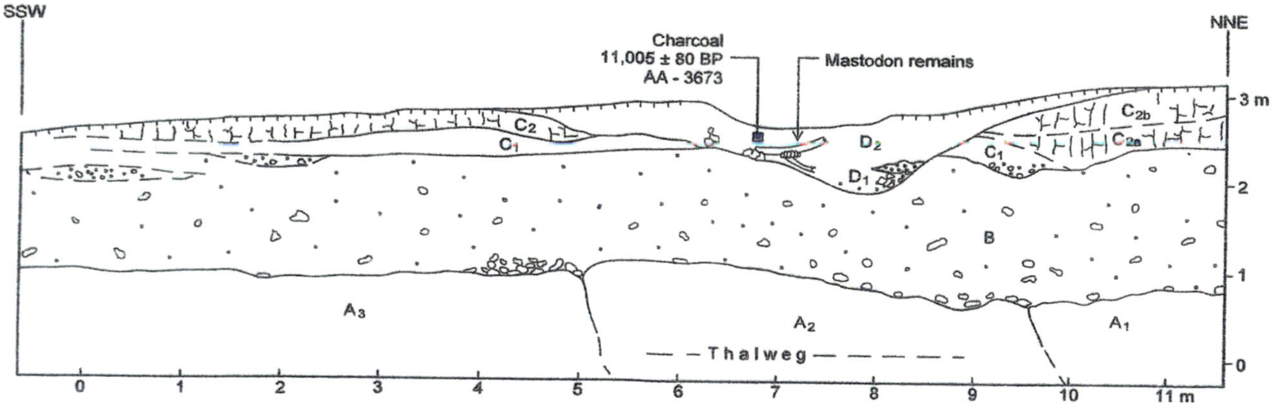

Geologic cross-section of arroyo wall showing mastodon skeletal remains in channel, Stratum D, and stratigraphic position of charoal dated by radiocarbon analysis. (Image courtesy of C. Vance Haynes, Jr.)

On the morning of November 2nd of 1985, I guided a group from the University of Arizona to the site of my discovery in Alamo Canyon. They were mostly graduate students, led by Geo-archaeologist C. Vance Haynes, Jr., and Paleontologist Everett H. Lindsay. A lot of concentrated effort by a dedicated group of people resulted in an entire excavation in a single day.

They uncovered the partial skull and tusk, along with another three or four molars recovered to go with my original sharp stick-removed specimen. Fragments of the femur of a deer-sized mammal were also collected from the deposit.

Watching the slow, painstaking process of applying plaster-soaked wrappings to create a sturdy "jacket" around the large heavy tusk, someone got the bright idea of breaking off a thick, curved piece of root from the bank to install with the plaster jacket as a carrying handle!

Excavation of mastodon tusk and molar (Photo by C. Vance Haynes, Jr.)

Earlier that morning, I remember Bruce Huckell—a graduate student—coming up from a survey of the canyon and surrounding area and handing me a stream-worn lithic that appeared to be black silicified limestone. A master flintknapper, lithics specialist, and archaeologist, Bruce knew my passion for stone after I had met him previously at one of his flintknapping demonstrations.

Much later and long after that memorable day, in October 1993, I received a letter from Dr. Haynes, in which he said, "I wanted to let you know that the charcoal we collected from the sediment burying the Billings Mastodon radiocarbon dated 11,005 ± 80 B.P. (AA-3673) on the Arizona—NSF accelerator mass spectrometer. The mastodon is either of this age or a bit older but definitely latest Pleistocene ..." A later Preliminary Report on the Mastodon goes on to suggest the probability that the channel fill ... correlates with the Clovis-age channel fills at the Murray Springs, Lehner, and Naco Clovis sites of the San Pedro Valley. Noting this—there was nothing observed or recovered indicating any human association with the Mastodon remains. In a more recently published article, Dr. Haynes added: "It is another example of the extinction of the megafauna at the end of the Pleistocene 13,000 cal. yr. BP [calibrated years before present]." (Haynes, et al., 2016)

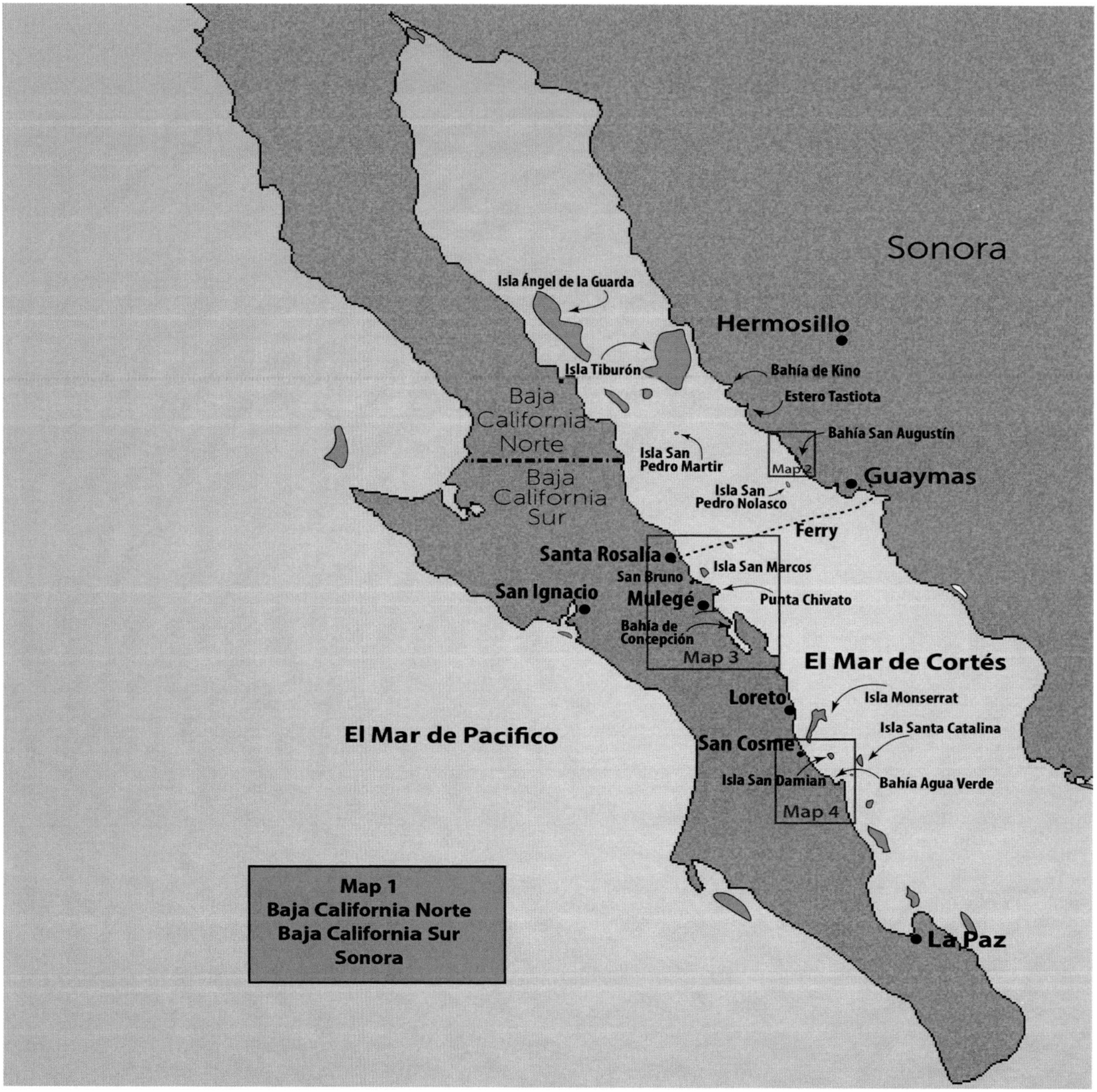
Sonora
Isla Ángel de la Guarda
Hermosillo
Isla Tiburón
Bahía de Kino
Estero Tastiota
Baja
California
Norte
Bahía San Augustín
Isla San
Pedro Martir
Map 2
Guaymas
Baja
California
Sur
Isla San
Pedro Nolasco
Ferry
Santa Rosalía
Isla San Marcos
San Bruno
San Ignacio
Mulegé
Punta Chivato
Bahía de
Concepción
Map 3
El Mar de Cortés
Loreto
Isla Monserrat
El Mar de Pacifico
San Cosme
Isla Santa Catalina
Isla San Damian
Bahía Agua Verde
Map 4
Map 1
Baja California Norte
Baja California Sur
Sonora
La Paz

Part 2: Sea of Cortez Expeditions

Chapter Six

Ensenada Rada El Pasito/Sonora

There seem to be fortuitous occasions that shift one's focus towards a whole unopened world of experience and discovery. Such was the case when I enrolled in a scuba diving class through a local Tucson dive shop in the fall of 1980. My instructor was the late Lane Larson, author-naturalist-wilderness guide, who led expeditions in the remotest parts of Mexico and Central America with many first-time descents of rivers flowing to the Pacific Ocean. Once I was certified as a diver, his experience was helpful in pointing me in the direction of the most remote and off-the-beaten-path sites along the coast of Sonora, Mexico. After a long existence as a land-locked Sonoran Desert

Jeepster Commando set up on terrace campsite above Ensenada Rada El Pasito

dweller living in Tucson, Arizona, I was finally going to venture south—for the first time—to examine where this familiar desert merges with the Gulf of California, otherwise known as the Sea of Cortez.

So began a succession of expeditions by four-wheel drive, outfitting the reliable 1968 Jeepster Commando for primitive coastal camping while undertaking explorations along the western mainland shores of Sonora and the eastern edge of the Baja Peninsula. The constant exposure through repetitive adventures allowed me to gain a good working knowledge of coastal desert environments on both sides of the Gulf. Packing a mini-library of sourcebooks likewise enabled my education of the natural history. (Shreve and Wiggins, 1964, Keen, 1971, Coyle and Roberts, 1975, Bowen, 1976, Thomson and McKibbin, 1976, Udvardy, 1977, Thomson, et al., 1979, Brusca, 1980, Eschmeyer, et al., 1983)

The standard routine went as follows: Secure at least a week off from work. Then, following a checklist: stock the Commando with ample supplies such as camping gear, tarps, water, non-perishable food (mostly), tools and emergency repair kit, basic dive gear (mask, fins, snorkel), and, of course, the essential "mini-library" of references and sourcebooks from the University of Arizona and Tucson public libraries, and cross border with adequate insurance, vehicle permit, and visa. Then settle into and enjoy the long scenic drive through Sonora and the small rural towns of Imuris, Magdalena, Santa Ana, and Benjamín Hill before reaching the metropolis of Hermosillo. Here was the last major gas fill-up before a long stretch across a vast desert plain to a distant turn-off.

Far south of Hermosillo, I left Mexico Highway 15, heading westward on a single lane road until, after about eleven miles, I arrived at an isolated brick building at *La Hermosura* (the beauty). This appeared to be the only store in a radius of many miles. So, whatever else I might need to add to my *comestíbles* such as potatoes, onions, peanuts, beer, ice, etc., I had better purchase them here at this *Tiendita*!

From this lonely outpost, the road swung southward, through an open patchwork of farm fields and plains. Beyond the low desert plain it gradually ascended upward into rocky hills, through brush and cacti. Then the road began dropping down towards the coast, winding through some very interesting canyon terrain that I had to stop and look at more closely. With the sun's heat radiating off volcanic boulders, the air smelled pungent and fresh. Here were *palo adán*, octopus-like jatrophas, and the exotic elephant and white-barked palo blanco trees I had read about, mixed in with familiar denizens like palo verdes and ironwoods.

The anticipation of the first distant sighting of a blue patch of ocean began with the earliest excursion and became an established ritual. Once a lustrous ribbon of blue appeared through a pass in the desert hills, it was time to pull over, stop, get out and relish the moment. Somehow, there's something magical about that first distant glimpse of *El Mar de Cortés*! As if all those years of never experiencing the desert ocean exponentially enhanced the sacredness and stunning beauty of this marvelous, mesmerizing sea.

The meandering road to the Sonoran coast passed a fork to the left and eventually emerged upon a wide, open terrace overlooking blue water stretching to the far horizon. I had arrived above the vast expansive bay of *Playa Jojoval*. Here, set well back from the coast was an empty, abandoned white-stuccoed adobe. An impressive, many-stemmed organ pipe cactus and large sprawling purple-flowered nightshade bush grew alongside what may have been the remains of the *Peña Blanca* settlement, as shown on the topo map. (I once took refuge here under the heaviest torrential rain I've ever experienced in this region). Farther along the track across this terrace area was a lone corrugated tin-roofed fishing shack, *Rancho Linda Vista*. This was a good spot to head into the surrounding dry hills and arroyos to collect firewood prior to arrival at a mostly barren upper beach campsite.

A couple more miles along the rough two-track seemed to end at a flat terrace above a small cove against a high hill. This spot—*Ensenada Rada El Pasito*—served as my main campsite for undersea adventures, extensive on-foot explorations up and down the coast, and far back inland—under the hot baking sun—roaming sandy desert arroyos and climbing up over volcanic crags. I learned to locate a particularly savvy herb in the desert here, that closely resembles oregano (*Lippia palmeri*). Once hung and dried, it served as an excellent seasoning for ceviche and grilled fish. I remember a Mexican *panga* fisherman named Francisco, who visited my camp on one of these early trips, pointing this plant out to me. On yet another visit with a companion during the winter, he suddenly came ashore decked out in full yellow-suited rain gear and dropped several freshly caught striped mullet upon my roaring campfire! This is a traditional Mexican style of cooking fish known as *pescado arrojado al fuego*.

View of Jeepster and El Pasito *cove from atop hill*

Francisco also confirmed the folklore behind the name attached to the coastal area north, beyond the hill, into the next bay and offshore rocks and "mini-island archipelago." Indeed, *Ensenada Julio Villa* had been named for a Mexican fisherman who illegally fished with dynamite and blew himself up.

The central gulf coast region of Sonora is one of the most arid of all the Sonoran Desert subdivisions. Only five inches or less of rainfall per year falls here on average. (Dimmitt, 2000) Despite this dryness, I found deer and coyote tracks in the arroyos, though wet waterholes and *tinajas* (rock water pockets) were extremely scarce. Once, on the 4th of July, I arrived here and was immediately swarmed by a large airborne colony of wild honeybees (*Apies mellifera*). Unbeknownst to me, a water cooler had been leaking during the rough, bouncy trip on the way in; saturating a floor carpet. Desperate bees seeking fresh water began accumulating inside the Commando. What had at first been a dozen or so now amounted to a solid mass of hundreds upon hundreds of crawling, guzzling bees! Realizing the urgency of the situation, I delicately lifted items coated with masses of bees and laid them gently down on rocks to dry. Then I carefully slid inside and maneuvered the Commando down a steep hillside. As I gained speed hurtling over the rough terrain, I whipped a towel vigorously behind me, clearing the remainder of bees from the back seat! Whew!

Returning to camp near sunset, I examined a badly dented hubcap, the only casualty of my sudden flight. I enjoyed a pleasant, peaceful night, but my deliverance was short-lived.

View northwest from hilltop overlooking Ensenada Julio Villa

View southwest past extended headland of Isla San Pedro Nolasco *and* Isla El Acero

Arising with the dawn, all seemed well the following day until the swarm suddenly reappeared en masse! This left me no recourse but to abandon camp and move operations several miles south to the aforementioned *Rancho Linda Vista*. This provided a unique opportunity to explore along the cliff faces set back from and along the full length of the *Playa Jojoval* shoreline. I encountered scores of large black witch moths (*Ascalapha odorata*) roosting in the shaded portions of the cliffs and, later, had a few of these same huge brown moths (seven-inch wing span) as company in the tarpaper *Rancho* fishing shack where I spent the night.

Coming down off the hill above the *Ensenada*, a stealthy desert fox was a frequent evening visitor, no doubt drawn to remains from campfire meals. Some of my favorite daytime camp guests were the raucous little brown towhees, who are always worth the price of admission for their amusing antics! The familiar cry of an osprey could be heard after sunrise, and occasionally seen hovering in mid-air before plunging, talons extended, in pursuit of fish. I always felt it was a good omen to have one around camp. Magnificent frigate birds soared and wheeled effortlessly high up in the sky. Closer to the sea, brown pelicans glided in unison, in single file, just above the surface. Zebra-tail lizards scurried about on hot sand in earnest pursuit of beach flies and isopods. My close companions, the yellow-footed gulls, became like second cousins. The sights and sounds of seabirds surrounding the cove and beyond were frequent: double-crested cormorants, brown boobies, diving grebes, unidentified brown and white sandpipers, and other small shorebirds. Here at the desert's edge, a pleasant, briny aroma permeated the nostrils, while I was soothed by the sounds of waves gently lapping against sand.

An even livelier abundance and diversity of wildlife existed under the surface waters of the *ensenada*. This was maximized by the variety of substrates and habitats ranging between the sandy-bottomed cove to the rocky shorelines, submerged benches, and offshore patch reefs. When I use the term "reef," it follows the ecological definition referring to rock, rather than a true coral reef which does not exist in this area. (Thomson, et al., 1979) Over one hundred fish species were found in a whole host of variable sand-to-rock niches, with occasional pelagic visitors from deeper offshore waters. Besides intensive fish watching, spearfishing was done strictly for day-to-day subsistence, and locally abundant, select predatory species were preferred. Among these were the leopard grouper, yellow snapper, dog snapper, barred pargo, finescale triggerfish, and even a small Cortez halibut. In the spirit of gratitude as a successful hunter, my reverence for the unique nature and beauty of each fish species was preserved in a series of photos taken of each one. I began referring to this portfolio as the *Fish File*.

I also waded out into the cove and with practice, became proficient at throwing my *tarraya* (cast net). This was primarily done for examination of local sandy bottom fishes rather than for sustenance. Schools of inshore fishes such as striped mullet, the silver-bodied machetes, flatiron herring, halfbeaks, and others were occasionally encountered in the open shallows of the *ensenada*.

All my underwater exploring, fish watching and subsistence hunting relied upon the maximum development of breath-hold diving skills, since I possessed no scuba equipment. This allowed for the most natural and least invasive entry into a silent underwater realm minus loud, noisy regulator breathing and constant discharges of bubbles! When I was just getting started on my first venture into this unknown marine realm, I was making do with the most primitive basic gear. This simplicity is a very good thing. I adapted to the underwater chill while wearing layers of long-sleeved tee-shirts and progressed with my diving under these conditions to the greatest extent possible. Then, at a future point, there was a sense of having "earned" my custom-fitting wetsuit. I have always followed this typical "primitive-to-advanced' progression. It naturally allows for a much greater depth of experience and knowledge of the elements to be gained than if one begins fully equipped, right from the start, with all the primo gear.

JB selfie with speargun at El Pasito

On most days, outfitted for the day's diving, I would enter the water in the shallow cove—in a straight line out from camp—and alternately swim and breath-hold dive further out into deeper water, while roughly following the *ensenada's* rocky shoreline. One very opportunistic vantage point was discovered in this manner, during my earliest dives.

I let myself be swept along with surface currents that flowed through a narrow channel between a near-shore chain of tabular reef rock and an extended headland. Here, you could stand on a bedrock platform, submerged behind a rock wall—breathing through a snorkel—and observe the almost constant activity and back-and-forth traffic of an amazing variety of colorful fish species! I began referring to it as "The Amphitheater of Fish."

Schools of graybar, Cortez and wavyline grunts, gafftopsail pompano, finescale triggerfish, scissortail damselfish, and the bright yellow-on-black or yellow band on purplish-blue Cortez rainbow wrasses provided a continuous parade passing through the channel. Distinctive multi-colored fish appeared, as if contestants on a midwater runway, in combinations of white, blue, orange, black, and yellow. These were individual specimens of the Cortez and king angelfish, and small aggregations of three-banded butterflyfish and barberfish. Several parrotfish species—azure and bluechin—displayed a striking blue-green-pink color combo, with the azure parrotfishes' long dorsal fin revealing vibrant blue and orange when expanded. Other regularly sighted herbivores and those that prey mostly on invertebrates were Mexican hogfish, various wrasses, Cortez chubs, opaleyes, and the occasional Pacific porgy, zebraperch, or burrito grunt. Of course, the predators such as leopard groupers, yellow and dog snappers, and barred pargos were always lurking within the channel and schools of jacks or other pelagic species made occasional appearances. One day while concealed behind the wall, I was surprised and delighted to see a pair of large yellowtail come cruising through.

The notion of a silent underwater realm—as previously alluded to—is not completely correct. While one is comfortably submerged over either rock or sand, there is a constant, resonating background of crisp, clear crackling sounds. This ever-present background sound is not unpleasant nor obtrusive and tends to merge with the diver's experience so that one becomes unaware of it at times, especially when entranced and absorbed into all the undersea wonders at hand. By contrast, the later return through the water/air barrier into the bright sunshine can be rudely shocking! Especially re-emerging in the midst of a loud raucous chorus of yellow-footed seagulls, "AWK—AWK—AWK—AWK—AWK!"

*Robust barred pargo—a snapper that hides in rock caves and crevices (*El Pasito *Fish File)*

Other, more momentary, undersea sounds are interesting to note, such as the low rumble like distant thunder when a large group of fish is suddenly startled, causing a massive "clear out!" Fish have very acute sensory receptors that detect minute vibrations in the surrounding water and can move in the blink of an eye and completely vanish! All you perceive is a blur! In fact, I don't think there is another group of animals that comes close to that ability of escape in reacting and moving that fast. Of course, as soon as the coast is clear, with no prevailing danger present, they soon return, settling back into normal routines. So, an awareness of fishes' sensitivity to their environment is helpful in adapting to their world. One practices and refines the art of smooth, fluid movements underwater, sometimes in deliberately slow fashion, to more easily integrate into the underwater piscivorous community.

There are, of course, a whole host of other denizens of that community that are sheltered and abundant along and inside of the structure of rocky shoreline and patch reef habitats.

Most are small, such as the numerous species of damselfish, gobies, blennies, and clingfishes and can be studied at close range. The brilliant iridescent blue juveniles of the Cortez damselfish are common and represent a species endemic to the Sea of Cortez. These perky little guys become chocolate-brown colored as adults and are fiercely territorial in defense of their rocky niches. The stone scorpionfish is a larger cryptic predator that blends into these rocky niches, though sometimes occurring over sandy bottoms. It resembles a seaweed-encrusted rock, and one learns to be very wary of this fish, since it possesses potently venomous dorsal fin spines. As I move into shallower reef waters, scattered schools of bright yellow and black-barred panamic sergeant majors are everywhere, just below the surface.

Within the in-between spaces bridging the sandy cove and rocky substrates, large four-foot wide diamond stingrays—semi-buried in bottom sediment—were frequently sighted. In the same vicinity, smaller round-shaped bullseye stingrays exhibited a characteristic fluid, undulating rhythm as they swam close to the bottom. There is, of course, a greater fish fauna occurring in the whole of this region beyond those described herein. The undersea domain within a wide extent of shoreline and outlying depths of the *ensenada* had been explored to a moderate extent during the initial series of Sonoran coastal expeditions. While one could never lack for areas to intently study and explore here within and just beyond the littoral zone, the time had come to venture out away from shore, across several miles of open water, to discover the world around a distant jagged *isla* of solid rock!

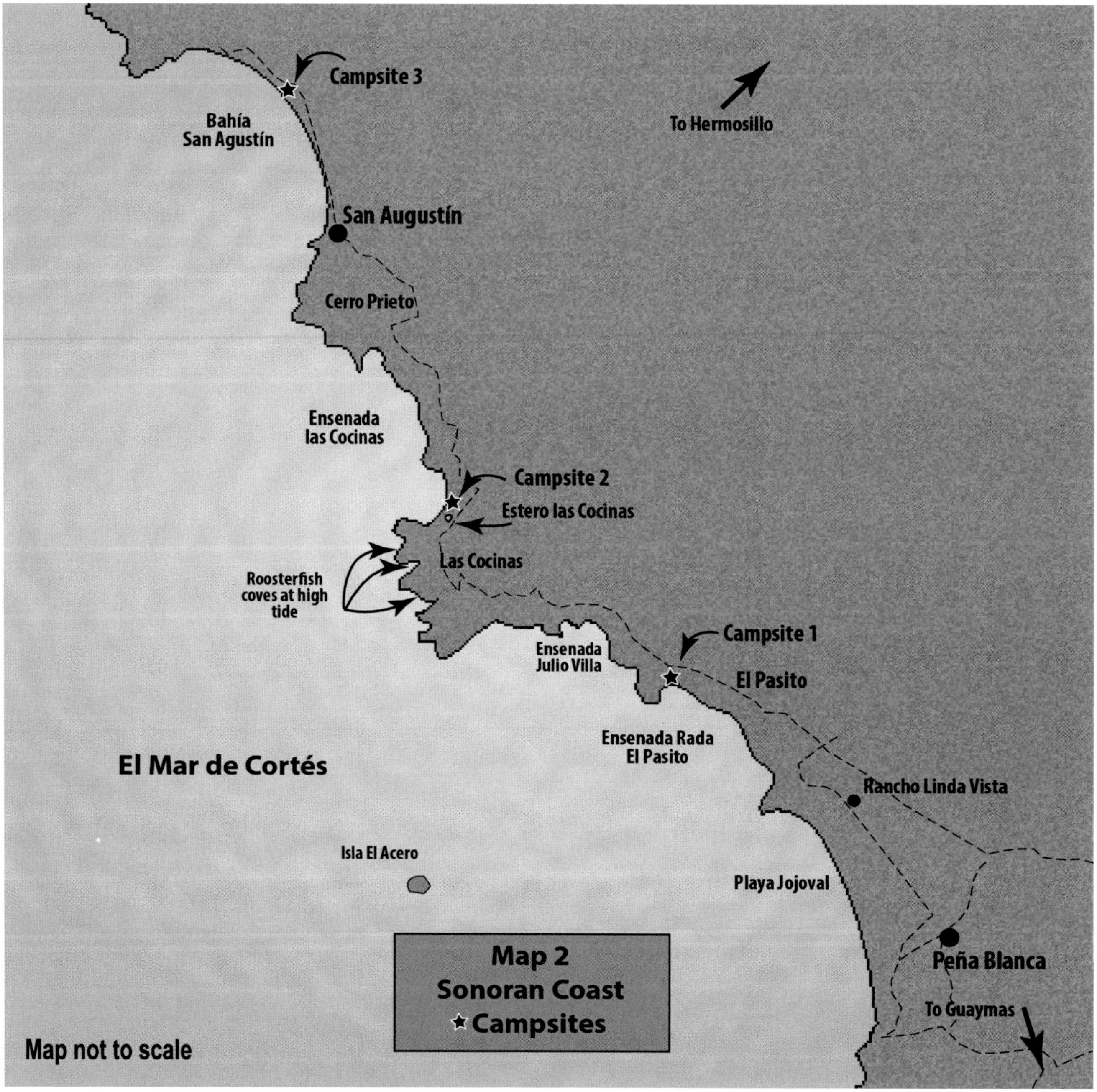
Campsite 3
To Hermosillo
Bahía
San Agustín
San Augustín
Cerro Prieto
Ensenada
las Cocinas
Campsite 2
Estero las Cocinas
Las Cocinas
Roosterfish
coves at high
tide
Campsite 1
Ensenada
Julio Villa
El Pasito
Ensenada Rada
El Pasito
El Mar de Cortés
Rancho Linda Vista
Isla El Acero
Playa Jojoval
Map 2
Sonoran Coast
Campsites
Peña Blanca
To Guaymas
Map not to scale

Chapter Seven

The *Isla El Acero* Raft Adventure/Sonora

From the first time I stepped onto the beach at *Ensenada Rada El Pasito*, I had been intrigued at the sight of the strangely-shaped, whitish apparition protruding above the sea, far out from shore. However, as much as I wanted to venture out to explore its environs, I was not equipped with suitable watercraft. One of my most memorable trips to the *ensenada* provided a possible breakthrough. On a last-minute impulse, despite limited space, I had loaded the box containing the small inflatable raft. Originally, it had been purchased for some long-ago lake fishing excursion but had never been taken out of the box. Once inflated, I took a hard look at the distant island that some call "White Rock" (i.e., *Peña Blanca*), and known as *Isla El Acero* on coastal sailing charts. Then I looked back at the puny raft. It looked a lo-

Close approach to Isla El Acero *through big, rolling swells*

o-ong way off, but wasn't this doable? The comparatively huge form of *Isla San Pedro Nolasco* was visible on the southern horizon, at a distance of between sixteen to eighteen miles away. Spanish seafarer Francisco de Ulloa sailed past and noted this island—northwest of Guaymas on September 20, 1540, during his historic voyage to the upper Gulf of California. (Bowen, 2000) This voyage led to the discovery that California was not an island, and Ulloa named this sea *El Mar de Cortés* for Hernán Cortés, his leader and the conqueror of Mexico. *Isla El Acero*, to the southwest of my campsite, I estimated to be at least one and a half to two miles from where I stood. So long as I got started early enough on a calm morning and returned before strong winds kicked up in the late afternoon, I'd be fine.

At first it seemed awkward rowing such a peculiar, barely seaworthy and misshapen little craft. But once I settled in and adapted my single oar rowing stroke to the most efficient rhythm, I began to make progress. I had brought along my dive gear and Sedic pocket camera with ample plastic wraps to protect it from sea spray. I prepared myself mentally for a long hard passage, and it certainly did not disappoint my estimation of that task! While relatively calm seas prevailed once underway, as I got farther offshore the raft bobbed up and down as gigantic undulating rollers of waves passed underneath. Once I drew nearer *Isla El Acero*, I gained a clearer perspective of these massive rolling swells against the stable position of the island. Yikes! (Oh shit—here we go!) As I began to close in, the *isla* that once appeared so far away, loomed up in front of me looking HUGE!

Nearing the sheer rock faces of the *isla*, I was amazed at the numbers of sea lions (*Zalophus californianus*) settled in different spots along the precipitous walls. It appeared

Sloping shelf of adult sea lions and view of mainland

Guano-encrusted shelf with brown boobies

Close-up of adult sea lions along central shelf of Isla El Acero

Looking up at boobies from raft, against rock wall of Isla El Acero

that the larger bulls and adults were mostly concentrated on one low accessible platform near the water's edge that led to a gradually inclined wider shelf area. The remaining smaller juveniles were packed together, one against the other, in a tight row higher up the rock wall along a narrow ledge. There was a great difference in size between the large adults of the lower rookery and the "kids" on the "upper floor" above. I arrived sometime around midday—*siesta* time—with all of them basking in the sun. Several larger bulls and adults with heads tilted back and chest out seemed to be the perfect picture of bliss and repose. A multitude of sounds reverberated off the rock walls: loud roars, coughs, trumpeting, barks, and other expressions. These magnificent large mammals do like to make themselves heard! Wow! The sights, sounds and smells all leave a strong impression on the observer and gives one a keen sense of their overall prowess, which can't be overstated.

Then I maneuvered around to make a close-in approach alongside a steep-edged roost of beautiful brown boobies *(Sula leucogaster)* who did not seem perturbed by my presence at all. These robust seabirds were spaced within a foot or more of each other, comfortably roosting on white guano-splattered perches, underneath a high overhang. Brown boobies are roughly equivalent in size to seagulls. They are a rich, chocolate-brown color, with contrasting white undersides, pale head and bill, with yellow feet. Unlike the raucous din of the nearby sea lion colony, the boobies were silent. They are phenomenal divers, plunging straight down from forty to eighty feet and using their wings to "fly" underwater to as deep as sixty-five feet in pursuit of small schooling fishes. (Schreiber and Norton, 2002) Their close relatives, the blue-footed boobies (*Sula nebouxii*), are found less than sixty miles away, towards the northwest. At a mid-Gulf refuge, they are known for their large breeding colonies on *Isla San Pedro Martir*. Here, there were also brown boobies and a few scattered Heermann's gulls perched higher atop the island's summit.

I'm not quite sure how I managed this, but I was able to find a way to secure the raft along the steep rock edge—at least temporarily—so that I could take a brief dive. Once I entered the water, it was "welcome to sea lion world!" I was greeted by a perky female and then another that suddenly appeared up close and just as quickly glided effortlessly away. Of course, just checking out the intruder. While possessing great speed and agility in the water, they are capable of reaching depths below 300 feet. I keenly remember a story told to me by a close friend about a diver off *Isla San Pedro Nolasco*—less than twenty miles away—who discovered on the bottom a sea lion carcass bitten in half, more than likely by a great white shark. As an earlier guidebook on Gulf of California fishes asserts, great white sharks are uncommon, but not rare in the gulf. (Thomson and McKibben, 1976) I did not see any sharks, and very little of the fish life around *Isla El Acero*. In fact, I did not have a chance to explore around much of the Island without a secure enough mooring to the rock.

View from Isla *back towards extended headland and campsite (center of coastline)*

Looking across the immensity of ocean now separating me from my distant campsite, it now seemed twice the distance it was prior to my maiden voyage. But neither the conditions nor the wind had changed notably, and I was gradually able to get into the same rowing groove as before. *¡Hasta la vista, amigos!* Perhaps, I can return another time and get to know your island a little better! I was especially comforted by the presence of a little brown-mottled juvenile Heermann's gull (*Larus heermannii*) who accompanied me for almost the entire journey back. Unlike the Mexican *panga* fishermen, I didn't have any treats to share with the lone gull in appreciation for its company. Perhaps it also enjoyed this leg of my adventure from the white "animal cracker"-shaped rock slowly becoming smaller behind me to my lonesome but very welcome desert seaside outpost appearing larger as I got closer to home base. When I got within reach of the *ensenada*, I recognized an arched window along the highest volcanic rock ridge, inland from the coast. It took about two hours rowing back on my return voyage. Entering the cove, I was not completely exhausted when the raft finally touched sand but sufficiently spent to sleep like a rock once I crawled into my sleeping bag. During the night, the weather changed, and it became very gusty. A strong wind squall overturned the raft, dumping its contents on the beach, and blowing it well out of sight.

Overlooking Ensenada Las Cocinas *from hilltop (July, 1983)*

Chapter Eight

Ensenada las Cocinas (Cove of the Kitchens)/Sonora

During progressive Sonoran coastal expeditions, I roamed overland to find and encamp at a number of other remote localities with ideal shoreline littoral structure and characteristics that provided fresh exciting opportunities for continued exploring, studying, and learning within the undersea and coastal desert environments. One of these sites was *Ensenada las Cocinas*. This was a beautiful, isolated cove situated roughly two miles to the northwest—as the crow flies—from my previous main campsite. Its discovery had not been easy, playing it by ear, following a very rough, steep dirt track over desert hills, from an unfamiliar coastal access main road. Finally, after the Commando made the last grinding four-wheel drive ascent, I reached a high overlook with a breathtaking view of the *ensenada*. A narrow, gleaming-white, fine sandy beach lined the innermost shoreline, with a unique and interesting feature—the *Estero las Cocinas*—linked to the ocean near the base of the prominent hill forming the headland. This negative estuarine lagoon alternately flows or turns into an enclosed saltwater marsh, depending on tides, ocean currents, and storm events. As a dry desert drainage system without a freshwater source, it is classified "negative" since the flow comes strictly from the ocean, except in the rare instance of a mega-rainfall event.

When I first set foot at *Ensenada las Cocinas*, in July of 1983, I found sand mounded up at the *estero* inlet, and a landlocked salt marsh. The high evaporation rate, salinity, and elevated water temperatures sharply reduced the life and activity here in contrast to the potential abundance of fish and invertebrate species. Upon my return the following summer, on July 20, 1984, I was stunned to view such a night and day difference! A strong current now flowed between the sea and an expanded, full estuarine lagoon teeming with small fishes and crabs! Wow! The Cove of the Kitchens was now cooking!

Saturday, July 21st:

> Got up in semi-darkness and entered the water in the cove before sunrise. The surface of the sea is absolutely calm, like glass. Observed usual fishes, shells, including a school of sierras [sierra mackerel]. Stalk with my *arpón* [speargun] around circle of rocks awash. Return along rocky south shore of headland. Saw juvenile spotted rose snappers in small aggregation [a first sighting: likely related to presence of *estero*]. Return to camp for popcorn and coffee. [JB Field Notes, 1984]

That afternoon, when I emerged from the water after spearing a *buen coche* (nice triggerfish), I prepared it traditional ceviche-style. Once skinned, filleted, and cut into thin strips, the fish is simply marinated in fresh lime juice. It's a great way to make a quickie meal, fresh out of the ocean, supplying a burst of energy and protein! Of course, this method is dependent upon how long your reserves of ice last to keep your limes fresh and chilled.

Sunday, July 22nd dawned on another morning of calm waters in the cove, following a clear, star-filled night sky, setting up favorable conditions for an underwater exploration into the lively, flowing *estero*:

> *Estero las Cocinas*/Fish Species: [most species were smaller juvenile forms; usually in small schools] Striped mullet (*Mugil cephalus*), machete (*Elops affinis*), dog snapper (*Lutjanus novemfasciatus*), Guaymas goby? [*Quietula spp.*-not confirmed], longtail goby (*Gobionellus sagittula*), mullet snapper [*Lutjanus aratus* - 3"], Pacific sardine? [*Sardinops spp.*-not confirmed], Yellow snapper [*Lutjanus argentiventris* -3"], flagfin mojarra [*Eucinostomus currani* - 7-8"], yellow bobo [*Polydactylus opercularis* -3-4"], stone scorpionfish [*Scorpaena mystes* -12"], bullseye puffer [*Sphoeroides annulatus*]-tiny 1" specimen. *Estero las Cocinas* / Crab Species: Blue crab (*Callinectes spp.*), common fiddler crab (*Uca crenulata*), ghost crab (*Ocypode occidentalis*). [JB Field Notes, 1984]

Even negative estuarine lagoons such as *Estero las Cocinas* are important refuges for many juvenile fish species and invertebrates. This is despite the lack of protective shelter that might be afforded them by mangrove stands, for example. Mangroves are absent here, though found in positive estuaries occurring much further south. (Brusca, 1980) It was exciting to record more "first" species I had not encountered before: a second snapper species (mullet snapper) to add to the spotted rose snapper found a day earlier, off the rocky shore. The ten

Estero Las Cocinas *open to the sea and fully expanded (July, 1984)*

confirmed fish species found in the *estero* were either sighted underwater through my mask or collected from casting across the lagoon with my *tarraya*. By "collected," I mean removed from the net, examined closely, measured, then returned to the lagoon. The other "first-timers" discovered were the longtail goby, flagfin mojarra and yellow bobo, with its peculiar long dangling pectoral filaments. A visiting great blue heron was also sighted in the lagoon.

Later that afternoon, I got in a long swim, exploring and hunting around a wide area south of the cove. I mixed in casting lures with a small spinning outfit but had no takers. I discovered a "mini-seamount" while going across open water between two rocky points extending off the headland. This was a small rock summit just under the surface, with greater visible depths surrounding its basal circumference. I managed to nail a nice four-and-a-half pound barred pargo that spun around on the spear shaft in a blur.

After viewing green glow of sunset once the sun passed beneath the sea to the west, I started back to camp, swimming past foraging moray eels and fishes finding their nooks for the night. After sunset, predatory fish (i.e. groupers, snappers) seem to vanish—possibly to unknown feeding grounds? Coming ashore in gathering darkness, I began preparations for a late evening meal of baked spuds and grilled snapper. A toast to another day spent fully alive. For the first time, I've seen several jewel morays (*Muraena lentiginosa*) so far.

Another dazzlingly clear starry night.

Monday, July 23rd:

Arose early to bathe and shave, eat leftover spuds, bee pollen, and head straight out for clam grounds. Added weight so belt is 12 pounds, plus carrying speargun. Few distinctive trails sighted and my capacity is down today—so need to take it slow and easy. While swimming above several patch reef margins, a small roosterfish comes into view. I give chase but the fish eventually vanishes into the gloom. A short while later, I'm looking down on a group of large sierras, but they too, are soon out of sight. (Maybe I can anchor the raft out here—cast lures + dive?) Eventually work my way in towards rocky shore [around headland] and into submarine canyons, where I discover I've got two huge roosters [*Nematistius pectoralis*] cornered but they elude me and I am hesitant because of their size. It's high tide, 11-to-11:30 a.m., so just as I noticed below *Rancho Linda Vista* in the submarine canyons facing out west [from the north end of *Playa Jojoval*], they like to slip in there at high tide (pursuing mullet?). After this sequence, I take a break in nice shady "Roosterfish Cove." Do a mental recap and set plan [mindset for hunting roosterfish] and cruise out of R-fish Cove and into next one where, lo and behold—there they are again! This time I'm [focused] having mentally prepared myself to get off a shot, but when I do one is at long range and unled [not able to get lined up with], my shot zings clear and above. Continuing around point [to the north] (probably should have continued around south point). Come up empty with a good shot at a leopard [grouper]. See *guaseta* [mutton hamlet—small sea bass species] (bites spear tip), pompano [gaftopsail], small jacks—probably black skipjacks. Did bring back a nice little *coche* [finescale triggerfish] for ceviche, beans, onions and green chiles—and rest. [JB Field Notes, 1984]

Dog snapper speared off southern headland of Las Cocinas

In retrospect, it's probably a good thing I wasn't able to spear one of those big "roosters." I might well have been towed out to sea! It's very exciting to encounter one of these spectacular, open water cruisers! They are a very distinctive, and powerfully-built pelagic species, reputedly with very good eating qualities. There's another side to spearing big fish: it's a LOT of work! One time at *Bahía San Augustín*, I was especially hard up to find something suitable to put on the dinner table and shot a huge bumphead parrotfish. This wound up becoming the most enormous and laborious task. It took much time and effort skinning out, filleting, and making sure to thoroughly prepare and make the best use of the whole fish. Never again! The thick scales were larger than conventional guitar picks and could be substituted for them. I suppose from an educational standpoint it was interesting to extract the pharyngeal mill inside the throat. This is literally a grinding mill. Parrotfish have beaks for scraping algae off rock substrates. They also ingest the rock fragments and sand as abrasives to help process what they consume against the enamel plates of this mill. (Thomson, et al., 1979) But...never again!

Tuesday, July 24th:

The gulls came by later to pick at the remains of my burnt popcorn from last night. They didn't have much else in way of handout [leftover meal scraps]. Stuck the only 'rooster' sighted this morning [minor penetration by speartip-fish swam away mostly unharmed]. Didn't take any other shots except I got 1 coche [triggerfish] to fry for lunch with coffee. Definitely located dog snapper hole but they were quite skittish. Spotted one small [green sea] turtle. Very murky today, probably from strong west wind of yesterday [late afternoon-early evening]. Light shower after getting out 7:00 a.m.—1:30, but didn't interfere with cooking. Quite calm this afternoon, so far. My little Coleman Stove has outperformed itself after being drenched in last October's flood and run over by me 3 days ago while moving my Jeep[ster] from my sleeping quarters to my cooking site. Hardships [conditions to adapt to and manage]: heat, *moscas* [mosquitoes], gnats, etc.,—make it difficult to fully appreciate experience of freedom and being able to hang out on the reef with fish, enjoy good simple pleasures and the slow passage of a day, each one full. Afternoon dive: 1 coche and a 4-lb. cabrilla. [JB Field Notes, 1984]

After I had experienced four days of solitude, a group of Mexican commercial divers out of Guaymas landed their *panga* (a fiberglass skiff) on the beach. We instantly hit it off and spent the evening sharing a meal and stories about our experiences in *El Mar de Cortés*. They invited me to join them for the next day's outing around their favorite fishing/foraging spots of this region of the sea. I arrived fully "wetsuited-up," with my dive gear (and dinky pocket camera) early the next morning.

On Wednesday, July 25th, a pleasantly cool morning upon calm seas, we headed out from the cove at seven o'clock. The water's surface was smooth as a mirror as we zipped along on the way to a vast expanse of beach to the southeast that I knew well. The *Playa Jojoval* was a familiar stretch of sandy coastline that I had hiked to and done offshore exploring at from my main campsite in the area. Once Leo—*El Jefe* (Captain)—found a desirable spot to anchor, perhaps several hundred yards out, the crew prepared for diving. *El Mundo*—(boat handler) and *buzo* (diver)—fired up the Briggs and Stratton compressor that would supply oxygen to their underwater air hoses. Another *buzo*, Francisco, prepared to dive sixty to one-hundred feet down to the sandy bottom. Here, the main quarry appeared to be *caracól burro*. This is one of the largest species of conch (*Strombus spp.*), that has traditionally been an important regional seafood item. Other than conch, the divers appeared to be opportunistically harvesting a few fish and other invertebrate forms, whenever possible.

I had been a guest aboard with local Mexican *panga* fishermen before, but this was my first adventure out at sea with a group of *buzos*. Once the divers disappeared down below, I slipped into the water, and began rhythmically hyperventilating in preparation for my own descent. I breath-hold dived down to where they were working, in multiple spots. Even inside their bulky dive helmets, it was easy to see their reaction when they spotted me lurking nearby. A surprised smile would be followed by a wave. Once, I was momentarily startled when Leo handed me an octopus! Whoa! (I later handed it over the side of the *panga* to El Mundo).

El Mundo *fishing*

This was one of my most interesting, enjoyable, and unique adventures to date and certainly a big highlight of the 1984 summer expedition. Perhaps the excitement of these circumstances may have had a positive effect on my diving capabilities? I don't know. But I *was* able to comfortably breath-hold dive with comparative ease down to

El Mundo *displaying large dorado caught with handline/jug method*

even deeper depths than I think I had before. While my limited Spanish was far from allowing me to converse well, my impressions from talking with my newfound dive mates is that they were permitted to harvest conch in these areas, and they were conducting their work properly. These guys were akin to primitive—though well-equipped—hunters harvesting selected resources and employing minimally impactful methods. Whatever they spear, catch or collect, they're putting in a lot of miles and hours to do so.

On the other hand, the history of the Sea of Cortez seems to have followed a parallel path of relentless over-exploitation of natural resources, beginning with the pearl oyster in the late sixteenth century and continuing, over the next four centuries, with successive episodes of whaling (mostly on the Pacific coast of Baja), harvesting bird guano and eggs (from the islands), slaughtering elephant seals and sea lions (mainly for oil), large-scale shrimp harvesting, and wasteful destruction of non-target fish and invertebrate species by bottom trawlers (Steinbeck and Ricketts, 1951), concentrated killing of sharks (mainly for livers and fins), large scale use of long lines and extensive purse nets depleting fish populations,and intensive overhunting of sea turtles and other undersea wildlife. (Bowen, 2000, Seminoff, 2010, Early-Capistrán, 2010)

The renowned underwater cinematographer Howard Hall returned to the Sea of Cortez twenty-five years after the making of one of his most popular films, *Shadows in a Desert Sea*, (Hall, 1992) to discover a bleak undersea landscape nearly devoid of the abundant life that once thrived there. That experience led to the making of a video sponsored by the SeaWatch Organization showing gut-wrenching scenes of overharvesting reef fish species, while conveying a strong message against this destructive trend. (Sea Watch, 2010) Fortunately, there has been a gradual counterbalance gaining momentum in more recent times, towards better and effective conservation and protection of these precious marine resources. (Erisman and Aburto-Oropeza ,2009, Brusca, 2010)

During the long ride back, Leo stopped the *panga* momentarily, to point out the location of an underwater seamount. This is essentially a steep-sided mountain arising from the seafloor, the summit of which lies under the surface at a relatively shallow depth. Therefore, it provides a rich structural base surrounded by open water that attracts many shallow water reef and deep ocean pelagic species, including larger fish and marine mammals such as schools of hammerhead sharks and porpoises. One such locality, in the lower Gulf near La Paz, became somewhat famous for the underwater documentaries filmed there. Unfortunately, like many once bountiful areas of the Sea of Cortez, it has undergone a drastic decline and the large schools of hammerheads are only a memory. (SeaWatch, 2010, Brusca, 2010)

We pulled into the cove at *Ensenada las Cocinas* at around 5:00 p.m. On the way in, while far out from shore, *El Mundo* had a solid strike on the custom, home-made feather jig he had been trolling. Employing the traditional Mexican milk-jug-and-attached-fishing-line method, it wasn't long before he pulled in a magnificent *Pesca de Dorado* or dolphinfish (*Coryphaena hippurus*) that was securely gaffed and hoisted over the gunwale. Glowing in resplendent multi-neon gold-green-blue color, it measured over 36 inches and "set the table" for that evening's feast on the beach. I lowered the tailgate of the Commando to provide a buffet table of sorts, with an array of side veggies and condiments to go with fresh and delicious grilled Mahi-Mahi!

Jeepster tailgate serves as buffet table for seafood fiesta with my mates

Thursday, July 26th: A bright sunny morning followed yesterday's high adventure and last night's fabulous feast. Leo Ramos and his mates were preparing to head back to Guaymas. I would also be packing up soon for my overland return to Tucson. Leo scribbled his address and *teléfono* on a slip of paper and

El Mundo, Francisco & Leo heading back to Guaymas in the Dulce María

handed it to me, while Francisco and *El Mundo* were busy wading out to load gear into the *panga*. The *Dulce Maria* (Sweet Mary) sat anchored a short distance from the beach. She measured roughly sixteen-to-eighteen feet from bow to stern, and perhaps six to seven feet abeam by my estimate and was powered by a sizable outboard motor. I brewed up an ample amount of coffee for all, and shortly after breakfast the Three Amigos were on their way seaward again. Standing in the shallows of the cove, I watched as their sturdy craft rounded the point and was gone. An interesting 'sun dog' of bright yellow and blue illumination shone down from the clouds, forming a rainbow-esque arch over the Sea to the west. Underneath the arch, about twelve feet away, a couple of little "gull-boats" floated contentedly in the shallows.

Aftermath of repairs on Jeepster at Bahía San Augustín

Chapter Nine

Bahía San Augustín/ Sonora

Bahía San Augustín is several miles farther northwest up the coast, closer to *Estero Tastiota*. The prominent, pointed pinnacle on the south end is clearly visible from *Ensenada las Cocinas*. It is accessible by a dirt road off the main road to Kino Bay from Mexico Highway 15, though still off the beaten path. This is a large, wide, expansive bay, comparable in size to *Playa Jojoval,* though not as open and exposed to the ocean, with extended headlands on the north and south. The shoreline is nearly an unbroken, endless stretch of sandy beach, with widely scattered patch reefs below waters of the Bay. *Bahía San Augustín* served as a reliable, more easily accessible campsite, especially in advance of preparing to board the Guaymas Ferry for an extended Baja coastal expedition. Perhaps most importantly, it offered the opportunity to explore and get to know a much different type of coastal marine environment in terms of the predominantly sandy substrate and limited reef structure.

An experience during one of my earliest visits here, set this site apart from all others. I had just settled in during a summer excursion and was slowly swimming out to explore the open shallow waters of the *bahía*. I was alternatively breath-hold diving to examine the mostly sandy bottom in addition to scanning from the surface. I took my time exploring the shallows and gradually ventured into deeper water, where the bottom wasn't so clearly visible. Suddenly, I became aware of an enormous shape directly underneath, blocking my view of the bottom! I could not believe my eyes! There, right below me was a gigantic Pacific manta ray (*Manta hamiltoni*), cruising through the water; its great wings flapping in rhythm! Its dorsal surface appeared to be a uniform brownish tone. I immediately dove down and closed in enough to put my hand against it momentarily. Its skin felt pleasantly soft, yet firm, unlike that of a fish. Whether the huge manta perceived my touch or not, I did not notice any reaction. But it continued moving slowly and effortlessly away, beyond my ability to keep pace with it until finally disappearing into the gloom of the bay's depths. Whew! It looked massive in width, perhaps eighteen to twenty feet across! In the Sea of Cortez, they have often been sighted over shallow reefs near shore and are considered to be primarily plankton feeders. (Thomson, et al., 1979) What an unexpected and exhilarating encounter!

On June 19th of 1986, I arrived at *Bahía San Augustín* from Tucson after driving on-and-off all night and into the wee hours of early morning. Upon reflection, it amazes me when I come across references in my notes of such unusual departure times for Sea of Cortez expeditions back then:

> What a fine afternoon of diving after taking a good catnap in Jeep[ster]. Slightly drained and weary from long, arduous but smooth drive with several stops along the way to nod off 5-15 minutes, last one several hours at least; finally getting back on road [Mexico Highway 15] between [Santa] Ana and Hermosillo at first light (Left Tucson 7:00 p.m. Wed). Water somewhat murky but it seemed to become gradually calmer during afternoon and water was surprisingly warm when first entered. Long 6" x 6" mesh net across bay encountered. While following its length came upon and eventually extracted a [green sea] turtle. A small one, it had "bagged" itself swimming into the net, becoming enveloped and twisting around. Fortunately, it was able to breathe since it chose a shallow area and I only needed to cut several strands to free it. A small turtle, maybe 2 feet long. It did not seem aggressively defensive towards me although I used caution while extricating cords around its head. Later on,

One of only a handful of tent olives collected from Sonoran coastal sites

The tent olive (Oliva porphyria) *is found on deeper, offshore sandy bottoms*

> I shot a fat trigger[fish] then picked up a smaller one; both out of large milling schools. Not difficult at all getting within range but rather deciding which one to go for. Experienced very few "clear-outs." Not sure how much to attribute to my deliberate ease and fluidity of movement. Sighted 2 small Pacific spadefish [*Chaetodipterus zonatus* -a first], a few [leopard] groupers, 1 large diamond stingray, schools of machetes at high tide near beach and many, many small schools of both silvery herring-anchovy types but also [juvenile] barracuda, [Cortez] chub, grunts, etc. Several octopi observed, stroked [petted] 1 small one in crevice. Typical large parrotfish but not too many [predatory] types. Osprey crying from top of big cardón [large columnar cactus-similar in form to saguaro] just after [my] arrival. [*Isla San Pedro*] Nolasco appears quite clearly and prominent to SE (? [south]. Saw several pangas (divers from Colorado? [Cove/outpost NW of Bahía]) going S from *Punta Lesna*. Osprey coming from that direction carrying fish, before sunset. [JB Field Notes, 1986]

The green sea turtle (*Chelonia mydas*), such as the trapped one I encountered, is the species of sea turtle most often seen in the Sea of Cortez, though it is uncommon. They can reach an adult size over three feet in length and weigh over 400 pounds. The upper and central Gulf serve as feeding grounds, with known nesting areas occurring much further south. Seagrass, marine algae, and various invertebrates are the primary diet of these beautiful and fascinating marine reptiles, known as *tortugas prietas*. (Seminoff, et al, 2002a, Seminoff, et al., 2002b) The Sea of Cortez once harbored a great abundance of five of the world's seven sea turtle species. But overhunting, egg collecting, nest site disruption, and incidental losses from large-scale maritime industries reduced all populations to threatened or endangered status by the late twentieth century. (Seminoff, 2010) Although happening at a late stage once population crash levels had already been breached, President Carlos Salinas de Gortari signed the 1990 decree outlawing the consumption or use of all sea turtle products in Mexico. (Early-Capistrán, 2010) Fortunately, efforts to protect beach nesting sites along the Michoacán and Oaxacan coasts had been underway much earlier, during the mid-1960s and late 1970s. (Figueroa et al., 1993) There have been positive signs of a gradual resurgence in the Eastern Pacific green sea turtle population, indicated by recent and thorough studies, based on both sides of the central Baja Peninsula. (Early-Capistrán, et al., 2017)

During another visit, I experienced a rare vehicular breakdown, while encamped at *Bahía San Augustín*.

Coincidently, during this episode, a long *panga* arrived on the beach. The occupants turned out to be a fishing family from Hermosíllo that I had become friends with years ago. Our first meeting had occurred on one of my first ventures into *Ensenada Rada El Pasito*. I came to their aid, helping to repair a boat trailer tire in the middle of the road, while on the way there. I carried a pretty handy emergency repair kit at the time, and used Loctite (a type of epoxy) to reattach a valve stem that had broken off the tire. Once the epoxy had hardened

My friends from Hermosillo preparing our seafood fiesta, left-to-right: Antonio, Ramón, Mariano, Arturo

securely, the next task was getting the tire properly reinflated. The combination of classic Mexican ingenuity together with my portable compressor plugged into the lighter of the Jeepster was our only hope for success. Antonio carefully tightened a piece of rope evenly around the middle of the tire's circumference, while Ramón was gradually twisting the ends of the rope with a stick. In this manner, as the rope was tightened, pressure was equally applied around the rim preventing air leakage. It took a concerted effort from all of us, but the pressure held and the tire inflated satisfactorily—we got the job done! In the case of the broken-down Commando, the situation was reversed. This time, Arturo, *El Mechanico* (the mechanic of the family), came to my aid. I had done some preliminary troubleshooting earlier without success. Now, with both our toolboxes close at hand and Arturo's greater mechanical knowledge and experience, it looked like we were on the right track. Somehow, he managed to make a breakthrough and resolve the problem. Arturo scribbled out a brief note to illuminate my understanding:

> *Falso Contacto bovina o posíble Condensador* [Bad electrical contact at the coil or possibly at the condenser]. [JB Field Note Files]

The Commando was back up and running! So, in the wake of our success, it was time for a fitting celebration. A couple years prior, I became the guest of honor aboard the family's *panga* for a full-blown fishing excursion. This time, the family turned the bow of their *panga* into a makeshift kitchen table, made lots of ceviche, and we had a big San Augustín beach seafood fiesta!

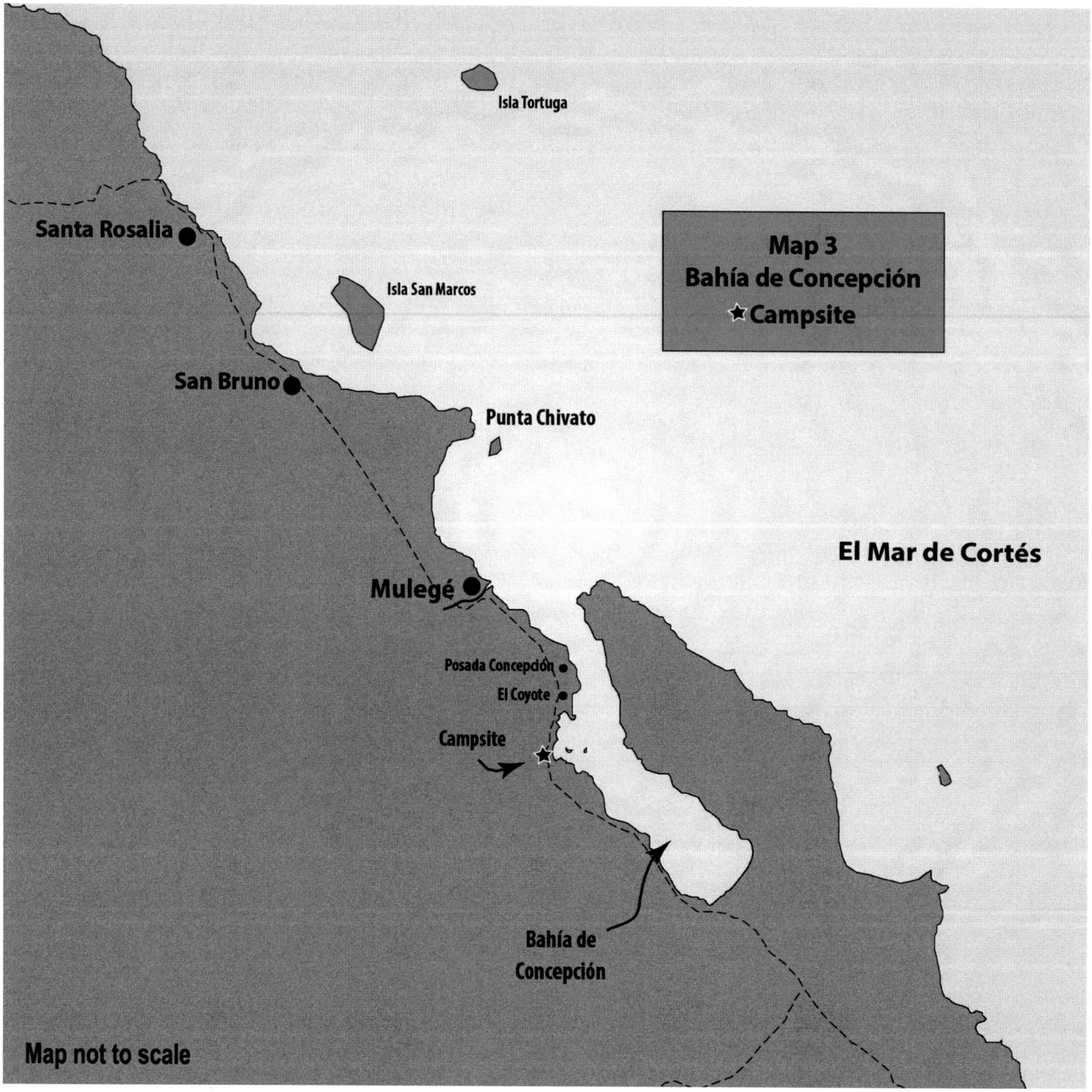
Isla Tortuga
Map 3
Bahía de Concepción
★Campsite
Santa Rosalia
Isla San Marcos
San Bruno
Punta Chivato
El Mar de Cortés
Mulegé
Posada Concepción
El Coyote
Campsite
Bahía de
Concepción
Map not to scale

CHAPTER TEN

BAHÍA CONCEPCIÓN/ BAJA CALIFORNIA SUR

With each succeeding Sonoran Desert coastal trip, gathering greater knowledge and familiarity of the sea, the visible, yet distant, Baja Peninsula became more and more irresistible. So, finally, in the late summer of 1983 or 1984, the first Baja expedition got underway. By this time, I was now slightly better equipped: thanks to the great generosity of the late Russell Davis, biology professor and field researcher of the University of Arizona, I had a custom-welded, stainless steel twenty-gallon water can, complete with faucet and hose. Maintaining fresh water supplies is an overriding concern when isolated remotely in desert coastal regions. On the occasions when I needed to resupply, I learned how and where to find the *Agua Purificada* (purified water) plants in the major towns along both coasts. Now, I could start out with an ample supply of perhaps 30 gallons or more—in total—and not have to be overly concerned about running low.

I had a full length "Farmer John" overall-type wetsuit of neoprene rubber covering chest and legs, as a primary insulating layer. Then, worn over that—depending upon conditions—a custom-fitting, long-sleeved wetsuit jacket with a "beavertail" flap pulled up, under crotch, and fastened in front. Of course, a 'sand-camo' tee-shirt worn over this completed the outfit. This multi-layered insulation would prove extremely useful considering the cold upwellings occurring along the Baja shoreline due to greater depths and prevailing currents. I did not wear neoprene booties for foot coverage, eschewing them for a couple pairs of cotton socks. Everything else I had in the way of gear was basic: largest-size hard rubber fins (IDI Power Fins), standard rubber snorkel, mask, and weight belt. My mask had my prescription lenses adhered on the inside; installed by a local Tucson optician who was also a diver (Richard Case Optical). Incidentally, out on the reef or offshore, I found the best way to clean and clear up my mask periodically, was by simply rubbing saliva over the glass, with a quick rinse of seawater.

The first step towards the next phase of the Sea of Cortez odyssey exploring the *Baja California Sur* coastline began with a reservation booked on the Guaymas Ferry. I learned it was essential to call months in advance to secure a reservation, especially during July through September, when the majority of Mexicans take their annual vacations. I chose the minimal economy class: parked the Commando below and just hung out or possibly catnapped upon the grungy upper decks below the giant smokestacks. The billowing stacks left a slight oily residue everywhere on top, but I didn't care; being content to get cheap passage to the Promised Land!

The great colossal, multi-story vessel rumbled slowly through the vastness of blue stretching across the open Gulf. The trip from Guaymas (around 90 miles) took a full day, close to twelve hours, before docking in the evening at *Santa Rosalía*. Once having disembarked, my priority was finding a convenient, though not too distant beach or desert camping site to pass the night because, on the very next morning, it was just as important to secure and book passage for the return trip. *Santa Rosalía* was an interesting town, so I took a little spin to have a look around, on foot around the block before heading out. According to historical accounts, the town was established by a French mining company (Boleo Mining Co.) after high-grade copper ore was discovered and a large-scale industrial operation began in 1885. (Bowen, 2000) The writer John Steinbeck did not sound very complimentary of the town in an account during his mid-twentieth century voyage:

> Much as Sparky and Tiny wished to continue their research and shore collecting at *Santa Rosalía*, we sailed on past it. Perhaps that was because we knew it was run by a French company. A Mexican town grows out of the ground. You cannot conceive its never having been there. But *Santa Rosalía* looked "built." There were industrial works of large size visible, loading trestles, and piles of broken rock. The mountains rose behind the town, burned almost white, and the green about the houses and the red roofs were in startling contrast. (Steinbeck and Ricketts, 1951)

Speaking for myself, I had just arrived here and was enjoying the novelty of kicking around in a Baja town yet to have formed any prejudice. I drifted close to a lively neighborhood club, drawn by sounds of live music. According to the marquee, "Los Absen Boys" were playing and I paused momentarily, tempted by the appealing sounds and pulsing beats from within. But I spurred myself onward through the night towards a good night's sleep and the excitement of greeting my first dawn upon the peninsula.

Once headed south along the Peninsular Highway, I was attuned to every side road, two-track and path into the surrounding desert or promising seaward route into an out-of-the-way coastal retreat. I had a rough idea of the "lay of the land," and wanted to get at least as far as the great *Bahía Concepción*. This was a prime area where I planned to encamp at and spend time exploring its underwater realm and shoreline environs. More than any specific objective, this was a preliminary scouting trip, to cover as much ground within a manageable stretch of the coast, to try to determine where the best prospects were for future, more in-depth expeditions.

Once I felt far enough removed from the vestiges of civilization, I turned off towards San Bruno. There was a small oceanside *ranchería* here that I continued on past. The dirt road went directly to the edge of the Gulf, with a view of the dominating contours of *Isla San Marcos*, before turning sharply back inland. From that point, I followed it a long way—mostly trusting my instincts—as it snaked back and forth repeatedly until I ultimately turned off towards the east, along a much more primitive two-track. My trust appeared to pay off when I finally emerged at the edge of a vast expansive, open seashore, completely deserted in both directions! Whew! What a nice relief after navigating endless *terra incognita*!

The nearly continuous sandy shoreline stretched far southeastward in a long, graceful curving arc, slipping underneath the lower portion of the far horizon-merged, unbroken ridgeline, which sloped off abruptly into the sea. Strewn across the sands were scattered dark volcanic cobbles, rock and occasional boulders, with a thicker coverage over the upper beach terraces. The same open substrate of scattered dark rock patches between open sandy bottom, was evident, while scanning across these shallow waters. Once I got my bearings, I realized I was northwest of *Punta Chivato*, the prominent point above a small settlement on the opposite side of the promontory I had been gazing towards, to the southeast. The undersea wildlife here was somewhat sparser than my familiar Sonoran haunts, as I might have imagined. I was well stocked with food, however, so having a quick "look-see" underwater took priority over hunting. Besides, I needed to prepare for a full day ahead. I would be passing through a lush palm-studded oasis and tropical lagoon, while on the journey to the enigmatic, crystalline waters of *Bahía Concepción*.

Navigating back out through the desert plain's crisscrossing maze of trackways, I arrived back on Highway 1; the One and only. One of the most enjoyable and exciting experiences is exploring unfamiliar territory for the first time, whether on foot, underwater, or by vehicle, though my preference would be the former two. There's only that one chance to experience the freshness, and fortuitous discoveries of going beyond the distant and forbidden ranges, descending into the mysterious hidden cove, or the irresistible lure around the next bend of a perilous road into the unknown! After about ten or twelve miles southward from where I re-joined the Peninsular Highway, a vision began to emerge of something in the distance that just did not seem to fit in the lowlands below harsh, arid cactus-studded desert hillsides.

View from Highway 1 bridge over the Río Santa Rosalía de Mulegé

I stood atop the highway bridge above the *Rio Santa Rosalía de Mulegé* (Mulegé River) gazing below at the most incongruously lush freshwater lagoon I had ever seen! Tall, dense stands of date palms, with mixed-in coconut palms, and solid mangrove thickets lined both sides of a wide swath of water. This is considered the northern limit of the coconut palm, and date palms have historically provided a cottage industry here, since naturalized by Jesuit priests in the 1700s. (Rebman and Roberts, 2012) I continued beyond this verdant oasis another 12 miles or 20km—according to Highway markers—before another spectacular vista was revealed.

At last, a gradual descent around a curve afforded an overlook of the shimmering blue-green waters of *El Mar de Bahía Concepción*, as far as the eye could see! "The Sea within the Sea," it might be called, with its tranquil waters largely protected from the waves and currents of the outer Gulf, along its twenty-five-mile length. The legendary Sonoran Desert resident-writer Joseph Wood Krutch described it in 1959:

> The first of Concepción Bay's superlatives is mere size, for it is some twenty-five miles across and that means nearly as big as our own San Francisco Bay proper. But it is also perfectly proportioned and in every other respect designed as if for maximum beauty and impressiveness. The water could not be bluer, the great sandy beaches could not be whiter, and their curves could not be more exquisitely right. The sky is almost as blue as the water and the few palms which here and there dot the open beaches are placed as though they had been put by design just where the eye finds them most effective. (Krutch, 1961)

Crystal-clear waters of estero *and mangroves around campsite*

Krutch went on, in his account, to add that "... no human habitation, no human being, was in sight." Well, that certainly wasn't true of my own experience, although in between the few concentrated trailer/RV-condo-marina-resort parks, there was a lot of open space among the greater proportion of beach, up and down the shoreline. The first of these bayside parks I came to was Santispac, after which I pulled over and stopped at the next cove, *Posada Concepción*. I think my motive for pausing here was likely to find a local person who might provide more specifics on "the lay of the land" and what kind of potential primitive camping spots might be found?

I entered the park, alongside a small harbor, and met a gentleman who turned out to be the park manager and also a diver. In fact, the conversation evolved into something quite a bit more interesting than where to go and where to camp. Don, "The Clam Man," was an experienced scuba diver with a good knowledge and a passion for local native clam species. He described how he had laid out plots and meticulously planted multiple species of clam varieties in beds within the harbor, literally underneath the moorings of boats. Whenever he had a hankering for a particular type of clam, he simply swam out to a plot, and harvested what he needed. The submarine equivalent of vegetable gardening, I suppose? Don also dispensed with a few good pointers on primitive camping in the local area, too. Before I headed out, I happened to mention my Sonoran coastal escapades hunting roosterfish. He stopped, his eyes lit up, and he said, "Hey, if you ever get a nice rooster, bring it right on over! Those are the best eatin', and I know just how to fix 'em"!

View out window of shallow, calm waters of Bahía Concepción *and large island*

In an area farther south, near *El Coyote*, I found a spot where I felt comfortable, even if it didn't resemble the typical, remote "middle-of-nowhere" locality I was used to. There were no traffic sounds, just the gentle lapping of wavelets upon the sand at the water's edge. There was a little mangrove-lined *estero* curving around behind my beach campsite with water so crystal clear, it looked like you could drink it. Gazing outward, there was much more open sandy bottom apparent, with a minimum of spaces showing a darker rock composition. The water had the appearance of being exceedingly shallow, as if you could wade right out to the nearest lump of an island, a half mile away.

From a geological standpoint, what is seen everywhere as glistening white sand, is not derived from weathered rock but is exclusively composed of grains of abundant shells and calcareous invertebrate fragments. The turquoise and aquamarine colors of the *bahía's* waters is produced by the colloidal lime derived from the endless bounty of shells and remains of marine animals. True sand as a lithic-derived source, on the other hand, is usually formed from weathering of granitic rock, which breaks down into mostly quartz and feldspar grains. Granitic rock is not known to occur in this region, which is dominated by volcanic geology. However, the detrition of volcanic rock produces a much finer grained material which becomes mud or fine silt, instead of sand. (Minch and Minch, 2017)

Everywhere along the Sea of Cortez is unique, fascinating, and worthy of taking note of, though my stay here was not destined to extend beyond three or four days. I enjoyed prowling the crystalline *estero* and covered a wide sweeping range of the waters off an extended perimeter of shoreline. While venturing into several adjacent areas of the *bahía*, I also met and enjoyed the company of campers from Riverside, Redondo Beach, and the San Francisco area of California. Overall, I didn't write up a series of notes or listings of species, and, as expected, the open, mostly sandy littoral zone and beyond did not offer up a very high diversity and abundance of marine life. So, it was time to say "*adios muchachos*" to the beautiful bay and head back out in pursuit of *terra incognita* with what little time remained on the current expedition.

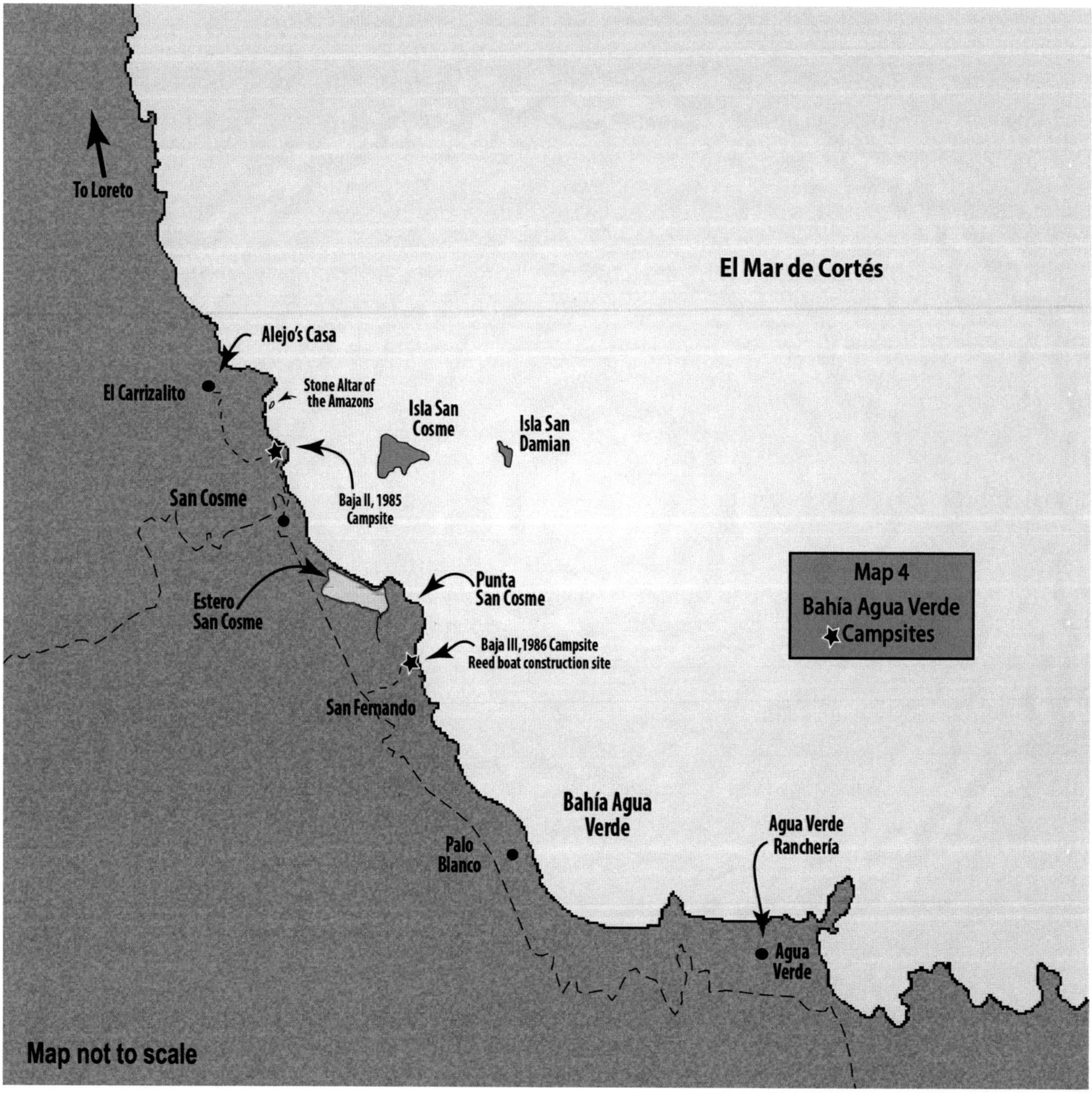
To Loreto
El Mar de Cortés
Alejo's Casa
El Carrizalito
Stone Altar of the Amazons
Isla San Cosme
Isla San Damian
Baja II, 1985 Campsite
San Cosme
Punta San Cosme
Estero San Cosme
Baja III, 1986 Campsite
Reed boat construction site
San Fernando
Map 4
Bahía Agua Verde
Campsites
Bahía Agua Verde
Agua Verde Ranchería
Palo Blanco
Agua Verde
Map not to scale

Chapter Eleven

Bahía Agua Verde/ Baja California Sur

In the summer of 1985, I had another opportunity to return to the Baja Peninsula, to explore further south, well beyond *Bahía Concepción*. I was well-prepared, had done some off-season research, and disembarked from the Santa Rosalía Ferry with a definite objective in mind: I would continue southward in much the same fashion as before, even taking advantage of the remote, open shoreline campsite northwest of *Punta Chivato*, along the way. Once beyond the southernmost limit of the previous expedition, I would head directly towards the town of Loreto. This picturesque town would be the prime stopping-off point for final preparations and stocking up on last minute supplies prior to setting out on the Second Baja Expedition's mission.

One thing became clear, the more I studied the maps and terrain across the entire central and lower Gulf portions of the Baja Peninsula: one of the most inaccessible, remote, and promising areas to explore lay in the greater *Bahía Agua Verde* region, between *Punta Candeleros* and *Punta San Marcial*. Of course, there was no clearly defined access road that jumped off the maps either. Certain areas to the south of this region seemed to be even more isolated from the nearest road or two-track, perhaps only reached by *panga* or burro?

Loreto was the oldest mission and the first permanent settlement established on the Baja Peninsula by the Jesuit priest, Father Juan María de Salvatierra, on October 19, 1697. (Bowen, 2000) I hoped at a future date to stroll about this pleasant seaside village and experience its sights and historic charms, but that would have to wait for now. The time had come to venture forth towards the unknown, precipitously high escarpments of the distant *Sierra de la*

Giganta, to the south. On the way there, I pulled off at *Juncalito*, just before *Bahía Escondido* (Hidden Bay). I just couldn't resist stopping to take in the breathtaking vista overlooking the sea, across from *Isla El Carmen* and the peculiar little island closer to shore.

Thirty kilometers further from *Puerto Escondido*, I sighted what looked to be a turnoff ahead. I was driving southwest along an ascending stretch of Peninsular Highway 1 after the sharp bend earlier past Ligüí. At the KM-Post 64 turnoff, I headed southeast off the main highway to begin what appeared to be the long, winding route through steep, columnar cacti-covered mountainsides to the fabled *Bahía Agua Verde* of Baja, California, home of mythical Amazons, according to ancient legends such as *Las Sergas de Esplandián* (The Exploits of Esplandián). (Bowen, 2000) Cultural anthropologist and marine biologist Michelle María Early-Capistrán provides an interpretation from the historical archives:

> Tenochtitlán had fallen. The Spanish *conquistadores*, blinded by the unimagined riches torn from the empires of the Americas, stood before a New World seemingly unbound by the constraints of reality. The lines between the tangible and the imaginary became blurred. Literature played no small role in this entanglement. The chivalric novel, beloved by the masses of medieval Spain, stimulated the ambitions of the sailors and soldiers (often freed from gallows and dungeons) who crossed the Atlantic. This genre, parodied by Cervantes in *Don Quixote*, inspired colonial fantasies thanks to the novel, *Las sergas de Esplandián* (The Sagas of Esplandián) from whence was born the myth of the Island of California. (Early-Capistrán 2014)

Pool and rock wall at La Última Agua*, between Peninsular Highway and coast*

History professor Robert Ryal Miller elaborates further on the effect these legends had on Hernán Cortés and the Spanish conquistadors:

> Rumors of pearls and Amazon warriors with gold-tipped spears also drew Cortés toward the northwest of New Spain. Some pearls were found along the west coast at Zacatula and in Colima, and in 1524 Cortés wrote the king that his men had heard of "an island populated only by women...they say it is very rich in pearls and gold." He added that he would try to discover the truth about the island. A romance of chivalry, *Las Sergas de Esplandían*, by Garcia Ordónez de Montalvo, published in Seville the previous decade and read by some of the conquistadors in New Spain, gave impetus to these reports. In that book there was an island named "California" where Amazon women lived and where pearls and precious stones were plentiful. (Miller, 1974)

Maybe my route was "mythical," too, since my 1981 *Mapa Turístico de Carreteras* (Tourist Road Map) showed no such coastal roads existing in this region.

The road went straight ahead for several miles, then entered a gap between steep-sloped mesas. As the scenery flattened out onto a desert plain, a familiar looking arid scrubland of dense vegetation lay beyond, with the occasional white-barked *palo blanco* revealed, along with tall multi-stemmed columnar cacti. No signs of any human habitation were evident anywhere across this vast landscape. The route gradually descended until it ran parallel with a dry sand and gravel arroyo, which soon arrived at a wide, flat confluence of adjoining desert washes. From here—close to the five-to-six mile mark—the track turned eastward, following an even larger, major, dry washbed. Another mile ahead, lay an inconceivable sight, reflecting the glare of the hot, baking mid-day sun!

Suddenly, I had reached a sparkling lowland oasis, a huge, lush shimmering canyon pool of at least two hundred or more feet long by perhaps a hundred -fifty-feet wide with patches of vegetation arising in a few spots. Steep-walled mountain escarpments and pinnacles rose up far from the oasis; nearby an imposing section of canyon wall overhung one side of the pool. Off in the distance, above the remotest edge of this flat, bottom expanse stood an elevated terrace of the most impressive *cardonál* (open forest of columnar *cardón* cacti). Baja, the land of constant surprises, continued to offer up these seemingly incongruous paradoxes! Rather than a "charco," or manmade water basin, such as is commonly found in Arizona cattle rangelands, this was a natural water impoundment. I later discovered the name of this locality, which was certainly true to its isolation: *La Última Agua* (The Last Water).

Beyond *La Última Agua*, the route followed the curving canyon floor, then angled off away and up gradually over a low rise, meandering back and forth for perhaps another five miles or so. Finally, after passing through the last rocky, sunburnt hills, the moment of truth arrived at the edge of a steep bluff: there, in all its incomprehensible glory, lay a boundless portal of deep blue stretching from horizon to horizon, only obscured by bold headlands jutting out from the edges. Misty, hulking forms of large islands could be made out through the distant haze: *Isla Monserrat* and *Isla Santa Catalina*. Gazing down the steep route traversing below to the coast, several intriguing smaller islands lay at a tempting distance offshore. The destination of the mission—an enchanting remote marine paradise—was now within reach, though a slow, grinding descent along a narrow, precarious route remained.

View from high above before first descent into Bahía Agua Verde

I engaged the hubs, then shifted the Jeepster Commando into four-wheel drive-high, before completing the arduous descent down to the coast. I did not disengage the four-wheel drive close to the beach, since I had scouted out—on foot—a rather unique route hugging the coast for about a half mile, to reach my appointed campsite. What made it unique and interesting was that the crux of the route went over a narrow rocky tidal bench, between sheer bluff cliff faces and the sea. It was only passable at low tide; fortunately, my timing was per-

Looking behind over tidal bench route on way to hidden campsite

Route ahead over tidal bench into "Devil's Head Cove" to campsite; "Devil's Head" on far right

fect! The tidal bench was strewn with boulders that had to be cleared from the route in several places. It was yet another "Oh shit—here we go" moment, but once underway, things proceeded smoothly and the Commando finally powered up the incline above the shore and came to a stop upon a gravelly beach terrace beyond a flat-bottomed arroyo outflow plain.

La Palmita was a great campsite, despite the difficulty in reaching it. This was certainly an out-of-view and well-protected spot. Situated near a large ironwood tree providing shade, limbs for hanging wetsuit, wet clothing and socks, as well as a possible windbreak. Other trees nearby, farther up the arroyo, would likely provide sufficient downed and dead branches for firewood. Perhaps most of all, it was an excellent strategic spot for multiple exploration purposes on foot over inland terrain, offshore undersea diving pursuits, and possible island hopping in the dinky inflatable raft. With or without the mythical Amazons, *La Palmita* (named for the small lone palm) seemed to have it all.

It was a great joy to finally enter the cove below camp, becoming immersed in the unknown waters of this enchanting, remote little archipelago. I could tell from a distant appearance that the inner shoal of the nearest headland, below precipitous cliffs, looked promising, with ample rocky reef structure. An imposing and sinister-looking, dark volcanic, "devil's head" formation—as if created by a master sculptor—arose above the surface at the point of the headland. Indeed, there were clearly visible dark, shadowy eye sockets, and a nose, with the mouth of a perfectly-shaped pointed head just above the surface of the water, with even the projection of an ear behind. So, I started using the term, "Devil's Head Cove," in my own descriptive nomenclature. Perhaps it was an eroded remnant of a volcanic plug, but it was unmistakable.

Swimming out towards the headland, the water seemed inordinately calm and smooth, with only a slight ripple. I recognized many of my favorite and familiar reef inhabitants, as I slowly glided over extended, parallel-running fins of rock, gradually working down into deeper reef formations. I started sighting small schools of yellowtail surgeonfish, which had not been present at my Sonoran coastal sites. These fish possess sharp-pointed retractible spines along the caudal peduncle (narrow part before tail)

Raft in shallows of Isla San Cosme*; mainland view of Sierra de la Giganta*

that can be used in defense by thrashing the tail section back and forth and inflicting slash wounds on potential predators. (Thomson, et al., 1979) Flag cabrilla, with their unique and striking color pattern, were recognized perhaps for the first time. These small to medium-sized sea basses were olive-green to red-brown in overall body color, overlain with a star-like pattern of bright small-to-large white spots. Returning to the cove, the tempting sight of *Isla San Cosme* loomed, perhaps a mile or more offshore to the east. It was time to take advantage of these nice, favorably calm conditions, and do a little island hopping!

Dawn arrived in the "Paradise of the Amazons" with the promise of another day's exciting adventures, under bright sunny skies shining down on tranquil seas. Casting off early after sunrise, the water looked flat as a mirror all the way out to the island. I thought about tossing in a spin casting outfit but talked myself out of it. Fishing with hook and line had certainly not been one of my strong points on these excursions. It was fun to sling a lure out into the water, every now and then, but undersea hunting with a spear put food on the table. This was a very different experience than my earlier journey rowing out to *Isla El Acero*. Divergent, if not opposite conditions and a very different type of island.

Most of the islands in the Sea of Cortez are considered "land bridge islands." That is, they are land bridge remnants that separated from the mainland, around four or more million years ago. (Case, et al., 2002) Geologist/zoologist Stewart Aitchison offers a concise perspective:

> ...islands can be classified as land bridge (continental) or oceanic. A land bridge island was once part of a larger land mass that became disconnected either through tectonic movements or rising sea

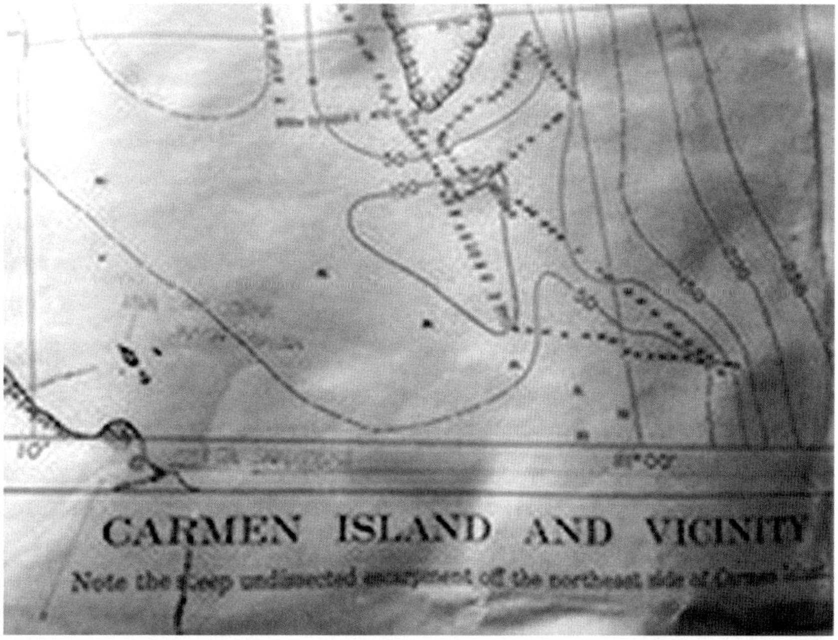

1875 Map of soundings by U. S. S. Narragansett; islands, Punta San Cosme, on lower left

levels (sometimes combined with subsidence and/or erosion). Most of the Gulf of California's islands are land bridge types, including the Gulf's largest island, *Isla Tiburón*. Oceanic islands are either the emergent summits of volcanoes and their attendant lava flows or sea floor faulted upward. *Isla Ángel de la Guarda* and many of the smaller Midriff Islands to its southeast are oceanic. Farther south, *Islas Tortuga, Monserrat, Santa Catalina, Santa Cruz, San Diego*, and *Cerralvo* are also oceanic. (Aitchison, 2010)

I'm not sure which classification *Isla San Cosme* falls into, but being so close to the coast, I strongly suspect it's a land bridge remnant. Unlike the whitish "animal cracker"-shaped rock of my earliest raft adventure, *Isla San Cosme* was a steeply-sloped chunk of land, covered with desert scrub and cacti. By comparison to *Isla El Acero* off the Sonoran coast, it looked enormous! Shaped in the form of an isosceles triangle with the point to the east, it had to be roughly a half mile across its long axis. It appeared to have over a mile of shoreline around its circumference, with a summit rising up over 300 feet on the west end. The soundings made during the historic voyage of the USS Narragansett in 1873-1875 suggest that the maximum depths occurring over the one mile-plus stretch of water separating *Isla San Cosme* from the shore below my campsite would be approximately 200-250+ feet. (Anderson, et al., 1950)

Entering the shallows close to *Isla San Cosme's* west-facing shore, I carefully maneuvered my rubber craft in between large boulders and stepped out upon a mixed large rock and cobble bottom. It had been an exhilarating row across the smooth, shimmering expanse, taking at least an hour. Once the raft was secured above the beachhead, I began the ascent of the steep slopes, donned in full "Farmer John" wetsuit and packing my Sedic pocket camera. The view looking back from the middle summit was beyond words to describe, once I climbed up past the last desert hackberry stand and *pitahaya agría* cactus (*Stenocereus spp.*). The spectacular vista made me oblivious to the fact that I was sweating buckets, sweltering inside my wetsuit under the scorching hot sun!

From my rocky perch atop the island, I had the most unique and stunning perspective, beyond what would be visible from a boat on the water. The impossibly steep-walled and articulated escarpments of the majestic *Sierra de la Giganta* marched across a vast, dominant portion of the mainland. To the south, bold, rocky headlands jutted out into the blue, with *Punta San Marcial* and its little offshore rock, just visible at the farthest end. Directly opposite my lofty outpost, the massive bulk of the *Punta San Cosme* headland loomed at close range; revealing dark cliff faces below seaward bluffs. Immediately on the north, run-

View atop middle summit of Isla San Cosme; Punta San Cosme *along mainland coast*

ning across a far-reaching, narrow strand, the brilliant white sheen of *coquina* sand streaked across the outer breakwater edge of the *Estero San Cosme*. From here, perhaps another mile or two farther north arrived at the familiar, though seemingly very distant "Devil's Head Cove." Scanning over the boundless, surrounding luminous expanse of blue—in all directions—there was nothing moving nor any visible watercraft manifesting itself. I embraced the radiant, mid-day heat, as I began my descent back down to the sea, in the form of a darkly absorbent "human solar panel!" Becoming refreshingly immersed in the shallows, once back to my raft, felt chilly and invigorating!

Imagine my shock returning to San Cosme's cobble beach and the raft to look out and see a beautiful white sailboat anchored out from the island's southwest edge! Impulsively, I entered the water and began swimming out towards it. Somehow the timing had to have been just right for its movement up from the south to have been obscured by the bulk of the Island until I made my descent. After several hundred yards, I neared the moored craft and called out. Surprised, yet friendly voices answered and invited me aboard. That's when I got to meet an ocean-going couple, Dale and Deborah Brasket, from Santa María, California, along with their two children, Kelli and Chris.

La Gitana (The Gypsy) was an elegant, 46-foot sailing sloop with a center cabin, manned by an adventurous family preparing to head out to the South Pacific; the first leg of fulfilling their dream of an around-the-world odyssey. I became comfortably relaxed upon the deck of this magnificent craft, enjoying our conversation and tales of traveling to far-off places in the western Pacific Ocean, such as the Marquesas Islands. Deborah Brasket's logbook entry of June 24th, 1985, describes our fortuitous encounter:

> As we approach Pt. San Cosme, we can't see the 3 islands charted off-shore, only the two. But it turns out Roca San Cosme curves in such a way to appear attached to the mainland. We pass the "Point" only to find it's an island! We anchor on the lee side and see an inflatable thrown up on the rocks and a diver who we invite aboard. He is Joe Billings, a lover of Baja and a lonely traveler. We talk for several hours and it turns out he is a friend of Trica and Marcos. He stays until 5pm, then the wind kicks up as he rows back to his camp ashore. It takes two hours! The next morning we go looking for the "lobster hotel" that Joe told us about, but the water is cold and full of seaweed--nary a lobster, scallop or fish to be captured. Disappointed we decide to head on. [Brasket, 1985—Logbook Entry provided in email of 10/08/20]

Over the passage of time, I began to think more and more about my long-lost sea-faring friends and wonder how they made out. In a remarkable stroke of good fortune I was able to locate and catch up with Deborah Brasket, after a thirty-five-year interlude. I learned from her writings, in greater depth, how much thought, preparation, fortuitous events and long-range, step-by-step planning had gone into making their dream come true over a six-and-a-half year circumnavigational adventure. And, especially, how they wrestled with the decision of wrenching their 8 and 11-year old children away from the mundane world to daily life on a sailboat far out at sea! As an accomplished writer, she provides a colorful retrospective of their journey in a seven-part saga on "Living on the Edge of the Wild" Blog (https://deborah-brasket.wordpress.com/2012/08/06/sea-saga-part-1/).

Meanwhile, back at the *Rancho La Palmita*, I was preparing for my first exploration into the desert areas skirting the coast. I've probably never thrown out an expired pair of running shoes that were still serviceable as beach wading shoes. That's what I set forth from *La Palmita* wearing the next day following the exploration of *Isla San Cosme*. I had my fins, basic dive gear and dinky pocket camera in a daypack, prepared for all the possibilities. Roaming

Looking north from desert plain towards "Hidden Cove"

inland through the thornscrub and organ pipe cactus-studded landscape, I came upon a familiar plant, finding it occurring "in habitat" for the first time. Roughly two to three feet tall with a similar spread, it is known here as *Rama parda*. Covered with showy, blue-purple flowers, *Ruellia peninsularis* is a compact and attractive shrub I had mixed into desert habitat garden projects in the past. (Jones and Sacamano, 2000, Starr, 2009)

I was totally entranced by the little cove where I found myself after emerging from doing "recon" across the coastal desert plain. It was a pretty well-protected little gem with a single small flat sand beach closer to the hills at the desert's edge. The entire cove, ranging far across and several hundred yards out, was incredibly shallow and could be waded with care over an uneven rocky bottom. I was drawn to an isolated oblong, sheer rock formation sitting on a raised platform of loose rock and sand, standing out in the middle of these shallows. It resembled a tall, chiseled giant stone altar, as if precisely placed there for sacred rituals. (Perhaps I had found the sacred altar of the Amazons?) Even more interesting than the sacred altar was what I came across next!

A pattern of stones visible above the surface, not far away from this monolith, drew my attention. The stones had been piled up to form a roughly circular outline, measuring around twelve feet long by ten feet in width. The top layer of stones above the surface was not continuous, with uneven gaps in between. Once I stood next to the mysterious circle, the abrupt change in water temperature revealed its nature. I had stumbled upon an active thermal vent, or hot springs. The water was pleasantly warm, certainly not hot. This was like-

Rock-ringed thermal upwelling in shallows of "Hidden Cove"

ly the site of a fault, where heated water arises from a considerable depth. A general up-to-date description of the process is offered by a longtime Baja geologist:

> **Hot Springs:** Hot springs are at least 10° C warmer than the mean air temperature. Hot springs do not normally require abnormal heat sources. The earth's temperature increases about 1.8° C per 100 meters of depth. As ground waters are heated to the temperature of the surrounding rock, the 10° warmer water need only come from about 550 m. below the surface. Faults provide an avenue for the rapid rise of hot ground water to the surface which results in hot springs. Most of the hot springs in the western United States are along faults. Some such as Yellowstone and Lassen are near volcanic centers and are due to magma near the surface. (Minch and Minch, 2017)

I could spend many weeks here at "The Archipelago of the Amazons," but time was running short. This paradise had lived up to its promise, since the first glimpse of its breathtaking expanse, from high above. The initial exposure to the undersea world on this side of the Gulf proved to be as anticipated: highly interesting and exciting, with much more ground yet to cover and ramparts to be explored. Despite my being a newcomer to these waters, I could already draw some initial impressions and comparisons with the Sonoran central Gulf reef-fish fauna and conditions in general.

For the most part, I've sighted virtually every fish species, at one time or another, as depicted in the primary sourcebook, "Reef Fishes of the Sea of Cortez." (Thomson, et al., 1979) within the central Gulf zoogeographical subdivision (the Gulf is divided into three subdivisions according to the book: upper, central and lower Gulf reef fish communities). I've yet to venture south to the lower Gulf, and had only one limited exposure to the upper Gulf region (*Puerto Lobos*). The greater *Bahía Agua Verde* is positioned farther southward—closer to the lower Gulf; therefore, it may have a slightly higher diversity of species, with overlapping affinities.

Thus far from my experience, the overwhelming proportion of familiar species seem to be present on both sides of the Gulf. There were a few, noted earlier, I hadn't seen before. There seem to be a greater abundance of schools of jacks, though I remember a "thundering herd of crevalle jacks" (clearout sound) offshore, north of *Playa Jojoval*, along the Sonoran coast. The yellow jack (*Gnathanodon speciosus*), was a new one encountered, here at *Bahía Agua Verde*. This is a wide-bodied, silvery fish with intense, zebra-like black bars and yellowish fins. Memories of unique encounters with interesting and unique species leave an indelible memory. The one and only time I discovered a Pacific seahorse (*Hippocampus ingens*) in a patch of seaweed at *Ensenada Rada El Pasito* was one such moment. This precious six to seven-inch creature hovered in the water while I examined it in amazement!

Yellow jack displayed on dark volcanic substrate

Another one-of-a-kind sighting—never repeated since—was the small school of Mexican lookdowns (*Selene brevoorti*) found around the far south side of the headland of *Ensenada las Cocinas.* They cannot be mistaken for any other species. These fascinating deep-bodied, silvery fishes with extravagantly long fins, were an impressive sighting in their own rocky reef habitat.

Apart from the reef-fish fauna, the conditions vary between the two central coast region areas in several notable respects: The cooler water temperatures along the Baja Peninsula, especially at depth, are noticeable. Overall, much calmer water conditions, extending far offshore, prevailed during the period of my encampment. Of course, I also may have been fortunate in the timing of my visit. The typical wind patterns occurring along Sonoran coastal sites were not present here. So, granted, my experience was limited, but there still seems to be a different weather paradigm operating along the Baja seashore in contrast with Sonora.

Most days on the Sonoran side of the central Gulf begin under relatively calm morning conditions. Then, the summer winds begin to intensify in the afternoon, usually out of the south and west. This pattern has a direct influence upon a particularly unwelcome phenomenon, that occurs in mid to latest summer: This is the seasonal influx of the infamous Portuguese man-of-war (*Physalia sp.*), or stinging jellyfish, otherwise known as *malagua* (bad water) by the natives. The small, bluish-tinted, bubble-like floats (usually 2-2.5") can be observed drifting upon the ocean surface. Trailing below these floats are tentacles armed with stinging nematocysts, up to two meters in length. With winds increasing in the afternoons, they begin to collect in shallow Sonoran coastal waters; having been blown in from open seas and riding the seasonal circulation pattern.

For the uninitiated, like myself, it can be a very alarming experience when you first unknowingly drift into these nearly invisible stinging tentacles! I distinctly remember those painful learning experiences. The stings are potent, and wherever a tentacle brushes across a skin surface leaves a line of stings. While in the water, I learned to adapt to being stung in several ways: Once I sustained stings, it was very irritating, but I found the effects wore off as I continued my normal activity, swimming and breath-hold diving without interruption. More importantly, I devised my own aversion training in adapting to these in-blown flotillas: First, I got into the habit of periodic surface scanning while out in the water offshore. Secondly, I developed a specific technique when ascending from a breath-hold dive: In the course of my ascent, I would spiral upward while intently scanning the surface. If I detected any tentacles or jellyfish floats, I would immediately dive back down and swim laterally for an effective distance—ten to twenty yards or more—before emerging well beyond the hazard. This became a very effective strategy, once I adapted to it, and the incidence of drifting into stinging tentacles became minimal.

Reed boat resting on beach cobbles at El Bajo *(Photo by Dorothy Coffman)*

Chapter Twelve

The Reed Boat Project/ *Baja California Sur*

During the off-season between Baja expeditions, a spontaneous study and selective research was initiated on primitive watercraft. This had always been a latent interest. Then—out of the blue—I received a very serendipitous, surprising and useful gift! Good friend, fellow diver, and kindred spirit Sharon Ann "Shari" Spear presented me with a large historic volume on the Seri Indians (or *Comcáac*) of the northern Gulf of California. (McGee, 1898) Within this immense volume were ethnographer W. J. McGee's descriptions of the reed canoes or balsas crafted by the Seris at the end of the nineteenth century.

All maritime native cultures of North and South America, and elsewhere around the world developed effective watercraft. These took the forms of canoes, kayaks, reed boats (or balsas), and rafts made from logs or palm trunks. (Quirke, 1952) In the summer of 1970, Thor Heyerdahl and his crew sailed across the Atlantic Ocean in a large boat formed of bundles of reeds that was based on an ancient Egyptian model. (Heyerdahl, 1972) After departing from Morocco, the RA II covered 4,000 miles of ocean in 57 days, before finally reaching Barbados. Interestingly, the

Ramon Blanco atop Seri reed balsa in Kino Bay, Sonora, circa 1922 (Photo by Edward Davis courtesy of Nathan Sowry of the Smithsonian Insitution)

main work force employed in the construction of the RA II, had been the legendary reed boat-building Aymara tribe of Lake Titicaca, Peru. These skilled boat-making fishermen were well-known for their large, sturdy craft formed from large reed bundles, that even occasionally included a pole mast and bamboo mat sail.

The native Chumash of California traditionally made a variety of reed boats according to size and function. Larger craft allowed for regular contact with tribal groups on the Channel Islands (twenty miles from the mainland). The knowledge of how to construct one of these craft was gained through interviews in the early 1900s with a Chumash Indian over 100 years old, who actually lived during the last Spanish Mission Period (early 1800s to mid-1830s) in California. This exacting design and knowledge was utilized and applied in the construction of a replica of a Chumash reed boat by an enterprising and inspiring instructor at Santa Barbara City College in the 1980s. (Miller, 1984)

Professor Dennis Ringer challenged his students to do the research and take on the task of constructing a vintage Chumash reed canoe. A small local lake's freshwater marsh provided ample stands of tule reeds (*Scirpus californicus*), gathered and then toughened by sun-drying. The well-formed, finished craft measured nineteen feet long at the waterline, four feet abeam, with eighteen inches of freeboard. The main thirty-foot long bundle running through the center of the craft had both ends pulled upward, forming a graceful curve, to a height of four and a half feet. The launch date arrived on June 5, 1982, when Ringer and one of his students, Larry Romero, walked it slowly into the surf below the college campus.

> Then, with a rush, [they] drove the canoe through the first wave and leaped aboard. They leaned into their double-bladed paddles and took her out into deeper water. She floated like a gull, light and responsive, as if born to the ocean. Cheers burst spontaneously from the throng of well-wishers assembled onshore. And here is the most remarkable feat of all: For the following three hours and more, repeated trips were made through the pounding surf, as various people took turns propelling the reed canoe out into deeper water and back again to the beach. The canoe took a terrific pounding, but in all that time, it remained perfectly buoyant and seaworthy even with inexperienced persons handling the paddles. In fact, the reed canoe was deemed to be so safe that parents even took very young children with them as they took the canoe through its paces. And not once was anyone lost overboard, nor did the canoe provide anything but a very stable ride. (Miller, 1984)

One of Dennis Ringer's former students, Jon Erlandson, and a friend had built and launched a similar Chumash reed canoe that accomplished an extended one-day voyage of twelve miles in an earlier project.

My own focus centered on aboriginal watercraft within the Gulf of California crafted from native or naturalized plant materials of the region. Both the *Comcáac* (Seri) of the Sonoran coast and the *Cochimí* of the Baja Peninsula were known for their seaworthy reed canoes, or balsas. (Bowen, 1976) Returning southward along the Baja coastline, following his exploration of the northern Gulf, Spanish seafaring captain Francisco de Ulloa made these observations of a *Cochimí* reed craft in 1540:

> They had a little raft which they must have used in fishing. It was made of canes tied together, the middle section being larger than the laterals. They rowed it with a slender oar, little more than half a fathom long [about 1 m], and two small paddles, badly made, one at each end. (Wagner, 1924)

The first historic description of the Seri reed balsa came from Jesuit priest and cartographer Father Adamo Gilg, of the Nuestra Señora del Pópulo mission of Sonora. (Bowen, 1976) As a missionary, Father Gilg had personally interacted with Seris and recorded these observations when he visited their territory in 1692:

> My Seris do not build their boats of planks, but of three bundles of reeds bound together, which are joined in a narrow point behind and before, and are widely separated from each other in the middle, forming a hollow bilge. In place of an anchor, they throw a good-sized stone into the depths when they want to stop. (DiPeso, et al., 1965)

In 1750, Spanish sailor Manuel Correa described similar Seri balsas sighted along Tiburón Island off the Sonoran coast, saying they were:

> composed of many small carrizos arranged in three bundles, thick in the middle and thin on the ends, joined together with plaited cord. These balsas were generally five or six varas long [4.2 m to 5.0 m] and about one and one-quarter varas wide [1.0 m] in the middle, tapering proportionally toward the tips. These balsas support the weight of three or four people and they slice through the water very rapidly.
>
> The paddles are wooden shafts about two varas long [1.7 m] with two blades fastened to the tips, and the paddler, holding it in the middle, paddles from one side to the other. (Bowen, 1976)

Sometime, during the early summer of 1986, I paid a visit to a Tucson landmark excelling in outdoor recreational equipment—camping, backpacking and climbing gear—located in midtown along Speedway Blvd. The Summit Hut, which was begun in a garage by high school student and legendary climber Dave Baker and a partner in 1967, had grown to become the local mecca for outdoor recreational enthusiasts. I was pleased to see Dave once I entered the store and proceeded to describe to him my newfound, off-the-wall project for the next Baja adventure. Without a word, he disappeared into the back. He returned a few minutes later, to hand me two broken pieces of a double-bladed paddle. "We broke this paddle on our last whitewater trip in the Grand Canyon," he explained. "Maybe you can find a way to repair it and make use of it?"

I had absolutely no experience working with fiberglass, but the impending necessity and mission imperative found a way to overcome that: I used the aluminum shaft of one of my dinky raft paddles as a splint, joining both broken ends of the paddle tightly together into a solid piece! Then, the paddle shaft was thoroughly and evenly coated with fiberglass for reinforcement and allowed to cure. Done! I now had a major item of equipment checked off the expedition list!

Fulfilling the other major items on the expedition list took place downtown at a very large warehouse building at the corner of Sixth Avenue and Seventh Street. Miller's Surplus had been a longtime Tucson mainstay for military surplus and all kinds of recreational gear and clothing. I purchased hundreds of feet of strong cord and bungee cord tie-down materials for both the reed boat construction phase and the loading operation, respectively.

I returned to Sonora in mid-June of 1986, for the beginning of another seagoing mission, during a brief re-acclimation period at *Bahía San Augustín.* On Sunday, June 22nd, I was crossing the great blue Gulf, heading back towards The Promised Land of Amazons, once again!

> Arrive Sta. Rosalia: Heading S [south] at first then turn around and drive N and W [north and west] towards San Ignacio. Find desolate extremely still campsite in desert S of [*Volcán*] *Las Tres Virgenes.* [JB Field Notes, 1986]

San Ignacio was founded by the Jesuits in 1728 and, unlike many failed Baja mission sites, has been inhabited continuously ever since. The Sonoran Desert inhabitant/writer Joseph Wood Krutch seemed to appreciate the town's historic charm when he passed through during his lengthy adventure across the Baja Peninsula in 1959:

> Then there is, of course, the plaza where generations have sat in the sun, and the now oversized church built of lava-stone blocks with walls four feet thick, completed nearly two hundred years ago, and still in a state of excellent preservation. See two black-robed nuns climbing the steps towards it and entering its doors or observe one of the equally somber widows, indistinguishable in any Latin town from her sister in any other, and the sense one gets is not of a primitive community but rather of a community where time has long stood still. (Krutch, 1961)

Monday, June 23rd: I arose to resume my travels inland to San Ignacio where I hoped to find abundant stands of reeds in the immense freshwater lagoon areas southwest of the town:

> Drive remainder of 45-50 miles to S. I. [San Ignacio]. Find spot along Rio San Ignacio outside town and start setting up camp. Begin cutting canes, keeping an eye on bird life [and listening to songs] (oriole singing "there's riches here, there's riches here"). Cut about 150 canes. Make acquaintance [with] Ignacio—craftsman who carves palm trunks. [JB Field Notes, 1986]

Tuesday, June 24th: No matter how remotely concealed you might think you are in any area of Mexico, you will eventually be discovered by a roving, curious army of small boys:

> Clean canes and bundle up. Meet lively group of young boys—Ignacio, Juan, Martín Javier, etc. Cut and clean 120 more canes and tie into bundles of 25. [JB Field Notes, 1986]

My encampment beside the Rio San Ignacio was semi-sheltered by palm trees, where I had a seemingly limitless abundance of *Arundo donax* (giant reed) or *carrizo* stands to harvest canes from. It is characterized by long-leafed stems, up to fifteen to twenty feet tall, with thick inflorescent plumes atop the tallest stalks. Originating from the Mediterranean region, giant reed has become widely naturalized throughout western North America and the

Harvesting Arundo donax *canes along* Río San Ignacio *lagoon*

tropics as an invasive species displacing native plant populations. (Chambers and Hawkins, 2002) It has been documented by field specimen collections of the late 19th and early 20th centuries, for Sonora and Baja, and presumably, was established in Sonora much earlier. (Van Devender, et al., 2006) The native species, *Phragmites australis* (common reedgrass), closely resembles *Arundo donax*, except for smaller stems. It has largely been replaced by *Arundo*—possibly by bird-introduced seeds—at most of the main Seri waterholes on Tiburón Island and the Sonoran mainland, and likely here, as well, along the *Rio San Ignacio* in Baja. (Felger and Moser, 1985)

Cane bundles strapped atop Jeepster prior to 170-mile trip south to Bahía Agua Verde

My procedure when harvesting *Arundo donax* canes was simply cutting them off cleanly, with a decurved pruning saw, close to the ground. Eventually, these cuts would all generate fresh bud shoots from the corms below, and regrow into tall, leafy stems. I selected the most robust, straight canes, and trimmed them all off at the top, for a uniform, roughly twelve-foot length. "Cleaning," or husking, the canes didn't require tools, just stripping all the leaves off each stem by hand. You do have to watch it though, because the leaves can cause sharp cuts if mishandled!

Wednesday, June 25th: Today would be the last day spent along the *Rio San Ignacio* for the final stage of harvesting and loading canes.

> Begin loading operation. After securely tying down with most of my tiedowns, bungee cord, rope etc., finally depart my campamento. Buy dates, beans etc. at local gasolinera at junction. Hot drive back to Sta. Rosalia. Very hot in town, not many people stirring. Many watching Copa Mundial soccer [with] Belgium vs. Argentina [World Cup semifinal match at Mexico City's Azteca Stadium]. Ferry office closed so head short ways out and drive down into long lagoon and camp. Swim all the way (1

> mile or so) out thru [estuary] mouth into clear cold currents; very strong, running S [south] over shallower smooth boulder bottom. Return to beach and walk back. [JB Field Notes, 1986]

The return trip to Santa Rosalía passed by the massive and imposing *Volcán Las Tres Virgenes* (Volcano of the Three Virgins). The *volcán* is a historically active volcano, with an eruption reported by a Spanish missionary in 1746. There was a later increase in activity, with smoke observed in 1857. (Minch and Minch, 2017)

Thursday, June 26th:

> Take care of Ferry [reservation] and head S [south]. Stop in Mulege for a few goodies then on to Loreto, where I: gas up, buy beer, fill water jugs from restaurant faucet (kindness of Miguel) and proceed S towards familiar territory [Bahía Agua Verde]. Country is very dry, and cañon [canyon] pool [La Última Agua] has dried up [wow!]. Camp at bottom of road at landing. Spear a couple triggers [finescale triggerfish] and fix dinner. [JB Field Notes, 1986]

Friday, June 27th: This day was marred by a very unfortunate mishap and loss that, ultimately, could have been avoided. I was preparing to relocate to an appropriate campsite, but just could not resist the urge to hike down and do a morning dive offshore that morning. Upon returning, I looked in the open window of the Commando and realized my wetsuit jacket was gone! In my haste, I had not thought to lock up the Jeepster before heading down to the water. So, someone not encumbered with the conventional notion of private property had found it irresistible, reached in through the window and stole it out of the back seat! So, there I was—infuriated—fuming—stomping around—crazed—and about to go ballistic! Once I was able to get most of that angst expended, I slowly but surely recognized being at fault for not being more protective of my vehicle and its life-supporting contents! It's always tempting to leave the windows down when it's this hot, but NOT away from a secure or attended campsite:

> Dive before moving camp. Unfortunate loss of *traje* [wetsuit jacket] occurs. Afternoon resituate at S [south] [*Punta*] *San Cosme* where woodland valley and wash meet arroyo. Climb hill and photograph sunset. [JB Field Notes, 1986]

Saturday, June 28th: After the previous season's expedition, I knew from doing 'recon' that I wanted to head south along the coastline, further into the heart of *Bahía Agua Verde*. So, my destination wound up being several miles true to that bearing and at the end of a little two-track cutover to an upper beach terrace overlooking the Gulf. It was favorably situated along a major arroyo outwash plain, just south of the *Punta San Cosme* headland. *Arroyo San Fernando* had galleries of ample mesquite and ironwood trees, in addition to the white-barked palo blancos. This setting would provide an ideal and abundant source of both downed and dead firewood and selected green wood for fish-smoking purposes.

White-barked palo blanco *trees* (Lysiloma candida) *along* Arroyo San Fernando

The next several days were spent attending to all the various tasks setting up the most ideal base camp and construction site that I would be living out of over a two-week period. The centerpiece of the site was a big, sparsely-foliaged ironwood tree made up of split multiple trunks, with a big gap in between. Besides the usual drying limbs for wet clothing, it offered structure that allowed for an overhead tarp fastened to branch tips that served as a small outside ramada of sorts. Under the constant blazing heat of the Baja coastal desert, every little niche providing respite from the sun is valued. At a close distance—maybe ten feet—across from the centerpiece tree were several adjoined, scrubby small trees with off-shoots that provided an open framework upon which tarps, brush and other materials could be installed. A large tarp was spread over the inside floor space, and care was taken, when entering, not to track in sand. This shaded brush hut functioned as my main

Bahía Agua Verde *campsite above* Arroyo San Fernando *outwash plain; shaded hut on left*

shelter and sleeping quarters. It roughly resembled a Seri *jacal*, as described by W. J. McGee. (1898) Water containers could also be stored under the shade here, instead of inside the hot Commando where the temperature would rise accordingly. The Commando itself, was parked up close to the hut side of the centerpiece tree, with the tailgate pointed seaward, for convenient access during evening meals on the beach.

Nature provided abundant material for my next major task: Dual dome-shaped fish smokers built out of rock. In advance of the expedition, I had given some thought to this: to be able to work on the reed boat as continuously and efficiently as possible, the plan was to gradually accumulate a large stock of smoked fish, that could provide regular sustenance for long stretches. Of course, it would require diligent hunting and preparation of a sufficient quantity of fish in the beginning stage and when supplies ran low, but eventually would reduce the time having to go out every day to put food on the table.

The beach was littered with tons of assorted sizes and shapes of a whitish, coarse-grained volcanic rock. The chosen spot for my fish smokers would be on the downslope edge of the upper beach terrace, just below the centerpiece tree of my campsite. I assembled two igloo-like, rounded forms, with precise stacking and placement of this rock. My largest, main smoker was perhaps five and a half feet long at the base, by five feet wide and about two feet high in the center. I had brought along a double grill measuring 16" x 18" and another one measuring 18" x 24." The key to proper construction was the placement of stone forming the opening in the middle of each smoker to precisely fit its selective grill. Once the structures were built, a damp basin of slick, gooey beach mud nearby provided the perfect grout to thoroughly fill in and seal the gaps between the stones.

With camp set up and most major tasks accomplished, it was time to return to twentieth-century hunter-gatherer mode. I enjoyed roaming the *Arroyo San Fernando* and cutting up short, green wood chunks by hand from mesquite trees to stack next to my smokers. Entering the rippling clear waters below the dry outwash of the arroyo and reappearing far out from shore felt like being baptized yet again by the spirit of the sea, with perhaps the blessings of the Amazons! It was such a profound joy being able to move through the water—at a decent speed—exploring depths penetrated by bright sunbeam columns illuminating a whirling multitude of dazzling fish forms.

Later, after taking an out-of-the-water break, my face shielded from the harsh sun by a "fin-visor," I enjoyed the moment of relaxing and reflecting on the morning. It was comforting to contemplate and appreciate my profound exuberance in light of the disheartening experience that occurred after my arrival at the *bahía* days earlier. It was pure bliss to imagine the vast extent of this paradise of open waters I was surrounded by—soon to be immersed in—and I felt gratitude for my health and vitality! I untied my beach wading shoes from my weight belt, slipped them on, and headed down the shoreline, fins and speargun in hand.

After expressing a prayer of gratitude for the bounty of fish I brought back, I began building small fires inside my fish smokers. This was my first cave man-style attempt to use this method of curing and preservation of freshly speared fish. Once my fires burned down to glowing coals, I then placed small stacks of green mesquite wood upon them. Skinning, filleting, and slicing the fillets into thin strips preceded laying a fully-covered grill upon each smoke hole. The smaller, double grill, could be fastened together for easy flipping, but the larger one required turning over all the pieces individually. In case dripping fish fat re-ignited the fire, I kept a bucket of seawater close by to contain occasional flare-ups.

The glorious dawn of the following morning illuminated the tranquil, mirror-like sea surface with a brilliant sun-lit sheen across the entire archipelago. To the northeast, the immense, crisp outline of *Isla Monserrat* looked nearer than ever. Eastward, *Isla Santa Catalina* rose up prominently, though smaller in profile, at over twice the distance away (eighteen to twenty miles) than *Isla Monserrat*. The tallest of *Isla Santa Catalina's* summits on its south end was also twice the height of its companion island, at 1,543 feet. (Anderson, et al., 1950)

All the yellow-footed gulls seemed to be stationed at their widely spread-out posts; white specks visible up and down both shorelines—to the north and south—and a few up on top of rocky outcrops of distant headlands. So, where do they all fly off to, before evening, in gathering to roost? Is there a preferred lofty perch on an island somewhere where they spend the night? And do the same gulls return to occupy the same beaches, every day? These are some of the questions I ponder, roaming over damp, low tide-exposed stretches of sand and gravel, as the overnight's coolness gives way to the sun's warmth. I love and enjoy the presence of gulls. I suppose I've gotten used to their constant companionship and gained a certain appreciation for them. Gulls are such an inseparable part of the oceanside experience. They are tough birds; very aggressive and competitive with each other. I realize their tendency to habituate to humans, becoming abundant at landfills and pests on certain public beaches, which has made them unpopular in some circles. But how can you fault an intelligent, adaptable, and fiercely competitive species for taking advantage of a greatly expanded resource base? Besides the loud, sometimes uproarious choruses, there's a softer, almost murmured, "kuk—kuk—kuk—kuk—kuk," in rapid succession, by an individual bird, that I find pleasing to hear. I've now reached my appointed dive destination and slipped into my fins with my wading shoes secured to the back of my weight belt. Farther south down the shoreline than the previous day, I enter the glistening depths enjoying the best visibility and calmest sea I've experienced so far.

Wednesday, July 2nd: It was time to begin working on the reed balsa in earnest. Earlier that morning, a playful group of bottlenose dolphins offshore were intermittently breaking the surface in graceful leaps, while swimming in formation. I was just preparing for my morning dive and swam out in their direction, but I never caught sight of them. Afterwards I settled in under my little centerpiece tree ramada where I had all my harvested cane bundles piled and got to work.

When ethnographer W. J. McGee visited Seriland in the northern Gulf of California in 1895, he took a keen interest in their capable reed balsas. Besides his own observations and interpretations, he relied upon firsthand information from a Spanish-speaking Seri sub-chief named Mashém, who lived apart from the tribe on a mainland Sonoran ranch. McGee's descriptions of balsas essentially served as my specifications:

> The manufacture of the balsa has never been seen by Caucasian eyes, but the processes are safely inferred from the structure, whose testimony is corroborated in part by Mashém's imperfect descriptions. The first step is the gathering of the *carrizal* from one of the patches growing about the three or four permanent fresh waters of Seriland, the canes being carefully selected for straightness, symmetry, and uniformity in size; these are then denuded of leaves and tassels, tied in bundles of convenient size (one seen on Tiburon contained 40 or 50 canes), and carried to the shore. In actual construction the canes are laid butt to butt, but overlapping 2 or 3 feet, the overlap being shifted this way and that with successive additions, so that the aggregate length of overlapping in the bundle reaches 10 or 12 feet—i. e., the full length of the body of the finished craft. The growing bundle is wrapped from time to time with lashings of mesquite root or maguey [agave] fiber, and kept in cylindrical form by constant rolling and by means of the lashing; though the cord used for the purpose is so slender as to do little more than serve the purposes of manufacture (only stray shreds of the interior cording could be found in an old and abandoned balsa on *Punta Antigualla*). As the bundle approaches the requisite size, the building process changes; the butts of the successively added stalks are thrust obliquely into the interstices extending beyond the butts of earlier-used canes, and the stems are slightly bent to bring them into parallelism with their fellows; and this interweaving process is continued with increasing care until, when the bundle is completed, there are no

> visible butts (all being pushed into the interior of the bundle), while the only visible tips are those projecting to form the tapered extremities. The finished bundle is then secured by a spiral winding of slender cord. Two other bundles are next made, the three being entirely similar, so far as is known; then the three are joined by a lashing of slender cord like that used for the separate bundles, which is twined alternately above and below the central bundle in such a manner as to hold the three in an approximate plane save toward the extremities, where the lashing is much firmer and the tapering tips of the bundles are brought into a triangular position, i.e., the position of smallest compass. The cordage is of either mesquite root or maguey fiber, the former being the more common, so far as observed (doubtless by reason of the dearth of the latter plant); it is notably uniform in twist and size, though surprisingly slender for the purpose, barely three-sixteenths of an inch, or 5 mm., in diameter, and limited in quantity. (McGee, 1898)

I took my time getting a proper feel for putting canes together, following the aboriginal process. It was important to visualize the correct symmetry and maintain a consistent uniformity in the manufacture of each bundle. It was going to be a slow, drawn-out process, but that is to be expected and that's OK. I had a great big beautiful blue sea to gaze out over, plenty of gulls and other sea (and land) birds to keep me company, and the wonderful, therapeutic cascading rhythms of waves rolling over the sands down below.

Thursday, July 3rd: The winds started to pick up yesterday and have really come on strong today! I'm seeing a lot of whitecaps, scanning across the whole *bahía*, and it's become very choppy out there! I feel so fortunate and grateful with the way my timing worked out while getting settled in days earlier and having ideal conditions to do so. While working on the balsa, I spotted a big yacht coming into view in the distance entering a cove to the south. (It left on the 6th.) Later in the afternoon, I became aware that my water supply was going to need replenishing or I would be running perilously low in another week. So, time to bathe and shave (lemon-fresh Dawn—the choice of hunter-gatherer/skin divers—in preparation for heading back to civilization; spending the 4th of July in Loreto, BCS.

Friday, July 4th: This morning it's still windy and choppy. I packed up all the essentials and secured everything around *Campo San Cosme*. On impulse, I headed down south towards Punta San Marcial first. I had spontaneously decided to stop in and visit the people at the little ranchería there. I introduced myself to Javier, his wife María and family, who turned out to be quite warm and welcoming, especially after I presented them with a package of my best, primo smoked skipjack! (I was really pleased with the flavor and how well this skipjack turned out). Then I got started on the long uphill grind, through the desert cacti and scrublands back to the Peninsular Highway.

Coming into Loreto, I drove towards the sea, then turned off and motored slowly along the *Malecón* until I arrived at the perfect lone shade tree and parked underneath. The *Malecón* is the term for the massive concrete seawall at the town's edge, running as far as the eye can see, overlooking boundless blue waters, only interrupted by the interminably long, low outline of *Isla El Carmen*. After a quick lunch I headed in towards the main town plaza and parked. I walked up and stood in front of *Nuestra Señora de Loreto Conchó*. I gazed up at the right-hand clock tower, above the open porticos. Father Juan María Salvatierra, the founding

Nuestra Señora de Loreto Conchó *mission church of Loreto (July 4, 1986)*

Jesuit priest, had departed from the Sonoran mainland, near the mouth of the Rio Yaqui, on October 11, 1697, on a sailing voyage southwest to the Baja Peninsula. He and the six soldiers accompanying him explored along the coast until ultimately founding the mission here on October 19th, where there was a "well-watered" area. (Bowen, 2000) During an earlier mission, in 1690, he had joined up with Father Eusebio Francisco Kino—the Patron Saint of the Arizona-Sonora Borderlands—in the *Pimería Alta* of northern Sonora. Father Salvatierra and Father Kino rode extensively throughout the region together, sharing similar philosophies as kindred spirits. (Bowen, 2000)

I entered through a high arched entrance, and removed my shoes, as is the acceptable custom here. There was a sign posted, with an arrow scribbled on it, pointing towards the church's interior, and written in plain English:

Mission of Our Lady of Loreto

→

The church is sacred

DO NOT ENTER IF YOU ARE NOT
IN PROPER CLOTHING

Be silent here

Pray a Little

Well, I had to stop and think about the clothing admonishment: I had come dressed in a decent pair of slacks, with a nice clean shirt. As close as I could get to my Baja "Sunday Best." Very peaceful, very quiet, and most assuredly a beneficial sanctuary for meditation and giving thanks for all of my blessings. Amen!

Saturday, July 5th: I had made the most of the brief interlude from reed balsa construction over an enjoyable town/errands day, returning with re-stocked freshwater supplies, Tecáte beer, and 1,000 pesos worth of beans, peanuts, etc. The welcome aroma of sea-brine returned to my nostrils as I caught up on all my tasks of undersea subsistence hunting, firing up smokers, working on reed bundles, and general camp chores. I discovered a small Baja rattlesnake in the rear of the brush hut that likely crept in during my absence. I captured and carried it well beyond Campo San Cosme before releasing it. The occurrence of rattlesnakes would be anticipated with the presence of favorable wildlife habitats surrounding the tree galleries of the arroyo outflow plain. Mice are also drawn to campsites, poking around gear and sometimes burrowing under tarps which can attract snakes.

Sunday, July 6th:

> New moon. Incident [with] speartip stuck in cave. Trigger [finescale triggerfish], 2 cabrilla and large pargo for smoking. Meet Eustadio who lands on beach and requests water—give him 2 gallons in bucket. [He's] from Javier's area [*Agua Verde Ranchería* near *Punta San Marcial*]—setting nets. [JB Field Notes, 1986]

A day of intensive diving and hunting—plus miles on foot along the shore. I walked a long way from camp to explore a promising, open area of the sea several hundred yards out and beyond from the shoreline. There were widely separated rocky-reef patches and very large boulder clusters at depths of around thirty to forty feet. I was actively hunting over this area, alternately scanning from above or roaming over the bottom and slowly stalking around rock features. I was down below in front of a cave under a big square boulder. I took aim but missed my target—probably a flag cabrilla—and the spear tip became solidly wedged in the rear of the cave. No matter how I twisted and yanked on the shaft, it just would not come free! It was stuck fast within the rock. A huge, panamic green moray eel emerged soon after, and remained in the right-hand side of the space under the boulder. So, now I was in a Mexican stand-off with a glaring eel whom I had no intention of harming nor of seriously disrupting the creature's lair.

While all this was taking place, I had to keep going up to the surface and back—making repeated breath-hold dives—to continue my efforts at a depth of at least 30-35 feet. I memorized the boulder cave's relative positioning with surrounding features and took note of where I was lined up with coastal landmarks. Then I left the speargun, line and shaft lying on the bottom, swimming back to the shore to return to camp for "Plan B!" Once I reached camp, I located the key tool for Plan B. It was a thick 4-foot piece of 3/4-inch steel rebar buried under everything in the back of the Commando. The long trek back along the sandy shore arrived at the precise point—marked in the sand—and wading shoes were changed out for fins once again. When I'd covered enough water straight out from shore, it was easy to recognize the location, though it felt weird swimming with a heavy chunk of rebar. I employed it, using leverage, and quickly freed the lodged spear tip. I was happy, the eel was happy (and relieved, no doubt), and I made it back to *Campo San Cosme* just in time for Happy Hour!

Monday, July 7th: "Houston, we have a problem." Borrowing from that time-worn message of alarm, I had a very sobering realization when I had most of the three bundles assembled prior to the next stage of finishing the primitive watercraft. Despite harvesting what I had presumed would be a substantial number of canes—close to 300—the reality I was now faced with was this: I had put the canes together in the proper manner, but the boat was far short of having enough width through the middle! If I continued in this fashion, a very unstable and tippy craft would result which is a difficult problem to resolve, since I had used up nearly all the remaining canes in forming the bundles. To the best of my knowledge, I was not within a reasonable distance of a source of reeds, either. So, I took a long, long walk up along the edge of the sea, hoping it would counsel me with my dilemma and maybe whisper a solution into my ear.

One of the most common items winding up in beach drift along Baja shorelines are palm frond stems. This is due to the abundance of palm groves occurring in so many seaside oases, such as the one I had observed above the *Río de Mulegé*, on the First Baja Expedition. Most of the ones encountered have a uniform length—around four to five feet. They are usually well battered as drift, so that the large-toothed serrations along the edges are sufficiently worn down. So, I set off northward on a dual mission: Roam as far as possible, foraging for driftwood palm frond stems, and make periodic stops for dives, hunting select fish species to supply the smokers. By the end of the day, I might have gotten my money's worth: an armload of palm stems, a nice triggerfish, a five-pound yellow snapper, a four-pound yellow jack, a net float, and tons of exercise!

Tuesday, July 8th:

Fish pile-up before 6! Swim out for 2 hrs. Tide way out. Collect palm stems from S [south] beaches. Very windy in afternoon. Put palm bundles together.

An exciting event occurred offshore at the beginning of another active and full day. This was the phenomenon known as a "fish pile-up," which is literally a feeding frenzy taking place, readily visible on the surface. The main cause of the commotion are large, dense shoals of smaller schooling fish such as anchovies and herring, that are targeted by a multitude of hundreds of predators from above and below! Even more conspicuous than the surface boiling with fish are the flocks of seabirds such as boobies, pelicans, cormorants, and terns diving into them, alongside the always opportunistic gulls floating nearby. Down below, undersea predators such as mackerels, groupers, jacks, snappers, and even sharks and porpoises are driving the frenzied shoals upward, to the birds' benefit! In my excitement, I impulsively swam out towards the pile-up, never having viewed one up close. It turned out to be a lot farther offshore, and had largely dissipated when I found myself in the approximate vicinity which was impossible to gauge.

I resumed foraging for palm frond stems, this time fanning out to roam the beaches far to the south of *Punta San Cosme.* Once this foraging mission was fulfilled, I seemed to have an ample quantity to work with, for enlarging my reed boat bundles across the center sections. The challenge before me now, was how to carefully spread open the reed bundles to insert the palm frond stem bundles inside the interior of each. This necessitated some disassembly of the reed bundles. Then, the next step was to re-install the outside layers of canes around the palm stems, following the same construction techniques, that would conform to the desired shape. Once this process was completed, cord lashings could be evenly wound around each bundle.

Wednesday, July 9th: Today was another day split between diving/subsistence hunting in the morning and working on the reed bundles later in the afternoon. I got started as early as possible venturing southward down the seashore, with the progressively farther and farther distances extended from camp, towards *Punta San Marcial.* I continued in the same mode, in what seemed to me, as a departure from my usual approach to diving. For the past week, I was way out in the middle of vast, underwater realms, with all my reference points below the surface. It was the continuing quest for the most prime underwater reef structure; sometimes found a long way out from shore. This was in sharp contrast to favorite areas in Sonora, where dives were mostly concentrated close along shorelines, littoral zone rocks awash, around headlands, and other such surface-emergent rock features.

Large Gulf grouper (Mycteroperca jordani) *with remora attached (Photo by Mark Conlin)*

I speared a species of grouper for the first time that I later resolved not to again once I learned about the current plight of this fish. (See full article in the Appendix on page 246.) I recognized the five-pound Gulf grouper (*Mycteroperca jordani*) when I encountered it, in the same open area of scattered patch reefs, in roughly forty to fifty feet of water. According to *Reef Fishes of the Sea of Cortez*, these groupers are usually found below 100 feet in deeper water, during the summer. (Thomson, et al., 1979) Being a breath-hold diver-hunter, it's far more practical for me to stay well above that range most of the time.

Friday, July 11th: I spent most of yesterday—Thursday the 10th— roaming far down the south end of *Bahía Agua Verde*, hunting and exploring. Then on Friday, I settled back into working on the reed boat and the last stage of construction. I was putting together the last one of my three bundles, when a lean, young *Bajeño* with a light scruff of beard and mustache showed up, riding a burro. Alejo came from a small *ranchería* to the north, and slightly inland from the coast. He had visited my first campsite in *Bahía Agua Verde* several times a year ago, when I was situated 3-4 miles north of *Campo San Cosme*. His gentle, friendly demeanor had put me at ease, and I had been able to communicate and share some of my Sea of Cortez sourcebooks with him, despite the language barrier. His curiosity drew him closer to my project, and he broke out into a broad smile inspecting the reed watercraft, while I petted his calmly uninterested burro.

The original inhabitants of this remote Baja landscape, disappeared over a century ago. Before any Europeans set foot here in the early sixteenth century, there were fierce indigenous tribes occupying the Peninsula, such as the *Pericú*, *Guayacura*, and *Cochimí* tribes. They were the ones who occupied what was truly "The Promised Land" when it was teeming with the most bountiful abundance, of both terrestrial and sea life. Of course, it was also a harsh arid desert environment, with scarce, widely scattered and not always dependable freshwater sources for the native inhabitants. The German Jesuit Priest, Johann Jakob Baegert, was fond of saying that out of the four basic elements, "[Baja] California received only two, air and fire." Father Baegert spent seventeen years (1751–1768) at the isolated *San Luis Gonzaga* mission in the center of the Peninsula, southwest of *Bahía Agua Verde* and due west, inland from *Isla San José*. In his Observations in Lower California he describes the landscape:

> ... Nothing is so common in California as rocks and thorns, nothing so rare as moisture, wood, and cool shade. It is not necessary to be afraid of drowning in California, but it is easy to die of thirst. A man only needs to lose his way, which can happen easily, and he may wander whole days or even weeks without finding a drop of water. Only a few years ago, several people whose ship had been wrecked on the coast of California died miserably of thirst, because in spite of their diligent search, they were unable to find water. (Baegert, 1979)

Father Baegert administered to the primitive and rugged *Guayacura* tribe that occupied this lower region of the Peninsula, over two centuries removed from the first European landing by the ill-fated Becerra Expedition in 1534. At the Bay of La Paz, 75—80 miles southeast of Mission San Luis Gonzaga, a party of 21 Spaniards sent by Hernán Cortés, from Acapulco, attempted to make landfall. Once ashore, they were furiously attacked by the *Guayacura*—armed with bows and arrows—and were nearly wiped out, except for a lone survivor who swam back to the ship and escaped. (Miller, 1974) From his firsthand *Observations in Lower California*, Father Johann Baegert goes on to describe the weaponry of the *Guayacura*:

> Whatever arts and crafts their ancestors might have known and exercised, whatever the tools they had once known how to use, in time they must have fallen into disuse and complete oblivion. This fact is found among all the American Indians, and therefore among the California natives also. Bows and arrows are the only things which have survived and have been retained by all the California Indians because they need these weapons for their protection and to obtain their food. The bows of the natives are more than six feet high, slightly curved, and are commonly made from the root of the wild willow. They are round, about five fingers thick in the center, and become gradually thinner and pointed at both ends. The bowstring or cord is made of strips of animal gut. The arrows are of common reed straightened by the heat of fire and are more than six spans long. At the lower end, they have a notch to catch the string, and three or four feathers as long as a finger, which do not project very much and are let into slits made for that purpose. At the other end of the shaft, a pointed piece of heavy wood is inserted, a span and a half long, bearing at its tip a piece of flint, triangular in shape, almost resembling a snake's tongue, and serrated at the edge like a saw. They practice with bow and arrow from early childhood. Consequently, many good marksmen are found among them. All science, work, and occupation of the male Indian, therefore, consists of making bows and arrows. The men always carry these weapons with them wherever they go. (Baegert, 1979)

I bid farewell to my friend, Alejo, wishing him a safe ride back northward to his *ranchería* at *Carrizalito*, and resumed working on the last bundle of canes. The day's progress culminated in winding the long strands of cord around the remaining bundle, then intertwining the cords between and around the joined bundles together. Finishing with a tighter, snugger lashing of both terminal ends of the three bundles, I had satisfactorily completed the reed balsa construction process. Now, I needed to start thinking of how my watercraft would be properly equipped. But that could wait until after a refreshing evening dive. I made an interesting find while prowling along the patch reef areas not far out from my beach terrace campsite: I picked up a small speargun laying on the rocky bottom in the shallows.

It was a small, French "Arbalete D.D.S., Crawl Marseille" speargun, with a 3/4-inch thick aluminum shaft and gun grip handle, measuring around three feet. There was no spear shaft attached, only six feet of thin nylon cord tied to a hard plastic "keeper." Seemingly a strange find in such a remote, rarely visited area. My one and only speargun had long since had the four foot by one and one-quarter inch aluminum shaft thoroughly covered over with "camo"green marine paint, obscuring the make and model. The one-foot extension beyond the trigger grip, on the bottom end, served as a handy spot to bungee cord-tie down a plastic dive knife scabbard. On the distal end, a T-shaped cross support allowed for the insertion of three rubber slings. The three-foot by three-eighths-inch diameter steel spear shaft propelled by these slings, loaded into the opposite end in front of the trigger grip, and was retained by a one-eighth-inch cord of approximately twelve feet to the keeper. The shaft by itself weighed at least one pound, perhaps slightly more. The number-one greatest shortcoming of these and all spearguns, is the short life and unreliable nature of the rubber slings, which are prone to rotting and deteriorating in the hot sun. The best long-term strategy, in my case, would be to adapt to the use of a custom-designed pole spear with no such liabilities in the future.

How one dives is reflected in how one hunts. In order to explain what I mean by that, requires both an admission—on my part—and a disclaimer—for the aspiring breath-hold or skin diver. Back in the early 1980s, I respectfully followed the PADI protocols during all the training sessions taught by my fine dive instructor, the late Lane Larson, of the Silent Experience Dive Shop. However, once I got acclimated and developed my own skills and approach—far from civilization—I naturally adapted to breath-hold diving without wearing a BCD (Buoyancy Control Device). I am not asserting that to be flippant or disrespectful of the PADI Dive Manual, or recommended procedures. I found the practicality of keeping the gear as basic and simple as possible suited my own approach where I could concentrate fully on my skill development, with the most minimal equipment. So, that's where the disclaimer comes in: my approach to diving in this manner is not recommended. While I don't recommend this approach, I personally assume the responsibility for the risks I take. I strongly believe that all of us should have that right, and I'm prepared to sign a personal responsibility affidavit form, if need be.

Skill, vision and stealth become uppermost in hunting underwater when you do not have the ability to camouflage yourself like the predatory stone scorpionfish (*Scorpaena mystes*).

Slowing down, a constant habit of scanning, roving awareness, and moving fluidly and deliberately becomes a regular practice. As a rule, I always had enough weights on my belt—sometimes up to twelve pounds—to be negatively buoyant while wearing the wetsuit. Sometimes I would just allow myself to slowly drift down to the bottom in a favorable location, curled up in kind of a compressed "sitting lotus" or "cannonball" position. Once on the bottom, I would very slowly unravel, while alertly scanning around me for opportunities close by. The element of surprise is always your best card, in nearly all instances, since you're clearly a strange creature that can't easily blend in. So, passive techniques like this can be very effective.

Another passive technique that worked exceedingly well was the wall-blind strategy I used at what I called the "Amphitheater of Fish" at *Ensenada Rada El Pasito* along the Sonoran coast that I described earlier. If you spend enough time, exploring widely along all sorts of rocky coastal and offshore reef structures, you're bound to discover some of these spots where fish naturally gather and where the underwater terrain offers advantages for the hunter.

Saturday, July 12th: Today, for the first time since all the reed canes had been harvested, they were finally going to be baptized in the Sea of Cortez, roughly 170 miles southeast—as the crow flies—from where they once grew. Measured along its full length, the craft was twenty and a half feet long. Its width abeam, across the middle, at close to two and a half feet, if that, still concerned me. Once totally immersed, sitting in the craft just above the midpoint, did feel a little tippy and unstable at first. However, it did not prevent me from shifting my weight to gain a better point of balance in the right spot, where I could get comfortable enough to assume a rowing position. There was not much freeboard; the water came right up through the canes, though the craft still was perfectly buoyant. This is due to the *Arundo donax* reed canes being composed of enclosed cylindrical air-filled chambers within each joint of a cane stalk. While this was true, the net surface area of the mass of canes also absorbed a lot of water at the same time, adding weight and resistance.

The most critical necessity for any voyage of any duration was going to be drinking water. So a balanced arrangement of at least six to seven gallons was secured along the craft's length: At the upper end, I fastened on a blue plastic pail that ensheathed and protected a two and a half-gallon plastic water storage container. Next, down at the lower end, in front of where my dive gear was stowed, was a two-gallon rectangular jug. Behind the blue pail, fastened on to the uppermost portion, were two one-gallon jugs with red screw-on lids. Lastly, and of prime importance, was a small, square plastic watertight cooler. Just prior to venturing to the Gulf from Tucson, my dear friend, Shari Spear, had graciously loaned me a camera, that was a huge improvement over the Sedic pocket camera! So, the watertight cooler was outfitted for the camera and lashed aboard. "Houston, all systems are GO!"

Sunday, July 13th: Launch Day. I woke up just before the little archipelago of small island clusters—*San Cosme, San Damian*, and all the adjoining *Rocas* (rocks)—were illuminated by a bright sunrise that presided over tranquil waters with only the barest breeze. Today was set for the inaugural voyage—the Trial Run—out to *Isla San Damian*. This small island lay about a mile farther east into the Gulf, beyond *Isla San Cosme*, and around three miles distant from my launch point on the beach, below camp. I was well-stoked with strong coffee and smoked fish (perhaps the gold-laden Amazons were watching over me as well): Oh—SHIT—here—we—GO! It was exciting to be finally shoving off, out into the beautiful blue Sea of Cortez. The sensation of moving through the water on this craft, after diligently working on it over the last several weeks, was exhilarating! Being equipped with a double-bladed paddle, rather than a single oar, made a big difference, too. However, the absorption of so much water by the reeds of the craft did not allow for much speed going forward. While it floated well enough, the sensation was somewhat comparable to imagining yourself rowing a log.

There's something intriguing about islands, and I find them irresistible to explore. Is there a remote, forbidden quality that contributes to their magnetic appeal, drawing us out to visit them? Most islands exist as such relatively small and insignificantly-sized pieces of earth, rock and sand, or in some cases just rock, swallowed up in the vast, incomprehensible immensity of surrounding blue. Perhaps they represent the isolated idyllic refuge for solitude and solace from the perpetual struggles of the mundane world. Islands clearly represent bio-geographical *refugia* for many wildlife and plant species, from north to south, up and down the Gulf of California. (Case, et al., 2002)

There are 922 islands and islets in the Gulf of California, including the smallest emergent, isolated rocks, according to the Mexican *Comisión Nacional de Áreas Naturales Protegidas* (CONANP). (Aitchison, 2010) Out of these, 244 have been designated by the United Nations Educational Scientific and Cultural Organization (UNESCO) as protected World Heritage Sites. The next classification narrows down to the forty-four major islands. This group is composed of all the largest islands with some of the smaller ones included that support significant seabird breeding or roosting colonies, such as *Islas Rasa* and *Patos*, *Roca Consag*, and others. (Aitchison, 2010) Islands in the Sea of Cortez are subject to the prevailing arid, hot desert climatic conditions, typical of both Sonoran mainland and Peninsula regions. Therefore, none have reliable freshwater resources except in a few rare cases, as on

Isla Tiburón in the northern Gulf, and the conjoined pair of *Islas Partida Sur* and *Espíritu Santo* to the south.

Sea of Cortez islands are refuges for a diverse array of tall columnar and smaller cacti, vascular plants, arthropods, numerous land and sea bird species, sea and terrestrial mammals, reptiles and even fish-eating bats. There are twenty-eight endemic species of plants (4.0 percent) found only on select Gulf islands, with cacti making up the highest proportion (11 percent), amounting to twenty-six percent of the family. (Rebman and Roberts, 2012) Birds might be the most conspicuous group overall, well-represented on all islands. None are considered endemic to the Gulf, with the possible exception of the yellow-footed gull . (Tershy and Breese, 1997) Out of the fifty endemic reptile species, several large two-foot long lizards—the piebald chuckwalla (*Sauromalus varius*) and spiny-tailed iguana (*Ctenosaura hemilopha*)—were food resources of the Seri Indians of *Isla San Esteban*. (Bowen, 2000) One of the most notable mammalian species is a black jackrabbit (*Lepus insularis*) occurring on the conjoined island pair of *Partida Sur* and *Espíritu Santo*. (Aitchison, 2010) On remote *Isla Santa Catalina*—in the outside perimeter of the *Bahía Agua Verde* region—a unique, rattleless rattlesnake (*Crotalus catalinensis*) exists on this island with giant barrel cacti (*Ferocactus diguetii*) over twelve feet tall. As crazy as it sounds, *Isla Santa Catalina* was at the top of the list of reed boat mission objectives, depending on how the "Trial Run" turned out.

The experience of rowing watercraft, once far offshore, has a hypnotic effect on the senses. One becomes both mesmerized by the steady, syncopated rowing rhythm, together with the sensation of merging as one into the massive entity of surrounding water. There is a constancy of views that almost seems static, since one's speed in this type of craft can only barely be perceived as progress as noted by incrementally passing distant landmarks. I knew I had closed out a considerable distance between *Campo San Cosme* and *Isla San Damian*. Making progress became less perceptible the closer I came towards reaching my destination, as if I was increasingly up against a greater resistance—or perhaps, currents? So, I picked up my pace and began rowing harder.

My perception gained greater clarity; my focus sharpened, as I became keenly aware that I was in the middle of some very strong currents that were affecting my forward progress. I could now line up directional landmarks, and clearly, I was NOT making any headway! So now, I really dug down and leaned into my rowing with an all-out intensity and strong rhythmic breathing. For what seemed a very long time, I kept that up, sustaining a furious intensity and rowing as efficiently and hard as I possibly could. I was not going to be trapped, stuck in cross-currents and prevented from reaching my objective. *Isla San Damian* suddenly entered my field of vision as if I was awakening from a trance. I maintained my rowing, coming ever closer, before I took stock of things. I looked behind me: OH SHIT! "Houston, we have a BIG problem!"

I couldn't believe it! The camera cooler was GONE! Somehow, during that long-sustained, furious episode of rowing, it had become unfastened from the craft and floated off, away and far out of sight! I felt completely crushed and devastated, an indescribable feeling of utter disbelief and shock! How could this happen? I thought I tied it on securely. (Yes, the usual self-talk and recrimination.) I was suddenly brought out of my despondency and self-absorbed admonishment by the sound of an approaching *panga*. The friendly fisherman that hailed me looked familiar. It was Eustadio, from Javier and María's *ranchería* at *Agua Verde*, near *Punta San Marcial*. He implored me to grab and tie on the ropeline he offered me. Which, initially, I was not prone to do, but then gained a better perspective on my situation.

There was no point in proceeding any further on the present journey, without being able to document the adventure with a camera. So, the "Grand Plan"—making the unthinkable, impossibly distant voyage to *Isla Santa Catalina*—was not in the cards for this expedition. I had to resign myself to that fact, while recognizing that I had at least reached my initial goal by arriving at San Damian. Besides, it's very discourteous not to accept a kindness offered by one of the local people in Mexico. So, I securely tied on Eustadio's rope, and off we went. For the first time that day, I experienced a wake behind my reed boat.

Monday, July 14th: The events of the previous day had abruptly shifted the Third Baja Expedition's mission into its final phase. This meant breaking camp and preparing to move on to the next destination. The reed balsa lay upon the upper beach terrace, drying out under the hot sun, while I attended to all the tasks of taking down my shelter and packing up gear. Late yesterday afternoon had been spent exhaustively hiking miles of shoreline, searching long and hard through endless piles of beach drift, though ultimately in vain for the lost camera in its watertight cooler. Then, not long afterward, a massive dark thunderhead moved in, unleashing the most powerful *chubasco* and torrential downpour I'd ever experienced in *Baja*! The storm eroded portions of upper sandy beach terraces, forming deeply incised rivulets crisscrossing them. The nearby *Arroyo San Fernando* poured into the sea, and the waters everywhere across the *bahía* were discolored with high turbidity and a greenish cast.

I made a solemn invocation of gratitude to this place, before resuming my nomadic ways. The reed balsa was securely strapped down, with one end extended well beyond the windshield and tied down above the front grill of the Commando. The lower section of the road was quishy and muddy, and the severe erosion foretold a more precarious and laborious trip covering the twenty miles back towards the Peninsular Highway. The worst areas of washouts encountered along the switchbacks above required getting out the army shovel for necessary roadwork to insure safe passage. It was good to see the desert below the *Sierra de la Giganta* having been drenched by a good rain, though regretfully, I wasn't going to be able to witness the emergent greenery to come.

Tuesday, July 15th: Sometimes there's a prescribed plan to follow; other times, things get flip-flopped, and plans are indeterminate and slowly become reconstituted and formulated along routes of travel. Such was the latter case, now in full force, immersed in deep contemplation of strategic options, while paying keen attention to instinctive impulses that might arise. I was beginning to hatch a plan for the next reed boat launching, while descending southward down Baja Highway 1 towards Loreto. Where would there be an optimum, off-the-beaten-path spot within access to coastal islands? I re-studied my beat-up 1981 *Mapa Turistico de Carreteras*. Then, after long consternation over a respectable length of Peninsular Highway, it clicked. The plan was hatched; the next mission objective was set!

Somewhere out beyond the outskirts of Loreto, five or six miles north, I turned off to the right. This road at this turnoff felt like the one that would bring me to the brink of the Gulf, opposite *Isla Coronados*. Meandering in and out of grayish-sandy flat washbeds, the dirt two-track headed east through a flat stretch of open desert. When I chanced upon a woodland thicket, I pulled over and stopped. Having been well-trained through my Sonoran coastal trips, I collected a mass of downed and dead branches for firewood. I wrapped some cordage loosely around the branches, before centering the whole massive pile atop the reed balsa and thoroughly lashing everything down with bungee cords. Then, onward through *terra incognita* back to the Sea of Cortez.

I can only imagine how the collective group of University of Arizona Marine Ecology students and staff must have wondered at the strange apparition approaching their field camp. As if the reed boat wasn't enough, the mass of firewood stacked on top, might have resembled antlers growing out of it! Quite unexpectedly, I found myself in the midst of a large summer field school encampment at the foundation ruins of an ancient resort at *El Bajo*. Directly across the water from the remains of the resort, lay *Isla Coronados*. An extinct volcano loomed close to 1,000 feet above sea level on the island, last active around 160,000 years BP. (Brusca, 2010)

I enjoyed the over-stimulation of so much human contact happening all at once after my arrival. This was in sharp contrast to the period of prolonged solitude spent at *Bahía Agua*

Verde that seemed closer to my normal experience. Of course, what would feel more compatible than hanging out with fellow "Sea of Cortez freaks?" I suppose I added something to their field school summer experience, and they certainly became part of the Third Baja Expedition.

Wednesday, July 16th: I watched two students in their river kayaks—boyfriend and girlfriend—rowing out towards the island together. With their minimal displacement, riding up high in the water, those kayaks could really scoot along at a high rate of speed! River kayaks tend to be shorter, and more maneuverable than sea kayaks, which are quite a bit longer. A reed balsa on the other hand, could certainly be constructed to have an improved potential for rowing speed and performance, beyond my prototype though never approaching the capabilities of kayaks. In the early 1940s, during the Steinbeck and Ricketts' Sea of Cortez Expedition, there are frequent references made to very efficient dugout canoes made by native Indians from the mainland below Mazatlán that they used in constantly crossing back and forth across the Gulf. Natives were welcomed aboard the Western Flyer, such as in this account of Indians and their Nayarit canoes:

> They were barefoot and carried the iron harpoons of the region, and in the bottom of their canoe lay a huge fish. Their canoe was typical of the region and was interesting. There are no large trees in the southern part of the Peninsula, hence all the canoes come from the mainland, most of them being made near Mazatlán. They are double-ended canoes carved from a single log of light wood, braced inside with struts. Sometimes a small sail is set, but ordinarily they are paddled swiftly by two men, one at either end. They are seaworthy and fast. The wood inside and out is covered with a thin layer of white or blue plaster, waterproof and very hard. This is made by the people themselves and applied regularly. It is not a paint, but a hard, shell-like plaster, and we could not learn how it is made although this is probably well known to many people. Equipped with one of these canoes, an iron harpoon, a pair of trousers, shirt, and hat, a young man is fairly well set up in life. In fact, the acquiring of a Nayarit canoe will probably give a young man so much security in his own eyes and make him so desirable in the eyes of others that he will promptly get married. (Steinbeck and Ricketts, 1951)

The reed balsa rested on the broken shell and cobble beach adjacent to my campsite. Here, with a majestic sweep of the northern shoreline and jagged mountains as a backdrop, it was photographed by student Dorothy Coffman. Then, once equipped with gear and provisions, I maneuvered the craft into the shallows and rowed around close to the point adjoining

UA staff member, Max Solo Summerdog, JB, and Dr. Donald Thomson alongside reed boat (Photo by Dorothy Coffman)

the field camp. Amongst a gathering of students and staff was the director and marine scientist, Donald A. Thomson, who happened to be the senior author of one of my favorite books I carted around, *Reef Fishes of the Sea of Cortez*. (Thomson, et al., 1979) Dr. Thomson waded out to inspect the craft as his rambunctious golden lab, "Max Solo Summerdog," swam out alongside. Then a female staff member wound up perched atop the bundles inside the craft, maintaining her balance, with Max positioned in the middle. A perfect "photo-op" was not squandered, thanks again to student Dorothy Coffman.

Fired up, refreshed and with renewed energy, I was excited to be seaborne again, in unfamiliar territory, moving steadily towards *Isla Coronados*. I was settling into my rowing rhythm over the tranquil surface of the sea with roughly two miles of water to cross between my departure point and the island. Rowing through calm waters becomes a deeply contemplative exercise, and I found myself reflecting on my gratitude for the events that had transpired over the last several days. How fortuitous to wind up here on the last leg of the trip, amongst this fine group, with no lack of cameras to solidly document the Reed Boat Project?

In exactly ten years following the Reed Boat Project, on July 19, 1996, the entire marine ecosystem archipelago spanned by the Third Baja Expedition, between *Isla Coronados* and *Isla Santa Catalina*, became established as a marine protected area (MPA) within the *Parque Nacional Bahía de Loreto*. Loreto Bay National Park (LBNP) was created for the conservation of natural resources, protection of marine habitats and vulnerable species, and the preservation of biodiversity across an area of nearly 800 square miles (1,837 km). The greater regional community as stakeholders was involved from the beginning, in pushing hard to exclude destructive and over-exploitive maritime industrial shrimp trawlers and purse-seiners from this region. An open process with the involvement of these user groups was instrumental to this MPA's founding. The Park management plan was completed in 2000, but not effectively implemented and enforced until 2003. (Rife, et al., 2013) This MPA is administered by the *Comisión Nacional de Áreas Naturales Protegidas* (CONANP) and became a UNESCO World Heritage Site in 2005.

A veteran team of marine scientists, divers and researchers, mostly from the Scripps Institute of Oceanography, did extensive monitoring and data gathering at LBNP sites and outside the park, for a thirteen-year period (1998-2010). (Rife, et al., 2013) The Scripps Institute has a long tradition of scientific work and research in the Gulf, dating back to the earliest E. W. Scripps Cruise of 1939. (Alvarez-Borrego, 1983) While industrial-scale fishing is prohibited inside the Park, some small-scale commercial and recreational fishing is allowed, with only 1 percent (1.27 km) set aside as "no-take" protected zones. One of the primary goals of the park is preserving reef fish biomass to allow for fish stock recovery with the resulting long-term objective of sustainable fisheries.

The results of the research team's monitoring and collecting data on fourteen LBNP sites and eight sites outside the perimeter over a thirteen-year period were disheartening: without the proper regulations, management plan and resources, Loreto Bay National Park appeared to be suffering from "Paper Park" syndrome, according to the team. Effective fish stock recovery was not occurring here; instead, the status quo of a degraded ecosystem was simply being maintained without much benefit to the community and local fisheries. (Rife, et al., 2013) The team's conclusions were summarized, in part, by the following statement:

> The goal of LBNP's management plan is to "preserve the natural resources," not explicitly to restore them, and to ensure "the social development of the communities," which we interpret as safeguarding livelihoods. The LBNP has met these objectives. We remain, however, concerned that this success is in the preservation of an already degraded environment, virtually indistinguishable from the unprotected areas nearby. This is not a positive outcome in any respect, nor is it how the LBNP is promoted publicly. One would hope to detect a significant recovery, especially in higher trophic groups that are the focus of fisheries in the area. We believe that in order to have sustainable fisheries and increase the benefits (ecological and economical) to the local community, recovery of depleted fish assemblages is essential and should be a focus for park managers in the future. Otherwise, one could also claim that the unprotected areas nearby have been as successful as LBNP in "preserving the natural resources"—which could render management of LBNP as irrelevant. (Rife, et al., 2013)

The revised management plan proposed by the research team called for expanding the total no-take area and specifically included areas known to harbor fish spawning aggregations which are critical for certain species, such as the endangered gulf grouper. These actions should improve prospects for the recovery of reef fish assemblages. Further recommendations were made for improved fish-catch quantification, revision of fishing regulations, management and increased enforcement, especially advocating the more effective community-involved enforcement. Lastly, the continuation of the monitoring and data-gathering program on reef fish assemblages of LBNP is critical for maintaining a data base and as an ongoing gauge of the effectiveness of the Park's management. (Rife, et al., 2013)

I eased my reed craft over the glistening rocky shallows closely skirting the shoreline of *Isla Coronados*. Whew! Made it, at last! It had been another exhausting grind rowing through anticipated offshore currents along much of the route! There were a few people already here, having arrived through much easier means. So, I joined in, wetsuited and in full dive gear. It felt great plunging into the refreshingly cool waters—after an hour plus of rowing—to explore the surrounding rocky reefs. The day was bright and sunny, and the views of the island's beauty were staggering to behold. Of course, as much as I wanted to go off into "never-never land" exploring, that nagging inner voice kept reminding me of the long arduous return voyage through the same gauntlet of currents. So, soon enough, I shoved off from the shallows and began the long row back to *Punta El Bajo* to join my new-found Sea of Cortez"'classmates."

It was a longer route going back, because of my perception of the tidal currents. I wound up making a wide arc from just past the halfway point in order to reach the shore close to the point. I gauged the sideways thrust of the currents against the craft and rowed opposing it to compensate and kept the craft from winding up a lot farther from my shoreline destination. I was a wreck after having finally run aground, however. My back felt tight as if my whole body was tied into a great big knot. I walked stiffly at first, but regained my stride, since my legs were only slightly cramped. The rest of me, as in upper torso, arms and back, was going to be really tight and sore for a few days. It was barbeque night, so I joined the group around a flat terrace area above the beach with a buffet feast and a roaring campfire.

Reed boat atop Jeepster Commando prior to departure west and north from El Bajo *(Photo by Dorothy Coffman)*

Thursday, July 17th: Packing-up Day. Slept hard after yesterday's adventures. Once I unfolded my sore limbs and painstakingly arose to greet the dawn, I felt glad, with much satisfaction and gratitude, to have been able to add this last memorable chapter to the Reed Boat Project Expedition. Of course, my profoundly sore arms and back would be continuously reminding me of my "gladness" all the way back to *Santa Rosalía*. More documentary photos of the reed balsa were taken, first lying flat against the cobble beach; then loaded up and strapped down atop the Commando. (Thanks, once again, to the kindness of photographer Dorothy Coffman.) I spied some thick, puffy cumulus clouds starting to build up in the far west over the rim of the mountains. So, I completed the remainder of my tasks, bid all my *campañeros del mar* farewell, and began slowly threading my way back through the gray sand and dirt track to Highway 1.

With the long, pleasant drive northward and an additional day camped out prior to boarding the ferry, I had a lot of time to reflect upon the Third Baja Expedition. To be truthful, it was a mixture of the joy of engagement in a vigorous new adventure of exploration and discovery, taking on the unique tasks, and implementation of a challenging project, mixed with moments of profound heartbreak and disappointment. Some of that "discovery" is inward with the recognition of one's own failures to pay close enough attention more of the time to avoid making critical mistakes. Self-honesty is always on the path to greater self-empowerment. Was the expedition a success? Without exacting specifications, I had followed a rough-laid mission of my own devising, along a reasonably well-charted path, in attempting to make my first primitive watercraft that bore a resemblance to the historic *Seri* balsa, but it was certainly not a replica. I was "learning by doing" and had to make adjustments since I did not have exacting specifications to follow, nor had I known the precise amount of canes required to fulfill the proper proportions. So, the result of an extended "labor of love" was a craft that was seaworthy enough to access several islands, covering minimal distances. Had I not suffered the critical loss of that camera, would I have attempted a marathon voyage of eighteen to twenty miles out to *Isla Santa Catalina*? Despite the hardship of rowing and assumption of risks, it would have been highly likely. Yes! Which would have been accomplishing "The Grand Plan," and would have felt truly fulfilling. But despite not achieving this ultimate goal, from my own best perspective, I consider the Reed Boat Project a qualified success.

Upon my return, a worn but solid and sturdy double-bladed paddle was presented to Dave Baker at the Summit Hut. The Reed Boat? It wound up its career being unceremoniously dropped off and left lying in the weeds alongside a Quonset Hut in the Rincon Valley. Later that fall, I was invited to a reunion of all my fellow University of Arizona Marine Ecology Field School *Campañeros del Mar*, where a big slide show presented all the highlights and photos of the field season. I had officially become an honorary member of "The Class of '86."

View across widest expanse of Rick Dailey Charco, from south to north

Part 3: Explorations Closer to Home

Chapter Thirteen

The Seasonal Phenomenon of Desert Tadpole and Fairy Shrimp

Rincon Valley cowboy and ranch foreman, Rick Dailey, beside his horse wearing his trademark black Stetson and white dress shirt (Photo by Elton Kerr, July, 1993)

Several years ago, I discovered a unique, isolated "charco" in the shadow of the Rincon Mountains, east of Tucson, Arizona, that I named in honor of a late friend and cowboy who worked for many years in the area. A "charco" is a common feature found upon historic ranges of Arizona and the southwest, providing a seasonal water source for cattle. These man-made water impoundments usually employed a small bulldozer or front end loader to scrape out a shallow depression. Then the quantity of soil removed would be mounded up as a berm along the edges with an overflow channel at the lower end provided for drainage beyond full capacity. Over time, as arboreal roots tap into the moisture below, these seasonal waterholes become "wildlife sanctuary islands," surrounded by lush galleries of blue paloverde, mesquite, acacia, and hackberry trees.

On April 24th of 2018, I walked into the bone-dry basin of Rick Dailey Charco while doing some exploring on the way back from a trail run. I thought at the time I could at least invoke the spirits of this empty salt-encrusted waterhole to bring forth bountiful summer monsoon rains, but I also found a few interesting things there.

Leaving footprints across the powdery-dry bottom, I followed the gradient down to the lowest point of the charco. Here, below the narrow inlet channel were densely packed deposits of desert snail shells that resembled beads! They even had holes through the centers. I had come across many isolated desert talus snail (*Sonorella spp.*) shells before, but had not found thick deposits like these. Several large, dark green beetle carapaces caught my eye. Examining more closely revealed them to be the remains of what, to me, was a long-lost mythical beast: *Hydrophilus triangularis*, the giant water scavenger beetle! I had not seen one of these big, impressive beetles since my childhood pond-exploring days.

Deposit of desert snail shells at lowest point of dry charco.

Giant water scavenger beetle carapace found in deposit.

My late spring invocation at Rick Dailey Charco produced the desired results, as strong thunderstorms swept across the upper Rincon Valley by mid-August. I returned to investigate, on August 22nd, under a light afternoon drizzle. Here, was a completely different world; unrecognizable from my first visit four months earlier. The football field-sized rim-to-rim watery expanse was almost incomprehensible. Fresh-made javelina and deer tracks through the mud led down to the edge of the rain-sprinkled pond surface. I hiked around over the top of the berm past tall mesquites above the east edge and back towards the inlet channel at the far north end. Be-

Dry basin of Rick Dailey Charco on April 24, 2018

cause here, I thought, might be a good spot to find a population of one of the most interesting and enigmatic creatures of the desert that magically appears during the summer monsoon season.

Rainfall accumulating and flowing down from a wide-reaching catchment area above the upper end of the charco had eroded a narrow inlet channel through a loosely-cemented conglomerate bedrock. When I hunkered down above the surface of the staggered pools of this channel, I was amazed at what I saw: teeming swarms of

Same scene across the rain-filled charco on August 22, 2018

what resembled dense schools of minnows—in the hundreds—make that thousands! They were not fish however, but dainty desert crustaceans known as fairy shrimp. I had encountered desert fairy shrimp (*Streptocephalus spp.*) like these before, mostly in small ephemeral pools or puddles, but never close to this staggering level of abundance. These creatures are not well-known because they only arise during the summer rainy season, from weather-resistant cysts deposited in the sun-baked mud. (Eriksen and Belk, 1999)

Once I returned to my original spot along the south edge, I slowly waded out, being painstakingly careful not to disrupt clay bottom sediments and cause cloudiness in the water. I got as far out as possible, just beyond waist-deep, and again encountered the thick swarms of fairy shrimp, at a shallow depth, within the main basin of the Charco.

Inlet channel at north end of charco

Swarm of desert fairy shrimp, inlet channel

Desert fairy shrimp examined in net before returning to charco

While I had been so deliberate and quiet in all my movements, several adult coatimundi had entered the tree gallery above the east bank and begun climbing one of the tall mesquites. Other wildlife could be heard within the dense thickets surrounding this oasis. Down below the west bank, a covey of rustling, agitated Gambel's quail were involved in a high-pitched family squabble, while the steady, rapid and melodic song of a Bell's vireo resonated from the trees on the opposite side. A bright, colorful, mostly yellow, male hooded oriole was sighted in the same mesquite stand after I honed in on his harsh, short call-notes. Later, as afternoon shadows lengthened, scores of mourning doves flew in, settling into their evening roosts. On my way out, huffing and grunting sounds came from the westside thicket where three or four javelinas had returned for the night.

On another day during the summer, in the late 1990s, I made a startling discovery along a seldom-used, rural dirt road in the Vail, Arizona, vicin-

Large, adult coatimundi in streambed of Cienega Creek

Tadpole shrimp (Triops spp.) *momentarily displayed on a rock*

ity. I had stopped at a large, linear puddle formed at the bottom of a long, gradual dip next to the railroad tracks. While I scooped up a couple five-gallon buckets of rainwater, two astonishing life forms I had never seen before emerged from the murky depths of one bucket. The first of these creatures resembled something long-extinct with a horseshoe crab-like carapace and a long, segmented tail trailing two filaments at the end. Two close-set beady eyes were visible at the front of the head end, above long, branched antennae, with a profusion of many legs underneath. The other one, in contrast, was considerably more delicate in appearance: It fit the image of an upside-down shrimp, long and sinuous, swimming with an undulating motion of its many legs (twenty-two). It was a beautiful fiery orange-red color with two distinctive black eyes. So, after many years roaming the Sonoran Desert, I had finally come face-to-face with something that had the aura of myth: the seasonal phenomenon of the desert fairy shrimp!

To be more exact, I had discovered both a desert tadpole shrimp (*Triops spp.*) and a desert fairy shrimp (*Streptocephalus spp.*): two distinct species of native crustaceans from the Class Branchiopoda,that arise from eggs or cysts in the dried mud,

Original desert shrimp discovery site east of Vail, Arizona

Tadpole shrimp in sunlit shallows of shrinking waterhole

Female fairy shrimp showing ovary filled with hundreds of cysts.

Desert fairy shrimp (Streptocephalus spp.) *from original discovery site*

grow, reproduce and live out their entire life cycle in the short time before their seasonal waterhole finally dries up under the baking sun. Both tadpole and fairy shrimps are considered among the most primitive crustaceans, and their paddle-like legs (phyllopodia), also function as gills. (Eriksen and Belk, 1999) Within the Branchiopoda, tadpole shrimp represent the Order Notostraca (noto: back; ostraca: hard plate or shell), and fairy shrimp as Anostraca (an: without; ostraca: hard plate or shell). (Eriksen and Belk, 1999) On another occasion returning to this puddle, I captured yet another member of the Branchiopoda: a smaller, clam shrimp species, with a distinctive clam-like shell (Order: Conchostraca).

After this experience, I never looked at large, rural roadside puddles in quite the same way. I began sampling other monsoon-filled, temporary waterholes I encountered in this region and consistently found both tadpole and fairy shrimp species present. It's useful to think of all these widely-scattered ephemeral pools and puddles, as "aquatic islands" in a "sea of land." It's likely that man's impact, through hard-compacted depressions along rural dirt roads, has created many more habitats for these creatures than this hot, arid desert would otherwise allow. Birds visiting these sites to drink are strongly suspected to be one of the main distributors, by transferring the cysts, attached to their feet, from the mud of one puddle, to another.

Examination of a mudflat in the late seasonal stage of one of these sites can resemble an ancient fossil bed with hundreds of embedded Notostracans, or tadpole shrimp, strewn across it. And indeed, they are derived from an ancient lineage, as one of the very oldest animals on earth, and have remained unchanged for over seventy-million years! (Sassaman, et al., 1997)

As an area of surface water evaporates and shrinks, the environment becomes increasingly oxygen-depleted. Under these conditions, tadpole shrimp can often be observed swimming upside down, their many swimming legs or phyllopodia rippling the more oxygenated water surface. They appear to be the most abundant species, at smaller-sized water impoundments and are omnivorous, frequently seen feeding over the bottom. The Anostracans, or desert fairy shrimp, are likewise omnivorous, filter-feeding on a variety of minute plant, animal, and detrital particles in the same environments.

The spadefoot toads emerging after the first ample series of summer monsoon thunderstorms and their offspring, cohabit many of the same desert mini-oases at the same time as tadpole and fairy shrimp species in southern Arizona. In fact, the tadpoles of these toads consume desert fairy shrimp as part of their diet. (Simovich, et al., 1991) There is a whole host of other animals that prey on desert fairy shrimp as a food source, including their contemporaries—the tadpole shrimps. (Eriksen and Belk, 1999) Several wading bird species, such as avocets and killdeer have been known to visit these sites to feed on them. The tracks in the mud of shrinking waterholes testify to the presence of other opportunistic predators as roadrunners, skunks, bobcats, raccoons, and javelinas. An array of freshwater insects such as backswimmers and dragonfly nymph are additional predaceous species consuming them in their own underwater environment. (Eriksen and Belk, 1999) Of course, the giant water scavenger beetle (*Hydrophilus triangularis*) would be at the top of the insect predatory list. I strongly suspect that these

Algae-stained mudflat strewn with expired tadpole and fairy shrimp

Large, sunlit mesquites mirrored in charco along east edge

beautiful, big diving beetles opportunistically arrive at Rick Dailey Charco when the area of surface water has considerably subsided, thereby consolidating the available swarms of desert fairy shrimp prey. Maybe sometime this fall, I'll get a chance to test that theory.

JB with freshly emerged gulf fritillary (Photo by Linda B. Millington)

Chapter Fourteen

El Fuerte/Tanque Verde Area Native Lepidoptera/Host Plant Project

The Stronghold. That's what "El Fuerte" translated from Spanish means in English. Rather than a fortification, I prefer the sense of a refuge, in the form of a natural area that has positively affirming qualities, where you feel well-grounded, have opportunities to grow, become stronger, and expand your knowledge and experience. The "Stronghold" of the mesquite-acacia woodlands, or bosque, of the Tanque Verde Wash floodplain was where I became situated in the early 1980s. This mostly intact native woodland expanse exists in a rural area far removed to the east from the urban metropolis of Tucson, Arizona. The Tanque Verde is a major wash tributary of the Santa Cruz River to the west. Its watershed extends over the northern half of the greater Rincon Mountains area, including Tanque Verde Ridge and Agua Caliente Hill. The Pantano Wash, gathering waters from the far southeast, joins the Tanque Verde to form the Rillito, before the confluence farther west at the Santa Cruz.

Indigenous mesquite bosques once formed extensive areas along the wide floodplains of all the major drainage systems of the Santa Cruz, San Pedro, and Gila Rivers of southeastern Arizona. The late biogeographer Charles H. Lowe provides a historical perspective:

> Mesquite (*Prosopis spp.*) formerly grew along many of the larger desert drainages, such as those along the Gila River and some of its tributaries, in dense forest-like stands called mesquite bosques. These valuable riparian trees reached heights of 40 to 50 feet, with some individuals having trunks 2 to 3 feet in diameter. Remnants of such stands are still present in scattered areas along San Pedro River and Santa Cruz River as well as parts of the Gila River and lower Colorado, and many smaller bosques still remain. (1964)

The ethnobiologist Amadeo M. Rea spent over thirty years among the Gila River Pima Indians, studying their traditional uses of native plants, with the mesquite being uppermost in importance:

> Bosques or almost pure stands of Velvet Mesquite (*Prosopis velutina*) occurred across Pima country on the lower alluvial plains of the Gila, Salt, and Santa Cruz Rivers as well as in spots along the major washes. Anglo-Americans usually described these bosques as being dense. The Pima resorted to these woodlands to collect one of their major wild foods, mesquite pods. Old bosques were the major source of the heavy construction posts the Gileños used in their round houses, ramadas, storage sheds and community meeting houses. (1997)

Mesquite trees in full bloom at Colossal Cave Park (5/09/2019)

The sweet, syrupy-tasting, dry mesquite beans, or pods, are well-known by most all Sonoran Desert natives who grew up chewing on these pods occasionally as children. In *At the Desert's Green Edge*, Dr. Rea expounds further upon the Gila River Pima tribe's usage of the sweet pods:

> Velvet Mesquite produced two annual crops, one early in the summer, the other late in the summer. When the dry pods fell, they were gathered in enormous quantities and stored in rooftop granaries. The flour produced from the pod mesocarp, rich in proteins and carbohydrates, was used to make bread, pudding, and a whole series of other dishes and drinks. (1997)

One enters a bountiful habitat, within the Tanque Verde area bosque. Scooping up a handful of the rich, dark, decomposed humus under the surface, below canopies, gives off a pleasant, slightly pungent hearty aroma. This layer also acts as an insulating mulch, more absorbent of rainfall with less moisture lost through evaporation. Other small, companion trees and shrubs persist here; the main one being catclaw or *Acacia greggii.* The elongated, creamy-yellow flower spikes give off a strong, sweet-fruity fragrance that attracts a diverse host of pollinators. Bees, flies, wasps, and beetles are some of those drawn to these thickly massed branches of blooms in early to late May, but especially butterflies: Leda and gray hairstreaks, pipevine swallowtails, queen, and funereal dusky-wing skipper were most conspicuous, with a wide assortment of blues, skippers, whites, and sulphurs usually seen.

Ironically, at El Fuerte, it wasn't the mesquite or the acacias, but the presence of several large, majestic non-native elm trees (*Ulmus spp.*) that served as the main catalyst for much of the Lepidoptera-related or butterfly-oriented activity which followed. These wonderful elms—something of a rarity in this region—were the dominant trees, with the largest one favorably situated close to the front door, on the north side of the duplex. Unbeknownst to me, a spectacular, more upper-elevational butterfly of the mountain canyons had taken a liking to and made visits to my elms.

At around the same time as the pleasant, fruity-scented essence of *Acacia* blooms permeated the air, I began to notice black and red-spotted, bristly caterpillars with white speckles showing up in the yard within close range of my duplex. Before I knew it, they were descending the branches and trunk of the biggest elm by the front door in droves! I did not recognize them, but knew they had to be butterfly larvae. So, I did the next best thing: I propped open my entry door, and invited them across the threshold en

Mourning Cloak caterpillars on coyote willows (Photo by Bob Gorum)

Mourning Cloak butterfly chrysalis (Photo by Rick and Nora Bowers)

masse! As the days passed, and the suspense began building, I began to see chrysalises all over the house. These, too, did not look familiar.

Mourning Cloak butterfly (Photo by Petr Ganaj)

Sarcostemma milkweed vine with flower clusters

It's hard to describe the freshness and iridescent glow of a beautiful, emergent butterfly, such as the mourning cloak (*Nymphalis antiopa*). This is one of the distinctive brush-footed butterflies, that you could not mistake for anything else: dorsally, a rich dark brown-maroon color overall, with an uneven cream-yellow band around the wing edges bearing a resemblance to a variegated, gold-leaf ornamental inlay, with brilliant, iridescent blue spots on the inside, along both wings. The butterfly became considerably well-camouflaged, its color tones subdued when its wings were folded. Freshly arisen butterflies sometimes appeared suddenly in flight inside the house. Most often though, they were found prior to emergence, becoming airborne after a brief release ceremony.

In the meantime, things were happening in different parts of the local landscape:

I had discovered where female queen butterflies (*Danaus gilippus*) were laying eggs on native *Sarcostemma* milkweed vines in a nearby thicket. The queen butterfly is a common, easily recognizable resident species, seen nearly on a year-round basis. The above darker brown coloration fades into a muted orange on hindwings and below with white spots, and black veins and wing margins. I had gathered milkweed seeds previously, along with a few tubers carefully excavated, and soon had the same milkweed vines growing indoors in containers. Whenever I found

Queen butterflies on desert broom

Pipevine swallowtail

Pipevine swallowtail caterpillar

a queen egg, I would carefully cut out a small round piece of the leaf surrounding it, and attach it to one of my indoor plants, applying a tiny speck of honey as glue. Afterwards, I wandered further into the mesquite bosque, where more surprising discoveries awaited.

Perhaps the most abundant large swallowtail of our region is the pipevine swallowtail (*Battus philenor*). Its larvae feed exclusively on a ground-trailing vine with peculiar brownish-purple flowers and strange, pungent-scented foliage. At first glance, dorsally, or in flight, an almost uniformly dark coloration is visible with only a hint of pale spotting along lower wing margins. However, when it is fluttering atop a flower—wings nearly folded—a bold pattern of iridescent metallic blue, orange, and yellow spots is striking, along with irregular, yellow spots lining the iridescent blue abdomen and thorax.

The pungent foliage of *Aristolochia watsonii*, or Dutchman's pipe, consumed by the caterpillars, renders the butterfly so distasteful to avian predators, that they avoid it. (Brock and Kaufman, 2003) In fact, one can smell the faint odor of the vine, when handling one of these swallowtails. These vines can be abundant within the bosque, and I had previously collected a few of the tubers while harvesting a small quantity of mesquite humus in another locality. When present on these vines, the large, dark brown-to-black caterpillars are hard to miss with variable-length black and red tubercles along the entire body.

While native milkweed vines and *Aristolochia* vines occurred in abundance in this area, I certainly did not expect to find native passion vines (*Passiflora spp.*) here, growing within the bosque to the east of El Fuerte! This is the exclusive host genera for yet another, very showy, and distinctive species of native Lepidoptera: The Gulf fritillary, which is colored bright red-orange with dark spots above, and elongated, silvery-metallic spots below—resembling liquid solder—with a sateen finish. (See photo on page 176.) While I located numerous vines in this vicinity, I periodically harvested fresh cuttings for my growing number of *Agraulis vanillae* larvae since I lacked seed or any starter plants grown from tubers. Things were beginning to get lively. I was accumulating an increasing collection of indoor host plants, for what was becoming the El Fuerte Native Butterfly Vivarium!

A LIST OF BUTTERFLY SPECIES OF THE LOWER SONORAN DESERT REGION	
Common name	**Species**
Skippers	
Common Sooty-wing	*Pholisora catullus*
White checkered skipper	*Pyrgus albescens*
Funereal dusky-wing	*Erynnis funeralis*

A LIST OF BUTTERFLY SPECIES OF THE LOWER SONORAN DESERT REGION	
Common name	**Species**
Acacia skipper	*Cogia hippalus*
Swallowtails	
Pipevine swallowtail	*Battus philenor*
Whites and Sulphurs	
Checkered White	*Pontia protodice*
Mexican yellow	*Eurema mexicana*
Sleepy Orange	*Eurema nicippe*
Metal marks	
Gray metalmark	*Apodemia palmeri*
Blues, Coppers, Hairstreaks	
Leda hairstreak	*Ministrymon leda*
Gray hairstreak	*Strymon melinus*
Marine blue	*Leptotes marina*
Reakirt's blue	*Hemiargus isola*
Antillean blue	*Hemiargus gyas*
Western pygmy blue	*Brephidium exilis*
Libythenes	
Snout butterfly	*Libytheana bachmanni*
Brush-footed butterflies	
Mountain emperor	*Asterocampa montis*
Camberwell beauty	*Nymphalis antiopa*
Texan crescent-spot	*Anthanassa texana*
Queen	*Danaus gilippus*

[Billings, 1982]

In the course of doing occasional research at the University of Arizona Science Library, I came across a handbook on Lepidoptera put out by a society of British entomologists. Interestingly, in the United Kingdom, they referred to my familiar household resident—the mourning cloak as "The Camberwell Beauty." In fact, it is not native to the British Isles, but a rare migrant from Scandinavia; according to a British lepidopterist and collector, who later wrote to me from Northumberland, England. His letter, and many more from Society members, some containing nectar plant seeds, were in response to a letter I wrote to the Society's Journal—*The Bulletin of the Amateur Entomologists' Society*—describing my activities, and including an up-to-date butterfly species list from my area.

I sent the letter in mid-summer and received the following reply, shortly thereafter from the General Editor of the bulletin, Mr. P. W. Cribb, in the form of a letter embossed with the official letterhead of The Amateur Entomologists' Society (Founded 1936):

The Amateur Entomologists' Society
1st July, 1982
355 Hounslow Road,
Hanworth, Feltham, Middx.

Dear Mr. Billings,

It was with great pleasure that I read your letter addressed to the Society and thank you for the donation to the funds. I am enclosing a prospectus of our Society and one of our Bulletins which are issued to members quarterly. Your new home sounds exciting and as one who was brought up on such writings as Gene Stratton Porter's 'Moths of the Limberlost', I envy you your opportunities. I act as General Editor for our Society in respect of our publications other than the Bulletin and we are about to publish a completely revised handbook on the silk moths (*Saturnids*, etc.), many of which are American natives. We have an exotic group within the Society, who breed all orders of foreign species. Personally I specialise in the *Rhopalocera* of Europe, particularly *montane* species, and spend at least part of my holiday each year in the mountains of Europe with net and camera. I breed butterflies for our various County Conservation Trusts for re-establishment purposes as well as Continental species for interest and information.

I have bred *N. antiopa* from France and would be delighted to try some from your part of the world. Ova or pupa would probably be the best method of sending (by air), remembering that the pupal stage is only about 14 days, and that for the eggs about the same. Hibernating females are usually unmated. My French ones were paired females taken in Var, France, and brought home in the fridge of my camper. They laid happily on a sallow (*Salix caprea*) in my garden. I was interested to know that with you they feed on elm—here we have lost all our elms in south England and Wales due to Dutch elm disease....

(P. W. Cribb letter of July 1982, from AES:1)

The pupal stage of the bulk of my indoor-raised *Nymphalis antiopa*, or mourning cloak butterflies, was remarkably consistent, at around twelve days, between chrysalis (pupa) and emergence (imago). So, that is not far off the fourteen-day pupal stage described by my British counterpart, Mr. Cribb. Given the much cooler weather in England, I would have expected a longer period. The main wave of my mourning cloaks occurred in the late spring—early summer period, during warm, but not typical hot summer temperatures. The mesquite bosque areas surrounding the major low-lying drainages, where cooler air masses sink, have somewhat lower temperatures than the outlying desert areas. While I had neither indoor heating or cooling at El Fuerte, the more consistent indoor temperature range may have shortened the pupal stage duration, in contrast with exposure to much cooler outdoor nighttime temperatures which hypothetically might have extended it.

Mourning cloaks are usually prone towards favoring native host plant trees growing in the canyons, as willow (*Salix spp.*) and cottonwood (*Populus sp.*), rather than non-native elms. (Bailowitz and Brock, 1991) While I never learned the exact species of my elms, the one prominent species listed as well-adapted to this region (*Ulmus pumila*), is native to eastern Siberia and northern China. (Jones and Saccamano, 2000) As far as sending any of my home-grown *N. antiopa* chrysalises overseas, I was not able to attempt it; all of my mourning cloaks had flown by then.

Mr. Cribb, the General Editor, went on to say that he would forward my letter to the Bulletin Editor. This resulted in a nearly two-page spread—letter and species list—titled, "ENTOMOLOGICAL THOUGHTS FROM ARIZONA" which appeared in the November 1982 issue of the bulletin. He also mentioned that his son, a taxonomist at Kew (Royal Botanic Gardens), might be able to provide assistance with legal requirements, in order to send me host plant seed. Clearly, with the rearing of species for re-establishment purposes, and other positive activities towards greater conservation, restoration, and study of native butterflies and their habitats, this Society seemed to be strongly committed and engaged in a great purpose. In reflection, I gained a much greater appreciation for my own region in contrast with the cooler, limited meteorologic diversity of the U. K., with southern Arizona's ideal and wide range of climatic conditions occurring across myriad environmental zones from lowest, burning cactus-studded deserts to highest, frosty sky island mountaintops covered in spruce-fir forests.

The Stronghold—Domestic Setting

My duplex and yard was accessible by a long, dirt driveway off the main street (also dirt), through an open stand of mesquite and acacia ending in a wide loop. I was in between a married couple, Wolf—a full-blooded Apache—and Cheryl, occupying the west half of the duplex, and two sisters in a large house a short distance away to the northeast. I enjoyed the presence of a menagerie of animals, despite not having pets of my own. They seemed to be drawn to me and my living space, so I had no choice but to temporarily adopt them, coming up with my own pet names.

The O'Meara sisters from across the way had at least four or five cats, besides their dogs and horses. One of my favorite visitors was a big, thick-furred male cat with an outgoing personality. His visits seemed to coincide with my weekly custom of cooking up range-fed beef, peppers, onions, garlic, and refried beans—all the ingredients that went into my staple burro mix. "Tommie Tucker"—the sisters' named him—after a favorite local Tucson musician. He then became for me, "Mr. FluffyCat," and he had an endearing ritual by which he announced his presence and desire to visit. I had a door on that side of the house with a high-set screened window panel. From the outside, he would take a flying leap and, with a resounding thump, latch himself firmly onto the screen with his claws! Whereupon, it was then my turn to take part in our little ritual, by slowly swinging the door open to the inside. He would then drop down off the screen and saunter throughout the house, tail held high and waving like a flag! On one occasion, Mr. FluffyCat accompanied me for a walk all the way out to our mailbox at street-side and back!

Mr. PestyCat was quite a different story. This lean, little black cat was the spitting image of "Fum," on the popular YouTube video series, "Fum and Gebra," the inseparably-bonded barn owl and cat playmates and their amusing antics. (Basora, 2011) I had to keep a watchful eye on him, especially through the fall, with so many butterflies emerging during that time. This frisky cat sometimes found the freshly eclosed specimens before I did, but I was always able to make last minute rescues, preventing any serious harm to the butterflies. Mr. PestyCat wandered in from Wolf and Cheryl's side of the duplex. One of their two friendly dogs had the most thick, bristly fur that reminded me of a javelina and was always hard to see at night. So, I re-named him "The Invisible Hog-Dog!"

The indoor rearing season continued through the late fall and into December. I had kept track of most of the butterflies that wandered away from their host plants to find pupation spots inside the house. But raising these native species began, more or less, spontaneously, rather than having been initiated to follow an exacting, data-gathering methodology. Of course, the incidental notes and limited data recording during this early period were a far cry from the intensive field procedures adopted many years later doing extensive monarch butterfly fieldwork and tagging. (Billings, 2019) But they still contributed to the learning process, nonetheless. Some of the entries on the lower part of a transcribed listing were water-damaged from the flooding that occurred a year later. This listing represents the last series of the fall through December period of 1982:

EL FUERTE / NATIVE BUTTERFLY VIVARIUM				
Species	**(# in Sequence)**	**Date of Pupation**	**Date of Emergence**	**Notes:**
Queen	(1)	10/08	10/23-24 (approx.)	16 days
Queen	(2)	10/10	11/08	28 days
Queen	(3)	(unk-found 10/16)	—	—
Gulf fritillary	(1)	10/15	11/19	34 days
Gulf fritillary	(2)	10/16 (a.m.)	—(unknown)	—
Gulf fritillary	(3)	10/16 (p.m.)	11/24	38 days
Pipevine S-tail	(1)	(unk-found 1st week of Oct.)	—	—
Pipevine S-tail	(2)	10/16	11/12 (eve)	26 days
Queen	(4)	10/16 (10:45p.m.)	11/12	26 days
Gulf fritillary	(4)	10/17	11/19(eve)	32 days
Pipevine S-tail	(3)	10/17	— (unknown)	—
Gulf fritillary	(5)	10/19	11/15	26 days
Gulf fritillary	(6)	10/21-24 (?)	11/23	29-32 days
Pipevine S-tail	(4)	10/26	(undec-water damaged)	—
Pipevine S-tail	(5)	—	(undecipherable-water damaged)	—

EL FUERTE / NATIVE BUTTERFLY VIVARIUM				
Species	**(# in Sequence)**	**Date of Pupation**	**Date of Emergence**	**Notes:**
Pipevine S-tail	(6)	—	(undecipher-able-water dam-aged)	—
Pipevine S-tail	(7)	—	(undecipher-able-water dam-aged)	—
Queen*	(5)	11/01 (1:30 p.m.)	11/25 (eve)	24 days
Queen	(6)	11/02 (9:30 p.m.)	12/09	37 days
Gulf fritillary	(7)	11/05 (eve)	— (unknown)	—
Gulf fritillary	(8)	11/08	12/12	34 days
Gulf fritillary	(9)	11/11	12/26	45 days
* 1st (and only) butterfly to emerge with deformed wings—that is; wings remained curled after drying out—inhibiting flight.				

[JB Fieldnotes, 1982]

The following fall, in late September—early October of 1983, Tropical Storm Octave hit full force upon El Fuerte! Early in the morning of the second day of torrential rains (three-day total = 6.5"), a foamy, rushing tide swept in through the front screen door of my duplex, inundating the entire space with floodwaters, up to a foot in depth. Many of my floor-shelf level record albums are still glazed with silt from the Tanque Verde Wash. In the aftermath, months later, I was climbing down, late in the day, from a favorite skinny-dipping pool in a rocky cataract off the Douglas Springs Trail of the Rincon Mountains. In the dim light, I caught sight of a butterfly that had an unusual appearance and flight. I stealthily approached, as it was fluttering around a desert willow tree, seeking a spot to roost. As it perched, I carefully caught it with finger-

Zebra longwing, a rare tropical stray (Photo by Volker Meyer)

tips—momentarily—gently clasping its folded wings. I was shocked, amazed and delighted! For here I beheld an exotic tropical creature, unlike anything I'd ever seen before: a blaze of yellow streaks upon black, zebra longwing butterfly! *Heliconius charitonius* was a magnificent beauty and rare stray from the far southeast; likely blown into southern Arizona with the tropical storm. (Bailowitz and Brock, 1991)

View south over Second Basin Wash area (Fall 1996)

Chapter Fifteen

Vail, Arizona/Native Pollinator Plant Survey

Several years after "The Great Flood of '83," I began making the transition from El Fuerte and the Tanque Verde Valley towards areas farther to the southeast. I eventually settled into a rental within a historic ranch in the heart of the Rincon Valley. Good fortune brought me, once again, to a grand and inspiring place that sparked continuous and extensive explorations all over the valley, nearby Rincon Mountains, and the greater Vail area surrounding Cienega Creek and Pantano Wash. The natural paradise as catalyst for a whole range of expansive studies, projects, inspiration, and growth, remained true to the pattern!

I became immersed right away in an intensive organic gardening phase amidst abounding resources of cow and chicken manure, free-for-the-taking hay mulch (thanks to the Vail Feed Store), and the presence of an open mesquite stand inside the yard. I grew squashes (zucchini, yellow, acorn, turban, Hubbard, butternut, etc.) with some of them climbing up into the mesquites and setting suspended fruits. There were cucumbers, cantaloupes, watermelons, and pumpkins. I collected dried desert spoon and agave stalks and wired them in place for convenient trellises. These provided nesting sites for the big, black female carpenter bees (*Xylocopa sp.*) that burrow into the stalks to create brood chambers and are virtually the only reliable pollinator for squashes and melons.

Six varieties of grapes were cultivated: Thompson and red flame seedless on the front porch overhead trellis, perlette, black monukka, muscat, and Concord in the mesquite side-yard, or uphill above the yard. A thick boysenberry vine covered the four-foot tall, wire horse fencing along the front and uphill portion of the side yard (the quail loved 'em).

Uphill, above the top fenceline of the mesquite sideyard, I built an enclosure of extended metal T-poles, framed with scrap irrigation pipe and covered over with chickenwire. (Thanks a bunch to good friend, the late Rick Dailey, La Posta Quemada Ranch Foreman, who gave me a big roll of it!) Within that enclosure grew okra, tomatoes, eggplant, peppers, Italian parsley, radishes, carrots, pear tomatoes (sweet!), with the Concord grape ascending over the framework. Once this phase ran its course, and things were well-established enough, my primary focus returned to hiking and exploring the length of the valley on both sides of Rincon Creek, roaming upper tributarial washes, canyons, and into the mountains beyond.

Granite dome atop skyline ridge, Rincon Mountains (Photo by Elton Kerr)

I slept atop a dome of solid granitic rock on occasion, at around 4,000 feet elevation, above the Saguaro National Monument boundary (before the transition to National Park). Nearby, along a cliff face, next to a small rock shelter, I had discovered a niche where an ancient hunter-gatherer had stashed a well-worn hammerstone and flaked-edge chopping tool, leaving them intact, *in situ*. I could envision a small band, or possibly individual, on a seasonal foraging mission along this rocky, canyon route into the mountains above. Lower down, across a wide expanse of the terraces above Rincon Creek, it was apparent that a sizable occupation of aboriginal residents had existed here hundreds or thousands of years ago.

Ancient hunter-gatherers likewise persisted along the main streambed and tributarial washes of the Pantano Wash/Cienega Creek drainage system. The combination of rich, riparian habitat, unique assemblages of native plants, rocks, and scenic "trainscapes," and railroad history made this area irresistible for my own eventual explorations. Of course, the contemporary character of steep cut-banked, sand and gravel watersheds across southeast Arizona, similar to Cienega Creek, bear little resemblance to what existed historically before the arrival of Anglo-Americans, even before the development of the mesquite bosques:

> Before 1900, the streams were sluggish, flowing through dense cienegas or bogs choked with tall grass. These ponds provided permanent and temporary homes for water-dwellers such as beaver and waterfowl. The grasslands, less affected by erosion, probably supported grazing animals throughout the past century. Grasslands mixed with oak and mesquite sheltered deer and javelina. In spite of the relatively rich supply of natural plant and animal foods available in the past, malarial conditions associated with the swampy areas may have been an obstacle to permanent human settlement. (Eddy and Cooley, 1983)

One could make the argument, that perhaps more than any other single factor, the trapping out and eventual extirpation of beavers was, by far, the most devastating in its overall impact on this watershed:

View from Rincon foothills toward Rincon Peak (Photo by Elton Kerr)

> Although North American Beaver are not usually thought of as desert animals, they occurred throughout the Gila drainage from the cool mountain meadows and canyons of New Mexico down through the hot country of Arizona to the confluence of the Gila and Colorado Rivers and beyond. Beaver build dams, thus impounding water, slowing runoff, increasing percolation, settling silt, halting stream degradation. (Stabler, 1985) They were an integral part of the Gila watershed system and had been so throughout the wetter Pleistocene, the last 1.8 million years. (Rea, 1997)

As an upper component of the Gila River watershed, Cienega Creek drains a vast area to the far southeast, between the Empire and Whetstone Mountains. Northwest from Vail, Arizona, it becomes the Pantano Wash, before its eventual confluence with the Tanque Verde Wash—as Rillito Creek—near Ft. Lowell Park, on Tucson's northeast side. Except in the aftermath of substantial rainfall runoff, it is rare to find much persistence of moisture along the Pantano Wash between Vail and Tucson. The upstream reaches of Cienega Creek, are mostly dry with only a few widely-spaced, trickling, minimal flows or wet spots throughout most of the year. Through the fall and winter periods, select wet patches have even been found along upper elevation wash tributaries to the south between the Creek and Interstate 10. It should be noted that it is necessary to secure day permits for hiking in these areas through Pima County Natural Resources. Pima County's long-term survey of the Cienega Creek Preserve area has recorded over 500 species of native plants. (Fonseca, 2022)

During earlier excursions, when my home base was situated in the Rincon Valley, I roamed over a great extent of the main Pantano Wash/Cienega Creekbed, while gathering raw materials for primitive weaponry projects. In the early 1990s, I was fortunate to get re-settled atop a high desert mesa, east of Vail, overlooking my entire study area. Now, from close range, I undertook a progressive survey over a three-to-four year-period—1993-1996—exploring widely over rugged terrain to discover and become familiar with the full range of endemic plant species. This covered native trees, shrubs, grasses and cacti, but especially areas of blooming nectar plant concentrations. Within this group, primary pollinator plants and specific butterfly host plant species were identified and

Second Basin Bebbia *thicket with many blooms despite June heat and dryness.*

studied. Areas of plant concentrations were systematically covered and photographed. There was also some follow-up fieldwork conducted in 1998, with additional findings.

The general site boundaries for the survey were Interstate 10 on the south, Marsh Station Road/Davidson Canyon to the east, and Colossal Cave Road and the Vail townsite on the west. For the most part, Pantano Wash/Cienega Creek served as the north boundary, though occasional hikes were undertaken up north-side tributaries, such as Agua Verde Creek. The elevation ranged roughly between 3,200 and 3,450 feet. In all other weather-related and climatic aspects, the study area closely matched the lower Sonoran Desert surrounding Tucson, despite the elevational difference. The areas of prime concentration were the open, deep-cut basin washes draining into the Creek from the south. These began one and a quarter miles upstream, east of the Colossal Cave Road Bridge, at the confluence of First Basin Wash and the creek, or more correctly, the Pantano Wash. A monumental, ninety-five-year-old concrete culvert provides entry from the north, passing under the railroad tracks.

View through First Basin culvert towards Pantano Wash confluence

Once entering First Basin Wash from this culvert, both banks are lined with an abundance of two of the primary pollinator species of the area: *Dicliptera resupinata* with its two-lipped, rose-purple flowers and translucent bracts (after seeds are expended) is thickly clumped on the left, or east terrace of the Wash. *Bebbia juncea*'s reflective seedheads are brightly illuminated by the sun on the opposite side. Thick clusters of stems topped with small yellow blooms occur in late spring, re-bloom in the fall, as does *Dicliptera*. These compact, round bushes are massed together along the west edge of the Wash. Periods of *Bebbia* bloom seem to attract more butterflies of every conceivable species, more so than all other pollinator plants in the area, except possibly desert broom and seepwillow. The well-known *Acacia greggii*, or catclaw, are likewise found along the terraces above the wash. First Basin Wash continues farther south, underneath the mainline railroad tracks, past the Southwest Gas pipeline route before trailing out southeastward, dividing into multiple rivulets, fanning out over desert scrub-covered ridges.

Winter-dormant First Basin Dicliptera *row of understory shrubs*

Mass of Bebbia *seedheads reflecting winter sun along First Basin Wash*

Pantano Wash officially becomes Cienega Creek above the Agua Verde Creek confluence, just over a mile upstream from First Basin Wash. Second Basin Wash merges into the main wash, roughly 300 yards below this confluence, through another historic concrete culvert. The most promising areas of pollinator/host plant concentrations occur in the upper reaches of Second Basin Wash to the south, beyond the mainline railroad tracks. This familiar primary core area of past studies was re-visited recently (by request of Pima County Natural Resources) during a one-day field "recon" outing. From the Pantano Washbed: First Basin Wash was covered, then after jogging a mile east, I returned to the prime area of Second Basin Wash in January 2020, after a twenty-plus-year absence:

> Once the descent down to the Wash is made, the familiar terrace of past studies here is relocated, albeit with a well-defined motorcycle path running along its length. This track skirts the edge of the thickest core concentration of *Bebbia* bushes, approximately 200 yards south of the RR culvert. There are roughly 70-80 of these bushes, which compares with a count of 125, during the earlier study period from 1993-1996. This terrace, above the Wash channel to the right or west, was always a high activity area during the fall blooming season. The abundant patches of *Dicliptera*

esupnata and *Bebbia juncea* upon this terrace area were the main attractants of a host of diverse butterfly species. Most conspicuous among these were pipevine swallowtail (*Battus philenor*), black swallowtail (*Papilio polyxenes*), variegated fritillary (*Euptoieta claudia*), southern dogface (*Colias cesonia*), cloudless sulphur (*Phoebis sennae*), queen (*Danaus gilippus*), gray hairstreak (*Strymon melinus*), metalmarks (*Apodemia* or *Calephelis spp.*), bordered patch (*Chlosyne lacinia*), and various blues. Occasionally, day-flying sphinx moths (*Hyles sp.*) were seen.

Billings, 2020 Brief Field Report:4

Left to right: Female dogface on Bebbia*, Pipevine swallowtail, Male dogface butterfly on* Bebbia*, Black swallowtail*

Overlook of Second Basin, south toward Mt. Fagan (Santa Rita Mountains)

It should be emphasized that all areas covered within this local watershed, excepting the main Pantano/Cienega Creekbed, are dry washes, with no running nor standing water. As one ascends further upstream in Second Basin Wash south of the railroad culvert where it becomes enclosed by conglomerate rock canyon walls, there are occasional wet patches, except during drier, hotter periods. This could be due to a much wider catchment area than the other side washes, or specific geological features. These are prime locations for concentrations of pollinator/host shrubs and trees along the upper section of this watershed area. Here, there are numerous large Bebbia and chuparosa (*Anisacanthus thurberi*) bushes, snake weed (*Gutierrezia spp.*), Aloysia or beebrush, catclaw mimosa (*Mimosa biuncifera*) thickets, as well as *Dicliptera*. Lush thickets of desert trees intermittently line both sides of this upper canyon arroyo: whitethorn (Acacia constricta) and catclaw acacia, desert willow (*Chilopsis linearis*), blue palo verde (*Parkinsonia florida*), and a few scattered mesquites.

A recent half-day "recon" of this section of upper Second Basin Wash in early June of 2020 turned up a surprising number of blooms in the main *Bebbia* patch, along with many flowering chuparosa bushes, and *Dicliptera* with bright bluish-purple flowers, nearby. Thickets of mimosa with little "white-ball" blooms were discovered further upstream, in the canyon. Here, a single, magnificent, lone hackberry tree with a lush, thick canopy provided the most intense deep shade imaginable. There were masses of bright, yellow "miniature fuzz-ball" blooms on branches of whitethorns throughout a wide range of the wash, though unattended by insect pollinators. A total of thirteen butterfly species were sighted and identified; most were photographed:

A LIST OF BUTTERFLIES AND NECTAR PLANTS OF UPPER 2ND BASIN WASH / PANTANO WASH—CIENEGA CREEK WATERSHED AREA / VAIL, ARIZONA / FROM JUNE 8, 2020			
Common Name	**Species**	**Nectar Plant(s)**	**Notes**
Fatal metalmark	*Calephelis nemesis*	*Bebbia, Sarcostemma**	
Texan crescentspot	*Phyciodes texana*	*Bebbia*	
Elada checkerspot	*Texola elada*	*Bebbia, Sarcostemma*	
Variegated fritillary	*Euptoieta Claudia*	*Bebbia*	
Queen	*Danaus gilippus*	*Mimosa, Bebbia*	
Checkered white	*Pontia protodice*	*Bebbia*	
Dainty sulphur	*Nathalis iole*	*Bebbia*	Free-flying
Southern dogface	*Colias cesonia*		Free-flying
Pipevine swallowtail	*Battus philenor*	*Anisacanthus*	Free-flying
Reakirt's blue	*Hemiargus isola*	*Mimosa, Sarcostemma*	
Ceraunus blue	*Hemiargus ceraunus*	*Bebbia*	
Funereal duskywing	*Erynnis funeralis*	*Bebbia*	
Empress leilia	*Asterocampa leilia*		Free-flying
**Sarcostemma hirtellum* (Climbing milkweed vine)			

JB Field Notebook 2020

Chuparosa (Anisacanthus) *with blooms*

Elada checkerspot on Sarcostemma *flower*

Anisacanthus is abundant in this upper Second Basin area and found scattered among both deep-cut basin washes, north of the mainline (south) railroad tracks. Sulphurs and pipevine swallowtails are especially drawn to the narrow, red or orange, tubular flowers, of these medium-sized shrubs. The little Elada checkerspot butterfly (*Texola elada*) is known to use this shrub as its caterpillar—host plant. (Bailowitz and Brock, 1991) *Dicliptera* is the prime host plant for the Texan crescentspot (*Phyciodes texana*); a distinctive resident, often seen nectaring in this area. A small-to-medium-sized butterfly, darker to light brown, dorsally, and dotted with white spots across forewings, in rows across hindwings, and soft reddish spots in the center of both—around thorax and abdomen. Ascending upward and outward from low-lying areas are unique and interesting plants of the slopes and mesas, well above the desert washbeds.

Thamnosma texana is a butterfly host plant semi-hidden on these slopes and mesas. This little plant is easily overlooked, diminutive in height, and blending in with grasses and low-growing vegetation. Look for dense clusters of gray-green, small-leafed stems, about a foot tall, with peculiar, little shell-like seed pods at the tips. If you're still unsure, crush and sniff the foliage: it is a member of the rue family (*Rutaceae*) with a distinctive and strongly pungent scent. It frequently occurs in small, shallow ravines, and is the primary host plant for the showy black swallowtail, whose black-yellow-white-banded caterpillars can frequently be sighted attached to the spindly stems. This is a brightly-patterned butterfly on the underside or, with wings folded, displays rows of iridescent yellow, blue, and variegated orange spots against an overall black coloration. The abdomen is uniformly lined with rows of tiny bright yellow dots, suggesting miniature lights. The males are "hill-toppers;" that is, they can

Texan crescentspot

Male black swallowtail on hilltop perch

Dicliptera *bush at edge of Second Basin Wash*

frequently be found patrolling hilltops. They'll fly out from favorite perches to drive off other butterflies, and sometimes other insects, like carpenter bees, while pursuing females that wander into their area.

Parthenium incanum, or mariola, is another indigenous plant not found in the Sonoran Desert proper surrounding Tucson but which occurs in abundance in the greater Vail area.

Thamnosma stems with black swallowtail caterpillar

Mariola in full bloom on upland desert plain

Blackfoot daisy (Melampodium)

Most of the time, it is found mixed with the whole range of low-growing, hardy desert shrubs covering flat mesas and ridgetops. Where moisture and landforms create favorable sites, massive hedgerows of these much larger, silvery-gray bushes can be found in lower-lying, open desert flats. Mariola casts strong, pleasant evening bloom fragrances during the late summer and fall, and likely provides nectar for moths among dense cream-white flower panicles.

Blackfoot daisy (*Melampodium leucanthum*) is another sought after perennial species occurring on upland slopes, with conspicuous white, honey-scented flowers, seen early in the spring. This little showy-blooming gem can be quite enigmatic. In a good year it springs up all over the landscape; at other times, is almost impossible to find. I have seen it in abundance during one spring above the upper southeast end of the Rincon Valley along the Arizona Trail inside Colossal Cave Park. It has been long-popular as a plant used in natural settings in the landscaping and nursery trade despite being short-lived.

Paperflower (*Psilostrophe cooperi*) is one of the most prominently flowering sunflower family plants (*Asteraceae*) during springtime in the uplands of the Pantano/Cienega watershed area. Mounds of gray-green leafed, whitish stems are covered with bright, soft yellow flowers in late spring, and later in the fall. They are visited by metalmarks and other small butterflies. *Thymophylla* or dogweed, on the other hand, is another yellow blooming composite, but diminutive in size, with delicate, fine stems and miniature flowers. Two species can be found across this area, though *T. pentachaeta* is much more common and widespread. Under a foot in height and spread, it is used as a host species by the smallest of the sulphurs, *Nathalis iole*, or dainty sulphur.

Paperflower on desert terrace with desert zinnia

The broad expanse of gradually sloping uplands and mesas above the Pantano Wash/Cienega Creek drainage system exists as a dense, highly diverse mosaic of many small-to-medium-sized shrubs. Some of the smaller denizens of this sun-baked realm: white-flowered desert zinnia and blackfoot daisy, elegant, pink-lavender blooming *Hibiscus denudatus*, gray-leafed *tiquilia*, fairyduster with mesquite-like foliage and delicate pinkish floral sprays, and yellow blooming bahias with their unique spheres of perfectly interlocked seed spikes. Among the larger shrubs that fit into this matrix are Lemony-scented *Aloysia* or beebrush, soft yellow-blooming *Menadora scabra*, Ephedra with its long, needle-like fo-

Thymophylla *or dogweed along railroad grade*

Large Menodora *bush in full bloom along railroad grade (Fall 1996)*

Close-up of Menodora *flowers*

White-flowered desert zinnia and yellow Bahias *amidst* Tiquilia

Flower of desert, Hibiscus denudata

liage, low mounds of *Krameria* or range ratany, with tiny rose-purple flowers and widespread white floral-clustered and fragrant mariola. Large, light-green prickly pears (*Opuntia spp.*) are conspicuous and well-represented within this community. Much of the uplands have open, stunted scrubby stands of creosote (*Larrea sp.*); in other areas towards the south, they are absent. Mixed in with all these shrubs and perennials are various seasonal wildflowers, native grass clumps, barrel cacti (*Ferocactus sp.*), chollas (*Cylindropuntia spp.*), stands of *Yucca arizonica* or Spanish bayonet, scattered agaves that send up tall stalks, ocotillos (*Fouquieria sp.*), desert spoons (*Dasylirion sp.*) that also put up showy floral stalks, and a variety of small, unique cacti species which fill in all the gaps upon the uplands. Tall saguaro cacti soaring skyward are scarce in areas south of the main wash/creek channel, but form solid stands in a few terrace spots along the north bank.

Slogging through vast expanses of sand, broken by occasional ephemeral, wet streambed stretches and tall, riparian tree galleries, it's quite a different experience roaming the Pantano Wash/Cienega Creek channel. I returned to relive that experience recently, on a clear, hot sunny day in mid-June 2020. Arriving early, I picked up a chunk of rock from the steeply descending two-track down to Second Basin Wash, and detached a series of dark flakes, creating a "one-minute-handaxe." Then I took a brief inventory of the main core *Bebbia* patch terrace, before heading north under the nearby, concrete culvert. The bed of this sidewash threads narrowly through dense thickets of mesquite, acacia (both whitethorn and catclaw), desert hackberry, and blue palo verde. It frequently splits, dividing into several divergent channels. Bright, showy rose-purple-flowered *Dicliptera* shrubs were encountered in many places; though largely unattended by pollinators, except an occasional sulphur butterfly. Blue palo verdes with few remaining "yellow star" blooms, drew in a few small butterflies. Soaring high above these thickets, a redtail hawk screamed, seemingly in dismay over my presence.

JB's "one-minute handaxe"

Passing under another cavernous, concrete culvert, I continued my course through more thickets of legumes, towards the main washbed. A great, wide area of distant space finally opened up ahead, where I could see across an immensity of sand. I emerged overlooking the east edge of the wash, between two thickets of trees covered with grape ivy. This was the precise spot where I had noted this unique plant, on August 10th of 1998:

Grape ivy (Cissus trifoliata) draped over tall mesquites

Close-up of blue palo verde flower with marine blue

Close-up of Dicliptera *flowers*

Cissus trifoliata/impressive vine growing over trees and shrubs along E [east] edge of 2nd Basin/Cienega Creek confluence. Inconsp.[icuous] flowers attracting many avidly feeding pipevine Sw-t's [swallowtails]. VITACEAE

JB Field Notebook, 1993—1998:50

I have never seen such a large concentration of pipevine swallowtails as those I observed draped over those grape ivy vines twenty-two years ago. I did not record any other butterfly species mixed in with them. As a resident Sonoran Desert butterfly, pipevines are drawn to perhaps the widest range of available nectar plant sources. The question in my mind is always, "What do they not feed on?" As I entered and began roaming the broad, dry washbed eastward, or upstream, I eventually found a nice pipevine to follow on its meandering flight over the wash. This was easy because it was stopping often to alight on the delicate, pinkish-white flowertops of clammyweed (*Polanisia sp.*). Known for its rank-smelling foliage, this plant might win the all-time, desert survivor award. It thrives in abundant, low stands across the driest, most exposed stretches of sandy washbed, in full, broiling summer sun. Like the grape ivy, it's another plant eschewed by virtually all other butterflies, except the lovely pipevine swallowtail.

I reversed course, and headed downstream, towards more riparian environs. A very large mule deer—still as a statue—studied me from the edge of a distant thicket to the south as I passed under the arched corridor of cottonwoods. A striking viceroy butterfly perched above me in one nearby tree. Despite the comforting shade, and close presence, or promise of water to come, there are many more butterfly species frequenting the drier, upper reaches of Second Basin Wash, where the day's journey began. One exception to this might occur while stands of seepwillow are in bloom. In areas farther downstream, along open, sunny exposures, I used to encounter a multitude of thick blooming stands with diverse butterflies drawn to the whitish flower clus-

Big desert mule deer at edge of thicket, with close-up showing him behind the latticework of vines

Arched riparian corridor of mostly cottonwoods

Viceroy butterfly perched above in cottonwoods

ters. But this foundation nectar plant—with its distinctive aroma—does not occur in the same places it used to:

> 10/30/96:...Go thru 70+ year-old tunnel (1925 stamped, both ends) [1st Basin Wash confluence] and enter lusher riparian growth, dominated by *Baccharis glutinosa* [seepwillow, changed taxonomically to *B. salicifolia*], willow trees *Salix sp.*, occasional walnut, cottonwood, ash, tamarisk, etc. *Xanthium strumarium* (common cocklebur) is everywhere. Water flowing in main channel is shallow, quiet but widens out in spots. Sahuaros on steep ridges and hillsides on N [north] side are impressive. Found a clearing, N of the main channel, surrounded by seepwillow; with a great stand of *Cassia leptophylla* [*Senna leptocarpa*]...
>
> JB Field Notebook, 1993-1998:41

Long pod senna with showy flower spikes (Rincon Valley)

Cabbage white on speedwell (Veronica spp.)

Cassia or (long pod senna) was another exciting and important find, since it served as the butterfly host plant for multiple species of sulphur. This is an attractive, lush-leafed shrub with showy, orange-yellow flowers. At a later date, I collected a small amount of seed that became commercially grown in a large Tucson nursery. Seepwillow, likewise, is a butterfly host plant (Fatal metalmark) as are other members of the riparian realm: willow, cottonwood, ash, speedwell (*Veronica spp.*), watercress (*Nasturtium* > *Rorippa sp.*), and others. (Bailowitz and Brock, 1991)

Returning upstream, through the heat of that mid-June afternoon, I froze—dead in my tracks—glimpsing brown furry creatures at a distance. I was privileged to observe a lively troupe of varying-sized coatimundi. Some scrambled up into the trees, while a large adult at mid-channel within the cottonwood corridor seemed unconcerned so long as I maintained my one-hundred-yard-plus distance. This robust adult was an impressive animal, with its magnificent, long tail held high:

Large adult coatimundi roaming Pantano/Cienega Creek washbed

Painted lady caterpillar

... Like baboons or javelinas, coatis travel in small, often noisy groups of five to 10, or even up to 20 animals, made up of sociable females and their young. They hunt for food in the open arid brushland, using their long flexible piglike snouts and strong webbed and clawed front paws to root up small rodents, insects, larvae, snakes, centipedes, and scorpions. Dry berries of juniper and manzanita, and occasionally small birds, also are eaten...In many parts of its range the coati is almost wholly arboreal, but in parts of southern Arizona, southeastern New Mexico, and northern Mexico it inhabits true desert areas, and at night and sometimes during the day climbs through the palo verde and mesquite thickets. In climbing, it uses the tail for both balance and support. (Jaeger, 1961)

Continuing further through open sandy stretches, I reflected on the day's observations. At least ten butterfly nectar/pollinator plants were recorded: *Bebbia*, *Dicliptera*, whitethorn, wolfberry (*Lycium sp.*), blue palo verde, chuparosa, milkweed vine, *Stephanomeria pauciflora*, speedwell, and clammyweed. I had covered the high and low spaces of the terrain, and these were the prime sources according to what I sighted, knew to look for, or what the butterflies guided me towards.

Once I returned to the familiar upper Second Basin *Bebbia* terrace patch, I added two more butterflies to the day's list. This required chasing around after tiny butterflies and hovering over innumerable, small yellow blooms, under full 107° sunshine, while training my mostly uncooperative Canon PowerShot camera, to get decent zoom photo IDs. The addi-

Common checkered skipper on Bebbia

Painted lady butterfly

tion of the little Elada checkerspot, and common checkered skipper brought my list up to seventeen species for the day. (Persistence pays off.) Feeling satisfied, I ascended the basin via the same steep route, recovering my custom-made, flaked-stone handaxe from where I had set it atop a road cut.

Butterfly "host plants" are the chosen plants upon which adult females lay their eggs, which eventually become caterpillars, or larvae, before reaching the pupation stage. What I had begun—similar to a tiny caterpillar—following my own path of discovery back in the 1990s—now seemed to be coming full-circle. The ongoing explorations and hands-on learning over the wild, native landscape had focused on the indigenous plants and butterflies. The relationships between both appeared to be reaching a fuller and more satisfying climax beyond the original survey results. Within this nearly thirty-year span, I had utilized much of this earlier knowledge in designing and constructing my natural habitat gardens as "The Landscaping Artist." I had pulled together my collective field notes and photos from the past, combining them with more recent field explorations and additional research of this region, and consulting sources by the most outstanding lepidopterists in the field towards the creation of a more comprehensive list:

A LIST OF BUTTERFLY HOST PLANTS AND THE BUTTERFLIES THEY ATTRACT/ PANTANO WASH—CIENEGA CREEK WATERSHED AREA / VAIL, ARIZONA

Plant Species	Name	Butterfly	Species	Location
Abutilon spp.	Indian mallow	Zampa skipper	*Systasea zampa*	D, E
Acacia constricta	Whitethorn	Reakirt's blue	*Echinargus isola*	B, C, D
Acacia greggii	Catclaw acacia	Marine blue	*Leptotes marina*	B, C, D
Agave palmeri	Palmer agave	Aryxna giant skipper	*Agathymus aryxna*	E
Ambrosia ambrosiodes	Ragweed	Bordered patch	*Chlosyne lacinia*	B, C, D
Anisacanthus thurberi	Chuparosa	Elada checkerspot	*Texola elada*	B, C, D
		Tiny checkerspot	*Dymasia dymas*	
Aristolochia watsonii	Pipevine	Pipevine swallowtail	*Battus philenor*	C,D
Artemisia ludoviciana	Western mugwort	Painted lady	*Vanessa cardui*	C, D
		American lady	*Vanessa virginiensis*	
***Asclepias linaria*[1]**	Pine-leaf milkweed	Queen	*Danaus gilippus*	E
		Monarch	*Danaus plexippus*	
Aster spp.	Asters	Sagebrush checkerspot	*Chlosyne acastus*	B, C, D
Atriplex canescens	Saltbush	Western pygmy blue	*Brephidium exilis*	B, C, D
Baccharis salicifolia	Seepwillow	Fatal metalmark	*Calephelis nemesis*	A, B, C
Bebbia juncea	Sweetbush	**Wright's metalmark[2]**	*Calephelis wrighti*	C, D
Boerhaavia spp.	Spiderling	Variegated fritillary	*Euptoieta Claudia*	B, C, D
Bouteloua curtipendula	Side oats grama	Sheep skipper	*Atrytonopsis edwardsii*	C, D, E
Calliandra eriophylla	Fairyduster	Marine blue	*Leptotes marina*	E
Cassia covesii	Desert senna	Cloudless sulphur	*Phoebis sennae*	C, D, E
Celtis pallida	Desert hackberry	Empress leilia	*Asterocampa leilia*	C, D
		Snout butterfly	*Libytheana carinenta*	
Celtis reticulata	Netleaf hackberry	Tawny emperor	*Asterocampa clyton*	A, B, C
		Snout butterfly	*Libytheana carinenta*	
Cirsium neomexicanum	N. M. Thistle	Painted lady	*Vanessa cardui*	B, C, D
		Mylitta crescent	*Phyciodes mylitta*	B, C, D

A LIST OF BUTTERFLY HOST PLANTS AND THE BUTTERFLIES THEY ATTRACT/ PANTANO WASH—CIENEGA CREEK WATERSHED AREA / VAIL, ARIZONA

Plant Species	Name	Butterfly	Species	Location
Clematis drummondii	Virgin's bower	Fatal metalmark	*Calephelis nemesis*	B, C
Croton spp.	Goatweed	**Tropical leafwing**[3]	*Anaea aidea*	D, E
		Goatweed leafwing	*Anaea andria*	
Cynodon dactylon	Bermuda grass	Fiery Skipper	*Hylephila phyleus*	A
		Orange skipperling	*Copaeodes aurantiacus*	
Dalea formosa	Feather dalea	Southern dogface	*Colias cesonia*	E
Dicliptera resupinata	Dicliptera	Texan crescentspot	*Phyciodes texana*	C, D
Eriogonum spp.	Buckwheat	Mormon metalmark	*Apodemia mormo*	C, D, E
		Acmon blue	*Plebejus acmon*	
Fraxinus velutina	Velvet ash	Two-tailed swallowtail	*Papilio multicaudata*	A
Gossypium thurberi	Desert cotton	Painted lady	*Vanessa cardui*	C, D
		Gray hairstreak	*Strymon melinus*	
Hoffmanseggia drypanocarpa	Sickle pod	Orange sulphur	*Colias eurytheme*	D, E
Janusia gracilis	Janusia	Funereal duskywing	*Erynnis funeralis*	D, E
Juniperus sp.	One seed juniper	"Siva" juniper hairstreak	*Callophrys gryneus*	B, C, D
Krameria spp	Range ratany	Mormon metalmark	*Apodemia mormo*	E
Lepidium spp.	Peppergrass	Checkered white	*Pontia protodice*	B, C, D
Mimosa biuncifera	Catclaw mimosa	Reakirt's blue	*Echinargus isola*	B, C, D
Phoradendron californicum	Mistletoe	Great purple hairstreak	*Atlides halesus*	B, C, D
Plantago spp.	Plantain	Buckeye	*Junonia coenia*	C, D, E
Populus fremontii	Fremont cottonwood	Mourning cloak	*Nymphalis antiopa*	A
		Red-spotted purple	*Limenitis arthemis*	

[1]***Asclepias linaria*:** This plant is very scarce within the area, but included since I personally found one large-sized blooming shrub. Potentially, it can be utilized by monarch butterflies, though I have never observed larvae on *A. linaria*.

[2]**Wright's metalmark** (*Calephelis wrighti*) is found over the western half of Arizona, despite an abundance of *Bebbia* in southeastern Arizona.

A LIST OF BUTTERFLY HOST PLANTS AND THE BUTTERFLIES THEY ATTRACT/ PANTANO WASH—CIENEGA CREEK WATERSHED AREA / VAIL, ARIZONA				
Plant Species	**Name**	**Butterfly**	**Species**	**Location**
[3]**Tropical leafwing**/Goatweed leafwing: One of these uncommon butterflies was briefly sighted on a flowering *Sarcostemma* milkweed vine, during the 1993-1996 study period. Low-growing Croton that are the preferred host plant genera were found in several spots along railroad utility roadways. Non-Native Species: Initially, I was reluctant to include non-native, naturalized plants such as "London rocket" mustard, but reconsidered that due to their widespread extent over the study area, and as significant butterfly host plants				
Prosopis juliflora	Velvet mesquite	Marine blue	*Leptotes marina*	B, C, D
		Ceraunus blue	*Hemiargus ceraunus*	
		Leda ministreak	*Ministrymon leda*	
		Palmer's metalmark	*Apodemia palmeri*	
Rorippa nasturtium-aquaticum	Water cress	Cabbage white	*Pieris rapae*	A
Salix spp.	Willows	Viceroy	*Limenitis archippus*	A
		Mourning cloak	*Nymphalis antiopa*	
Sarcostemma spp.	Milkweed vine	Queen	*Danaus gilippus*	B, C, D
Senna leptocarpa	Long-pod senna	Sleepy orange	*Eurema nicippe*	A, B, C
		Cloudless sulphur	*Phoebis sennae*	
		Boisduval's sulphur	*Eurema boisduvaliana*	
Sida procumbens	Sida	Desert checkered skipper	*Pyrgus philetas*	D, E
Sisymbrium irio	London rocket	Checkered white	*Pontia protodice*	D
		Pearly marble	*Euchloe hyantis*	
		"Pima" desert orangetip	*Anthocharis cethura*	
		Sara orangetip	*Anthocharis sara*	
Sorghum halepense	Johnson grass	Eufala skipper	*Lerodea eufala*	A
Sphaeralcea spp.	Globe mallow	Zampa skipper	*Systasea zampa*	D, E
		White checkered skipper	*Pyrgus albescens*	
		Gray hairstreak	*Strymon melinus*	
Thamnosma texana	Desert rue	Black swallowtail	*Papilio polyxenes*	E

A LIST OF BUTTERFLY HOST PLANTS AND THE BUTTERFLIES THEY ATTRACT/ PANTANO WASH—CIENEGA CREEK WATERSHED AREA / VAIL, ARIZONA				
Plant Species	**Name**	**Butterfly**	**Species**	**Location**
Thymophylla acerosa	Shrubby Dogweed	Dainty sulphur	*Nathalis iole*	D, E
Thymophylla pentachaeta	Dogweed	Dainty sulphur	*Nathalis iole*	E
Verbesina encelioides	Cowpen daisy	Bordered patch	*Chlosyne lacinia*	B, C, D
Veronica anagallis-aquaticum	Speedwell	Buckeye	*Junonia coenia*	A
		Dark buckeye	*Junonia nigrosuffusa*	
Viguiera annua	Annual goldeneye	Bordered patch	*Chlosyne lacinia*	B, C, D
Yucca arizonica	Arizona yucca	Yuccae giant skipper	*Megathymus yuccae*	D, E
Yucca elata	Soaptree yucca	Yuccae giant skipper	*Megathymus yuccae*	B,C,D,E

Left to right: Reakirt's blue on Mimosa, *Mormon metalmark on* Bebbia, *Funereal duskywing on* Bebbia, *Queen butterfly on* Mimosa

Left to right: Bordered patch on fleabane, Variegated fritillary, American painted lady, Cloudless sulphur

LOCATION CODE / HOST PLANTS OF PANTANO—CIENEGA WATERSHED AREA:

A) Main Pantano Wash—Cienega Creek channel: wet riparian zone.

B) Main Pantano Wash—Cienega Creek channel: open, mostly dry sandy wash zone.

C) Upper tributarial washes and low-lying terraces; south of main channel.

D) Mesquite bosques and thickets of trees, shrubs, etc., set well back (closer to base of slopes) from edges of main channel or tributarial washbeds.

E) Upland slopes and open, mostly flat desert mesas to the south of main channel.

(Bailowitz and Brock, 1991, Stewart, et al., 2001, Brock and Kaufman, 2003, Bailowitz and Brodkin, 2007, Cary, 2009, Rose, 2012, Verrier, 2018, Brock, personal communication, 2020, Verrier, personal communication, 2020)

From the lowest stretches of the main Pantano/Cienega channel, to the highest parts of desert ridges and mesas to the south, the Union Pacific Railroad tracks represent an "in-between zone" of sorts, cutting a roughly level grade at a midpoint across the landscape from the northwest to the southeast and along the south edge, above the main channel. During the early period (1993-1996) of study, in the last years of the Southern Pacific's domain, these areas were open, accessible and unrestricted. I observed, photographed and learned a significant amount just from some of the plant specimens concentrated in places along the railroad utility roads. I regularly ran long loop-course runs over these same routes beginning in the late 1980s. The utility roads allowed for greater access to some of the more remote sidewashes and upland terrain.

Union Pacific train crossing trestle, re-emerging near Second Basin

The Pantano Wash/Cienega Creek watershed area reeks of railroad history. The earliest camps of construction workers blasted through road cuts and left behind rusted artifacts such as twenty-five pound black blasting powder drums along with beverage cans opened with one or two stabs of a buck knife. Catastrophic earthquakes and floods in the late nineteenth century resulted in major line-change construction projects, raising the railroad bed above the existing gradient of the watershed. Of course, this was long before erosional down cutting changed the topography of the entire landscape from what it resembled when the first tracks were laid, as described by pioneering rancher Edward L. Vail of the Empire Ranch:

> There was no deep wash through the bottom as at present but a succession of meadows thickly covered with sacaton and salt grass. A number of springs fed the main stream that ran down the valley. The mesquite did not cover the country as at present but grew in the gulches that drained into the main wash with occasional groves in the wash itself and a few hackberry and china-berry trees.... The track was laid on the bottom near the stream. (Myrick, 1975)

Historically, the Pantano Station served this section, and was situated roughly four miles southeast of the watershed and main study area from the eastern boundary of Marsh Station Road and Davidson Canyon. The effects of ongoing environmental degradation converged with a savage, two-pronged series of natural disasters during the late 1880s:

> Nature was unkind to Pantano in 1887. In the widespread earthquake of May 3, some chimneys fell there. Then on November 11 both Pantano and Total Wreck were shaken again; this time the force was so great that it cracked the wooden depot building. Pantano was the site of a major washout in September 1887 just a month after the train robbery. A reporter ventured up the creek to find a wooden bridge washed downstream from its moorings and a second bridge, which had withstood previous storms, washed away. From that point eastward, the road was in bad shape; a spectacular sight was one rail bent double around a cottonwood tree. The worst damage was two miles ahead, east of the double span bridge. High water carried many crossties all the way down to Fort Lowell on the outskirts of Tucson. Two weeks were required for repairs of this segment. (Myrick, 1975)

As if natural catastrophes weren't enough, the human variety intervened during the same period of 1887: two train robberies took place, one in April and one in August within the present study area eight to ten miles west of Pantano approaching the present Vail townsite. (Myrick, 1975) In the first instance, a passenger train—the Sunset Express—was on its way to San Francisco late in the evening of April 27th:

> At the head end was Col. William Harper, sitting on the right-hand side watching for possible trouble as the headlight parted the darkness. On the firemen's side was James Clancy. Running 45 minutes late, Harper had left Pantano Station, 28 miles

> east of Tucson, and was now working his way through the cuts and over the fills of Cienega Canyon. Passing through a cut nine miles west of Pantano, Harper saw a red lantern and then heard the warning noises of track torpedoes. As he brought the train to a stop short of an obstruction on the track, the engine received a shower of bullets; then two masked men stepped into the cab and gave their instructions. (Myrick, 1975)

Uncoupling the engine and express car from the passenger cars, the robbers drove them further down the track. After getting very little loot, the robbers vanished into thin air. They returned, however, for a repeat performance three months later, at nearly the same location. In the second incident, the train derailed, after hitting an obstruction on the track, turning the engine and tender over, leaving it lying sideways above a steep embankment. While the engineer and fireman escaped without serious injury, the results were similar to the first. The masked gunmen got away with the contents of the safe inside the Wells Fargo express car and disappeared into the night. An interesting find shortly thereafter added legendary lore to a local tourist attraction. A sheriff's posse in close pursuit had picked up the robbers' trail, and followed it to the Rincon Mountains. Soon after, they came upon a campfire, with a sack of $1,000 in Mexican silver left behind; likely abandoned as excess baggage. (Myrick, 1975) Close by was Colossal Cave—suspected as a hideout—which eventually was developed into a major venue to visit and explore in the mid-twentieth Century. I was never fortunate enough to stumble across any pieces of Mexican silver during all my wanderings around these parts. However, on one occasion roaming the desert south of the northside tracks, I got lucky: I reached down to pick up a black disc embedded in the desert pavement. It turned out to be an

Large Trixis *bush near railroad tracks (fall 1996)*

Summer poppies (Kallstroemia) *near railroad tracks*

Desert holly (Acourtia nana)

1875 seated liberty half dollar, tarnished but otherwise in good condition! The date on the coin was five years before the Southern Pacific tracks were laid and trains began running up and down the Pantano Wash/Cienega Creek canyon.

The railroad utility roads afforded access to ridges and roadside swales above the drainage areas, where interesting plants were found. Many of these concentrations of flora have long since disappeared or been sharply diminished. This is likely due to a change between the annual rainfall regime occurring during the main study period (1993-1996) and the prevailing drought conditions at present. Large, impressive full-flowering bushes of *Menodora scabra*, Perezia (*Acourtia sp.*), and *Trixis californica* were often encountered, along with abundant annuals as gilias (*Ipomopsis longiflora*), caltrop (*Kallstroemia spp.*), morning glory vines (*Ipomoea spp.*), *Bahias*, purple-flowered *Allionia*, and desert marigolds (*Baileya multiradiata*). Several adjacent low-lying grassy, thicket areas were explored off these utility roadways. One such spot became known as the "Vail-Powerline Thicket".

It is surprising what one encounters when roaming over wide stretches of desert. You begin to adapt, expecting the landscape to resemble a given pattern when viewed repetitively over continuous terrain. Then—all at once—that pattern abruptly changes. That is how I would preface walking into the "Vail-Powerline Thicket" for the first time. The first thing that caught my eye were big mule deer, in this "mini-oasis." The powerline-thicket area is roughly centered along the north-to-south-running power corridor, and in close proximity to the twin limestone hills that are set back about a mile east of Colossal Cave Road. Impressive, thick stands of tobosa grass (*Hilaria mutica*) carpeted a wide, expansive swaled area, where desert rainfall runoff became trapped. Large, robust desert hackberry dominated the grassy flats, with Bahias, *Acourtia nana* or desert holly, and several other native grass species. The elegant, large pink-flowered desert hibiscus (*Hibiscus denudatus*) was found in stands upon and between the two limestone hills, where a small amount of seed was collected.

Farther west, several miles outside the study area, another even more interesting dry, grassy desert swale area was discovered. South of the mainline tracks, this area became known as "Rocket Road Arroyo," being a short distance from a remote dirt extension of the namesake road. Here, the discovery was made of a hidden little gem of a perennial wild flower known as desert petunia or *Ruellia nudiflora*. From a basal rosette of dark green leaves, several short erect stems arise to deliver the desert's "Best of Show:" two to four or more of stunning, large violet to light purple flowers that attract nectaring sulphur butterflies. Ruellias tend to grow in clusters around the drip ring of tree canopies, such as mesquites, where they benefit from concentrated rainfall and semi-shade. When I began collecting native seed, I learned firsthand that *Ruellia* seed capsules were explosively dehiscent:

> 11/3/96 Early afternoon. Park in usual spot and head over to same area in main gully, where I was examining *Ruellia* seed capsules on 11/1/96. These seed capsules are "spring-loaded;" when ripeness is attained and capsule dries out, it splits open along its length, snapping open to release 16 disk-shaped seeds, 4 pairs on each side. In order to effectively collect these seed, therefore, an effective seed trap had to be devised. So on 11/3, I came prepared with a series of mesh cylinders (9) produced from a 24" x 26" piece of window screen (each cylinder made from 9" x 8" piece).Securely stapled and fastened together, 2 x 4" pieces of baling wire, secured cylinders to rebar stakes. A site was found, where a side channel branched off main arroyo;

with enough *Ruellia nudiflora* specimens with a good quantity of potential seed and also I could maintain a fairly tight cluster on one site. Care was taken to fold mesh up (triangular fold, parallel edges meet in middle) from bottom to seal it securely, without damaging stem(s). Several cylinders enclosed 2 stems, with up to 25 potential seed capsules. Regular traffic of local cattle along trail nearby necessitated building protective brush corral along those borders, enclosing gaps between bushes.

JB Field Notebook, 1993—1998:42 and 43

Ruellia*, cloudless sulphur amidst* Pectis papposa

There was a peculiar, though attractive little annual sunflower family (*Asteraceae*) plant I discovered here, *Sanvitalia abertii*, that sprang up following summer monsoon rainfall. I collected a small amount of seed from it, too. A bountiful display of post-monsoon bloom occurred closer to Vail, across a great expanse of desert clay flats, adjacent to the I-10 frontage road. A blazing sea of bright yellow *Pectis papposa*, was nearly unbroken, except for an occasional *Ruellia*, another summer annual—*Tidestroemia lanulosum*—and a few widely scattered shrubs. Yes, I scraped up a quantity of *Pectis* seed too, beyond season's end. It is also known as chinchweed. This plant gives off perhaps the most uniquely pungent aroma found on the desert, which I certainly do not find unpleasant. In fact, as the cactus wren is the Arizona state bird, *Pectis papposa* might qualify as the official scent of the Sonoran Desert. (Don't knock it till you've tried it.) Besides serving as a medicinal plant, it is used as both a traditional dye and as seasoning by the Hopi. The Zuni are said to rub it on their bodies as an aromatic perfume, in addition to usage as a seasoning. (Kane, 2006)

There used to exist a small, linear, micro-habitat thicket in the far southwest corner of the study area between The Shrine of Santa Rita in the Desert and the mainline railroad tracks before the paved road crossing. However, one would never know of its existence there, having been scraped clean off the landscape years ago. During the study period, it was simply referred to as "The Vail Thicket."

"Vail Thicket" on left, pale blue trumpets (Ipomopsis) *in foreground*

"Vail Thicket:" Between Success Dr. and RR#1: Begins W [west] of the cutover from RR#1 to Success Dr. Thins out before Vail/Wentworth Rd. This small thicket of several med.-large mesquite, *acacia constricta*, and desert hackberry (one very large; tree-sized specimen), is recessed into a basin that collects rain run-off, which helps to sustain a dense cover of shrubs, perennials and annuals. On the sunniest exposure—S [south] side—several blooming desert broom, one overgrown with a flowering *Sarcostemma* milkweed vine. Butterflies were actively feeding as of 10/3/96 when several photos (Roll II, 28-30) were taken in p.m. (C [cloud]-less sulphur, queen, snout, gr. [great] purple h [hair]-streak etc. possibly sighted goatweed b-fly [*Anaea spp.*]) Also amongst *gutierrezia* [snakeweed], *parthenium* [mariola] and other shrubbery are patches of *dicliptera pseudoverticillaris* Fl. [flower] 1/3—1/4th the size of *D. resupinata* [Rickett, 1970].

JB Field Notebook, 1993—1998:22

The *Dicliptera* specimen I discovered here clearly differed from all the other patches of *D. resupinata* I had observed in widespread locations. However, further research seemed strongly to suggest that it was a varietal form of *D. resupinata*, rather than a distinct species. Still, it was interesting that this once-thriving, little micro-habitat refuge would be a site for such an unusual discovery. Of course, every habitat fragment lost adds up in the grand scheme of things across the natural world.

A distinctive regional biotic plant community such as the Sonoran Desert is represented by a core of dominant or indicator species. Conversely, the absence of these same species serves to characterize a neighboring plant community for what sets it apart. Two of the prime indicator shrub species of the Sonoran Desert of southern Arizona are brittlebush (*Encelia farinosa*) and triangle-leaf bursage (*Ambrosia deltoidea*). (Lowe, 1964) Brittlebush is hard to miss, with its stalked yellow-flowered, springtime displays on sites around the greater Tucson area; especially upland areas closer to the Santa Catalina Mountains. Within the Pantano Wash/Cienega Creek watershed study area, these two plants are either entirely absent or uncommon, or absent over much of the area. Brittlebush occurs atop the rocky hills and ridges along the northernmost fringe of the study area, above the Pantano/Cienega channel. The southeast-to-northwest running channel seems to serve as a boundary. Beyond this boundary, progressing southward, a desert of a different and unique character arises.

Within the study area, the plant that comes the closest to filling a "keystone" role, as an abundant, widespread understory shrub species, is mariola (*Parthenium incanum*). Beyond that, there exists a highly diverse mix of variable-sized desert shrubs and perennials, as has been described. Other plants of interest encountered within the study area that are not previously covered in text, or shown on lists, are represented briefly below:

TREES / LARGE SHRUBS		
Species	**Plant**	**Notes**
Condalia warnockii	Mexican crucillo	Common in mesquite bosques.
Hymenoclea monogyra	Burrobush	Widespread; open Pantano Washbed.
Lycium spp.	Wolfberry	Creek terrace thickets; mesquite bosques.
Morus microphylla	Texas mulberry	Uncommon; east-end mesquite bosque.
Nicotiana glauca	Tree tobacco	Scattered in spots close by main Wash-Creek channel. Tubular flowers attract hummingbirds and moths. Naturalized.
Parkinsonia microphylla	Foothills palo verde	Hill slopes; northwest side of study area.
Zizyphus obtusifolia	Graythorn	Common in mesquite bosques.

YUCCAS		
Species	**Plant**	**Notes**
Yucca elata	Soaptree yucca	Uncommon; wash terraces to uplands.

SHRUBS / PERENNIALS / ANNUALS / VINES / MISC.		
Species	**Plant**	**Notes**
Apodanthera undulata	Wavy leaf gourd	Widespread; roadsides and flats after rains.
Argemone pleicantha	Prickly poppy	Large white flower with yellow center.
Asclepias nyctaginifolia	Mojave milkweed	Only found in First Basin Wash; pipeline.
Ayenia microphylla	Ayenia	Uncommon; small upland area, west of First Basin Wash; pumpkin-shaped pods.
Brickelia spp.	Brickelia	Along washes and in thickets; lush leaves.
Chamaesaracha spp.	Greenleaf five eyes	Widespread, low-growing, in uplands.
Cucurbita digitata	Five finger gourd	Widespread, washes and terrace thick-ets.
Datura wrightii	Sacred datura	Huge white flowers with strong evening fragrance. Washes, thickets, roadsides.
Encelia frutescens	Button brittlebush	Rare; only found in spot on mesa, northwest of First Basin. Green ovate leaves.
Equisetum laevigatum	Horsetail	Clumps of vertical, segmented stems in wet areas of main Wash-Creek channel.
Ericameria laricifolia	Turpentine bush	Uncommon; desert flats and uplands.
Erigeron spp.	Fleabane	Widespread in most areas; roadsides.
Euphorbia albomarginata	Sand mat	Widespread; desert flats and roadsides.
Euphorbia heterophylla	Wild poinsettia	Found along utility roadsides, thickets.
Froelichia arizonica	Snake cotton	Only found on upper 2nd Basin terrace.
Happlopappus spinulosus	Spiny daisy	Occasionally along utility roadsides.
Heterotheca subaxillaris	Camphorweed	Along roadsides and in disturbed areas.
Hymenothrix wislizenus	Thimblehead	Dry washbeds, flats and utility roads. Resembles goldenrod. Pollinator plant.
Isocoma tenuisecta	Burroweed	Scattered; wash terraces and roadsides.
Juncus torreyi	Torrey's rush	Main Wash-Creek channel. Sandy, wet spots; or with moisture close to surface.
Machaeranthera spp.	Purple aster	Scattered; washes, thickets, roadsides.

SHRUBS / PERENNIALS / ANNUALS / VINES / MISC.		
Species	**Plant**	**Notes**
Mandevilla brachysiphon	Rock trumpet	Rare; isolated patch between 2nd and 3rd Basins. Incredible tubed flower with jasmine-like fragrance. Exciting find!
Maurandella antirrhiniflora	Snapdragon vine	Occasionally found in washes, thickets. Flowers in purple or red color phase.
Mentzelia spp.	Blazing star flower	In patches along utility roadsides.
Nicotiana trigonophylla	Desert tobacco	Sidewash terraces, and rocky slopes.
Penstemon parryi	Parry penstemon	Scattered stands on terraces above utility roadways and on desert flats.
Physalis spp.	Ground cherry	Dry washbeds, thickets, roadsides.
Plantago spp.	Indian wheat	Widespread: desert flats and uplands.
Porophyllum gracile	Odora	Unmistakable pungent aroma of foliage. Roadsides, flats, and uplands.
Proboscidea althaeifolia	Unicorn plant	Large orange flower. Widespread on desert flats, along washes and roadsides.
Proboscidea parviflora	Devil's claw	Smaller, purple flower. Both use 'claw' seed dispersal technique* Unique claw-shaped pod latches on to hoofed and other animals; as well as humans.. Same areas.
Schoenoplectus americanus	Chairmaker's bulrush	Clumps along edge of main Wash-Creek channel; surface or subsurface wetter streambed areas.
Solanum elaeagnifolium	Silverleaf nightshade	Common along roadsides, desert flats and disturbed areas. Striking blue flower.
Typha domingensis	Southern cattail	Main Wash-Creek channel; persistent wet spots or ephemeral stream flows.
Vitis arizonica	Canyon grape	Woody vine climbs over trees, large shrubs; main Wash-Creek channel.
GRASSES		
Aristida longiseta	Red three-awn	Perennial bunchgrass. Southside utility roadsides, near gasline/fence.
Bouteloua chondrosioides	Spruce top grama	Widely scattered over desert flats, roadsides and uplands.

SHRUBS / PERENNIALS / ANNUALS / VINES / MISC.		
Species	**Plant**	**Notes**
Bouteloua curtipendula	Side oats grama	Common; along washes, in thickets, roadsides and uplands.
Bouteloua eriopoda	Black grama	Occasionally found mixed in with other grasses on desert flats and roadsides.
Enneapogon desvauxii	Spike pappusgrass	Mesa west of First Basin Wash. Prefers calcareous ground. Seed spikelets resemble tiny "swimming octopi".
Heteropogon contortus	Tanglehead	Widely scattered. Found in roadside swales in solid stands and along washes.
Hilaria mutica	Tobosa	Perennial bunchgrass. Forms solid patches on mesa above First Basin, in Vail-Powerline Thicket and elsewhere.
Muhlenbergia porteri	Bush muhly	Widespread; from washes to uplands.
Muhlenbergia rigens	Deergrass	Lush bunchgrass found along main Pantano—Cienega channel; especially east-end. Scattered in sidewashes.
Pappophorum mucronulatum	Pappusgrass	Widespread in low-lying spots; found in south utility roadside ditches with tanglehead and plains bristlegrass.
Scleropogon brevifolius	Burrograss	Short perennial. Fringe patches in Vail-Powerline Thicket swale area.
Setaria macrostachya	Plains bristlegrass	Occurring in same areas as Arizona cottontop. Slopes and upland areas.
Trichachne californica	Arizona cottontop	Patches south and above gasline road, halfway down to First Basin Wash.
Tridens muticus	Slim tridens	North sides of open, sunny slope above First Basin Wash/gas line road. Plant suggests cowboy name ("Yeah, I remember ol' Slim Tridens!").
Tridens pulchellus	Desert fluffgrass	Widely scattered in desert pavement of flats, slopes and uplands.
NOTE: Non-native/naturalized grasses such as bermuda (*Cynodon dactylon*) and Johnson grass (*Sorghum halepense*) were not included on this list, though occurring in the study area; especially along the main Wash—Creek channel.		

SMALL CACTI		
Species	**Plant**	**Notes:**
Coryphantha robustispina	Pima pineapple cactus	Rare; most plants concentrated on mesa, west of First Basin Wash, but occasional single specimens found over a wide area. Yellow flowers.
Coryphantha vivipara	Beehive cactus	Uncommon, clump-forming. Two-toned pink-purple and white flowers are spectacular. Atop mesa, west of First Basin Wash. Blooms in July.
Cylindropuntia leptocaulis	Christmas cholla	Common, though semi-hidden in thickets. Roadrunners consume red fruits (examined stomach contents of roadkill, harvested for feathers).
Echinocereus fasciculatus	Hedgehog cactus	Widespread over flats, slopes and uplands. Large, showy magenta flowers, March-April. Edible fruits.
Mamillaria microcarpa	Fishhook pin cushion	Widespread; desert flats, slopes and uplands. Striped pink flowers form circular bouquet around stemtops.
Neolloydia erectocentra	Needle spine pineapple	Uncommon; open clusters of stems found over a wide area. Up to one foot tall. Snow-white flowers appear in March—April.
NOTE: The botanical names during the study period (1993-1996) were retained for the CACTI though taxonomical changes should be noted: *Escobaria* (*Coryphantha*) *vivipara*, *Mamillaria* (*Microcarpa*) *grahamii*, *Echinomastus erectocentrus* (*Neolloydia erectocentra*).		

(Kearney and Peebles, 1951, Gould, 1951, Humphrey, 1958, Rickett, 1970, Lamb, 1977, Bowers and McLaughlin, 1987, The University of Arizona Herbarium, Epple and Epple, 1995, Johnson 2004, Kane 2006, Verrier 2018, Joseph, personal communication 2020, Makings, personal communication, 2020)

Small collections of selected native plant seed began to take on greater importance over time, and field-collected/labeled seed packets were passed along to local native plant growers in the greater Tucson area. It was hoped that over time these regional natives would be cultivated among native plant growers, especially the pollinator and butterfly host plant species. Seed samples were occasionally provided to Civano Nursery, Desert Survivors Nursery, and Plants for the Southwest:

A BRIEF LISTING OF MINIMAL FIELD-COLLECTED SEED SAMPLES / NATIVE PLANTS PANTANO WASH—CIENEGA CREEK WATERSHED STUDY AREA / VAIL, ARIZONA:

Acourtia nana (Desert holly) / *Acourtia wrightii* (Perezia) / *Bahia absinthifolia* (Bahias) /*Bebbia juncea* (Sweetbush) / *Clematis drummondii* (Virgin's bower) / *Coryphantha robustispina* (Pima pineapple cactus) / *Dicliptera resupinata* (Dicliptera) / *Echinomastus erectocentrus* (Needle spine pineapple) / *Escobaria vivipara* (Beehive cactus) / *Hibiscus denudatus* (Desert hibiscus) / *Hilaria mutica* (Tobosa grass) / *Janusia gracilis* (Janusia) / *Machaeranthera spp.* (Asters) / *Menadora scabra* (Menadora) / *Mamillaria grahamii* (Fishhook pincushion) / *Pectis papposa* (Chinchweed) / *Porophyllum gracile* (Odora) / *Proboscidea parviflora* (Devil's claw) / *Ruellia nudiflora* (Desert petunia) / *Sanvitalia abertii* (Sanvitalia) / *Senna leptocarpa* (Long pod senna) / *Thamnosma* texana (Desert rue).

JB Field Notebook 1993—1998

The whole notion of "pollinator plants" gets complicated. In the desert, as elsewhere, effective cross-pollination between plants of the same species is critical, in order that successful reproduction takes place. There is a high diversity of creatures drawn to the nectar and pollen of flowering plants of the Sonoran Desert. (Buchmann and Nabhan, 1997) I, myself, hand-pollinated my squash plants in the Rincon Valley until I began seeing black carpenter bees (*Xylocopa sp.*) showing up. Some of these floral resources become critical for migrating pollinators of the night skies such as nectar-feeding bats. (Howell, 1974) One of the benefits of cattle removal from the Pantano Wash/Cienega Creek watershed area in 1988 was pointed out to me by friend and mentor, James T. Verrier. Over the course of a rigorous, full day exploring remote northeast backcountry of the Santa Catalina Mountains one July, he constantly pointed out agave or century plant stalks chewed off by cattle, thus preventing them from arising to bloom and set fruit. These agave flowering stalks are one of the migrating bat's prime food sources, in addition to providing nectar for moths and diurnal pollinators.

One sunny summer day, I was crossing a calcareous desert flat in Vail, Arizona, on my way out for a trail run. Suddenly, I became aware of a large moth—having freshly emerged nearby—skittering low along the ground. I ran after it and caught it just as it was gaining momentum over a graded dirt road. I carefully cradled it in my hands, returning back home to retrieve my camera. Once there, it posed perfectly for photos upon a colored mat, atop my desk; and then was released outside. What had crossed my path, was *Manduca rustica*, a large hawkmoth, with a wing span close to five inches, of the family *Sphingidae*. These beautiful moths are usually found feeding on desert willow trees (*Chilopsis linearis*), as large, hornworm-type, mostly light green caterpillars that blend into the foliage. As adults, they actively visit night-blooming, usually white flowers, such as Datura, employing tongues (pro-

Hawkmoth (Manduca rustica)

White-lined sphinx moth

Black-chinned hummingbird

boscides) as long or longer than their bodies. (Buchmann and Nabhan, 1997)

Moths, such as *M. rustica*, can closely resemble hummingbirds in flight. They share the same ability to hover steadily in front of a flower, while nectaring. I truly think they might possess the most highly concentrated energy output per unit of body weight of perhaps any creature on the planet? Many years ago, I once discovered one of these moths roosting, perched outside a phone booth, during the daytime. I carefully slipped it into a small paper sack and brought it home, where it was left lying on a table and forgotten. Sometime later that same evening, that sack was literally bouncing up and down off that table! I quickly released the moth outside to go about its nightly rounds. The white-lined sphinx moth (*Hyles lineata*) on the other hand, is commonly seen feeding diurnally in the study area, on blooming plants such as *Allionia*, chuparosa, *Dicliptera* and even *Bebbia*!

Hummingbirds are drawn to many of these same flowers, in addition to bright orange-red ocotillo blooms (*Fouquieria splendens*). Certain species migrate along "nectar corridors" from south-to-north, in a similar fashion as bats. There are at least seventeen species of hummingbirds in Arizona, more than any other state. (Buchmann, 2015) Besides the tubular flowers of ocotillo, chuparosa, calliandra, penstemon, and the like, I've observed them feeding readily at a variety of other flowers, too, such as thistles (*Cirsium spp.*). Other birds that play a pollinating role are woodpeckers, orioles, cactus wrens, verdins and especially white-wing doves that flock to saguaros during their flowering season.

One of my earliest childhood memories is roaming through the thick stands of burroweed

(*Isocoma tenuisecta*) in the desert areas I grew up in northeast of urban Tucson, Arizona. I wasn't much taller than these bushes, topped with masses of yellowish blooms. They were always covered with the same long-horned, orange beetles frequently with mated couplings, one atop the other. As I would bend down to get a closer look with the dusty-sweet pollen scent swirling into my nostrils, the beetles made a peculiar squeaking sound by bending their head and thorax segments up and down. I haven't seen any of those types of beetles since that early time. I certainly hope they're still around. According to Dr. Stephen Buchmann, beetles make up the largest proportion of pollinators worldwide. (Buchmann and Nabhan, 1997)

The more you look for beetles on flowers; the more you find. One of the most conspicuous is *Cotinis mutabilis*. These are the beautiful, velvety-green fig or June beetles, with bright, reflective metallic green undersides. They frequently show up atop the white flower clusters of desert broom (*Baccharis sarothroides*) during the fall blooming season, as well as the earlier blooming *B. salicifolia* or seepwillow. I've also observed their competitive "battles" in groups, foraging for sap underneath a willow branch. Green buprestids (*Gyacutus sp.*) are a favorite beetle that shows up during warmer weather within stands of whitethorn. These wood borers seem to become conspicuously abundant, with characteristic buzzing flights, from Acacia to Acacia. If you can sneak up carefully enough and grab them off a twig, you get to appreciate the unique beauty, up close, of these metallic green, narrow-bodied, big-eyed beetles. They appear to have a residue of yellow pollen dust, but do not be fooled! This is a waxy substance they exude, not pollen. (Brummermann, personal communication, 2020) Then you can re-launch them, buzzing up and away, to another bush!

One of the revelations of field research conducted at both the Arizona-Sonoran Desert Museum and the Tumamoc Desert Laboratory in recent decades has revealed a staggering number of native bee species attracted to the abundant blooming palo verdes and local floral resources. The high diversity of plant species and ideal climatic conditions provides environments where an estimated 1,000 native bees find

Green buprestid beetle on whitethorn

Underside of green buprestid beetle

specific habitat/plant niches within this region of the Sonoran Desert. (Buchmann and Nabhan, 1997) These well-adapted desert natives have been largely overshadowed by the introduced, omnipresent European and Africanized honeybees (*Apies mellifera*) that tend to outcompete all other species for precious nectar and pollen resources. A highly skilled artist and landscape designer on Tucson's west side has found a creative and innovative way to assist these important pollinators of our desert flora.

Metal/wood sculptural piece by Greg Corman

Greg Corman does his own style of wood and metal sculpture, but with a unique, personal twist: his knowledge of many, various-sized native bee species has combined art and conservation into a single piece of work. According to Greg, the majority of our native bees are solitary, and nest in cavities in the ground or in dead trees. Unlike honey or "killer" bees, they tolerate human presence and sting only if molested—and even then, it's mild compared to a honeybee. Greg's sculptural pieces have pre-drilled holes to accommodate leafcutter, mason, and resin bees of varying sizes. The females pack these brood cells with pollen and nectar, lay eggs, and seal off each cell in sequence. Once the eggs hatch, they develop into adults while being sustained by the pollen and nectar reserves. Reaching maturity, the bees chew their way out during the following season. Greg's fine work is on display at Tohono Chul Park and the Arizona-Sonora Desert Museum.

May 11, 2015: Peering over a low masonry wall, I detected activity on the ground, within the loop of a faded green garden hose. I zoomed in close with the Canon PowerShot to capture images of some very busy, gray-brown bees entering and emerging from underground burrows. One of the more robust and active pollinators of the yellow-flowered palo verdes and several other desert legumes is the digger bee, *Centris pallida*. The females harvest pollen and nectar that they cache in underground brood chambers at a frenetic pace from these seasonal masses of blooms. One day while standing next to a Mexican palo verde tree with Trica O. Hawkins, Tumamoc Desert Laboratory researcher and education specialist, she made a comment regarding an observation of the tree's blooms. She noted that some of the flowers revealed a change in the color of one of the petals, displaying a bright red color and implying that those flowers had been pollinated or fertilized. It was much later before I realized the connection between that comment and the symbiotic relationship between palo verdes and the industrious *Centris pallida* digger bees. Entomologist John Alcock, in his studies of *C. pallida*, noted these distinctly-colored banner petals alert the bees to fertilized flowers, thus helping to maximize their furious efforts harvesting pollen and stocking underground brood cells while continuously excavating new ones. (1985)

Beyond bats, moths, beetles, birds, and bees are mostly lesser pollinators such as wasps, flies, butterflies, and even squirrels. Large, orange-and-black-winged tarantula hawk wasps are conspicuous pollinators of milkweed plants (*Asclepiadaceae*), and are frequently observed on the mass fall blooms of *Asclepias subverticillata* in Cochise and Santa Cruz Counties. Butterflies—while my prime focus—are not usually very effective pollinators, except where flowers are more favorably adapted to them. (Brummermann, 2019) The little Harris antelope ground squirrels get in on the action, foraging over an abundance of cholla, barrel, and hedgehog cactus flowers. Some of these cacti they pollinate may be the varieties they also harvest and consume the fruits of.

Centris pallida digger bee near excavated brood chamber

A LIST OF SELECTED PRIMARY AND SECONDARY POLLINATOR PLANTS / PANTANO WASH—CIENEGA CREEK WATERSHED STUDY AREA / VAIL, AZ.	
Species	**Plant**
TREES / LARGE SHRUBS	
*Acacia constricta**	Whitethorn
*Acacia greggii**	Catclaw acacia
*Baccharis salicifolia**	Seepwillow
*Baccharis sarothroides**	Desert broom
*Chilopsis linearis**	Desert willow
Condalia warnockii	Mexican crucillo
*Larrea tridentata**	Creosote bush
Lycium spp.	Wolfberry
*Mimosa biuncifera**	Catclaw mimosa
*Parkinsonia florida**	Blue palo verde
*Parkinsonia microphyllum**	Foothills palo verde
*Prosopis juliflora**	Velvet mesquite
Salix spp.	Willow
*Zizyphus obtusifolia**	Graythorn

CACTI / STALKED SUCCULENTS / OCOTILLOS	
Species	**Plant:**
*Agave palmeri**	Century plant
*Carnegiea gigantea**	Saguaro
Cylindropuntia spp.	Chollas
Dasylirion wheeleri	Desert spoon
Ferocactus wislizenii	Barrel cacti
*Fouquieria splendens**	Ocotillo
*Opuntia spp.**	Prickly pears
*Yucca arizonica**	Spanish bayonet
*Yucca elata**	Soaptree yucca

SHRUBS / PERENNIALS / ANNUALS / VINES	
Species	**Plant:**
Acourtia wrightii	Perezia
*Allionia incarnata**	Trailing four o'clock
*Aloysia wrightii**	Aloysia
*Anisacanthus thurberi**	Chuparosa
Apodanthera undulata	Wavy leaf gourd
Bahia absinthifolia	Bahias
*Bebbia juncea**	Sweetbush
*Calliandra eriophylla**	Fairyduster
Cirsium neomexicanum	Thistle
*Cissus trifoliata**	Grape ivy
*Clematis drummondii**	Virgin's bower
Cucurbita digitata	Five finger gourd vine
Dalea Formosa	Feather dalea
*Datura wrightii**	Sacred datura
*Dicliptera resupinata**	Dicliptera
Ericameria laricifolia	Turpentine bush
*Erigeron spp.**	Fleabane
*Gutierrezia microcephala**	Snakeweed
*Hymenothrix wislizenus**	Thimblehead
Isocoma tenuisecta	Burroweed
*Melampodium leucanthum**	Blackfoot daisy
*Parthenium incanum**	Mariola
*Penstemon parryi**	Parry penstemon
*Polanisia dodecandra**	Clammyweed
Porophyllum gracile	Odora
*Psilostrophe cooperi**	Paperflower
*Sarcostemma spp.**	Milkweed vine
*Senna leptocarpa**	Long pod senna
*Thymophylla acerosa**	Shrubby dogweed

SHRUBS / PERENNIALS / ANNUALS / VINES	
Species	**Plant:**
*Thymophylla pentachaeta**	Dogweed
*Trixis califórnica**	Trixis
*Veronica anagallis-aquaticum**	Speedwell
*Zinnia acerosa**	Desert zinnia

NOTE: *Primary pollinator plants. In some cases, plants (*Dalea formosa, Ericameria laricifolia*, etc.) were not given primary status, or entered on the list due to limited-size populations and distribution within the study area.

Pollinator plants, apart from the process of cross-pollination, have their principal value in providing ample nectar and pollen resources (and sometimes exuded resins) to the whole world of avian, mammalian, lepidopteran—insectean visitors and all other creatures of the day and night that have come to depend on them. They are differentiated from "Butterfly Host Plants" (see list above), serving primarily as food resources for adult lepidoptera.

In closing this chapter, I've saved the most challenging task for last: selecting out the plants over the study area with the highest forage value as pollinator plants. These selections are mostly based on years of personal observations and experience, supplemented by shared knowledge with other field researchers, and follow-up research. It's not written in stone, with a degree of variability and uncertainty embraced as a necessary element of the process. Over time, the picture will become clearer. I plan to continue this quest forever, in exploring and expanding my knowledge of our magnificent desert world.

I hope you will join me on this quest, someday. It is very good for the soul...

ACKNOWLEDGMENTS

Throughout the course of all my wanderings, I never could have imagined I would someday be bringing forth these adventures in print to share with my readers. I was merely following my own internal directive—living in the moment as the pure naturalist—from day one through each phase of my development and experience. I was extremely fortunate to work with a great book and cover designer, mapmaker, and photo editor—Sharon K. Miller—whom I felt compatible with right from the start. Her excellent work and attention to detail allowed these journeys to be revealed and magically illuminated with countless historic photographs.

Charting each of these paths beginning with the Galiuro Mountains Wilderness and beyond: Special thanks to and much appreciation for Mike Isley and the Isley family, Dave Mehalic, Jim Tenney, Peta-Anne Tenney, Kathy Klump, Chuck Duncan, Dan Lackner, Johannes Von Trapp, Daryl Mitchell, Cameron Trejo, Heidi Osselaer, John Holcomb, Ron Olding, Bill Roe, Brian Hickerson, Joe Tomelleri, Sam Negri, Anthony Lunt, Major John Rhodes, Carol Broeder, Faye Sadlon, Melanie Garcia, Jerry Foster, Susan Sorg, Bryan Neumeister, Martin Turner, Jack R. Goodhart, Daniel Baker, Peter Else, Scott Wilbor, Mitzi Sassé, and others. I recalled my friendship long ago with close neighbors Pat and Jim Corbett, listening to Jim's stories of walking goats in the Galiuros. Thanks also to Lucy J. Billings for providing a key article. On my earliest quest to find the Powers Garden journals, I met up with hikers Sean Farris and Michael Udervich from the opposite side of the range for a memorable campfire at Powers Garden.

Re-tracing the thread of stone tool-making and encounters with Pleistocene megafauna: Much gratitude for shared field time and friendships forged with C. Vance Haynes, Jr., Everett H. Lindsay, Bruce Huckell, William Peachey, Michael Faught, Kevin Moody, Jeffrey Saunders of the University of Arizona and property owner John Schannep. I'm grateful also to have worked with Mary Lou Heuett, Laurie Slawson, Ron Maldonado, Susan Beacom, and John Wenaas. I'm indebted to friend and photographer Elton Kerr for his documentation of the Rincon quarry site and views of the surrounding landscape. I will also never forget the lively early morning meet-ups at the Sonoita Cafe—on similar topics—with James H. Davis, Juanita Bostick, and the late Phil Van Strander, who gifted me a soft calfskin knapsack for my flintknapping tools.

Heading into the Sea of Cortez and past expeditions along both coastlines: I'm profoundly grateful for Dorothy Coffman's superb photos, taken on the last leg of that journey. Much gratitude as well for the hospitality and companionship of University of Arizona Marine Ecology Field School staff and students. I was inspired by Thomas Bowen's masterpiece, *Unknown Island*, and appreciated his gracious and kind comments. Many thanks to friend and mentor Rick Brusca, who was always willing to provide technical guidance and positive encouragement. Looking back with fond memories for the wonderful friendship and generosity of Sharon Ann "Shari" Spear. Thanks to Dave Baker and the late Lane Larson, as well as Aaron Flesch and Sky Jacobs (who, along with me, are devout "Lane Fans"), also Peggy Larson, Sonya Norman, Deborah J. Brasket, Mike McGettigan, Michelle María Early Capistrán, Andrea Sáenz-Arroyo, Jeffrey Seminoff, Octavio Aburto-Oropeza, Brad Erisman, Jon Erlandson, Lauren Harrison, Danielle Morley, Mark Conlin of Blue Ocean Art, and Nathan Sowry of the Smithsonian. Early on, I gained knowledge reading the inspiring books by the pioneering skin diver and underwater naturalist Hans Haas, too—those books are still around.

Returning to the familiar ground of the Sonoran Desert realm closer to home: At El Fuerte I appreciated my neighbors there, especially Suzi Mendoza and the Mendoza family. I'm thankful for my time in the Rincon Valley, engaging in many good chats along the pasture fence line with late friend and cattle rancher Kenny Ethridge. W. Anne Gibson and her late husband Howard were wonderful, supportive friends. Thanks also to Deb Peckham, Rick Hannaman, and Kathy Sampson. Farther to the southeast, perched above the Pantano Wash/Cienega Creek corridor, I was fortunate to settle into another optimum environment thanks to Ralph Hurd, Craig Bohme, and the Desert Hardwoods mesquite sawmill collective.

Throughout all the explorations, surveys and studies undertaken from each of these prime rural home bases, I've been fortunate and thankful for the friendships formed and knowledge learned from and shared with so many kindred spirits, many with great expertise: John Alcock, C. Vance Haynes, Jr., Karl Flessa, Jim Brock, Rich Bailowitz, Mary Belk, Liz Makings, James T. Verrier, Iris Rodden, John Rhodes, Matt Johnson, Jillian Cowles, Mary Darling, Doug Mullins, Dave Wikle, Bob Behrstock, Marie Simovich, Justin Schmidt, Gene Joseph and Jane Evans, Margarethe Brummermann, Janine McCabe, Homer Hansen, William Peachey, Frank Rose, Charles W. Kane, Jon R. Weeks, Marcus White, Dennis Caldwell, and Don Carter. Special thanks to James T. Verrier and Iris Rodden for assistance on several botanical charts in PART 3. Thanks also to Linda B. Millington for the *El Fuerte* heading photo. Thanks to contributing photographers Rick and Nora Bowers, Petr Ganaj, Bob Gorum, Volker Meyer, and Elton Kerr.

Cathy and Dan Arnit are at the top of the list for longstanding friendship and support during current twenty-first century expeditions, monarch butterfly fieldwork and projects. I will never forget the late Maria Segura Hoopes, an elegant, kind and dedicated central reference librarian who assisted me with my earliest research in the University of Arizona campus libraries. Others generating the most cherished and positive memories who have passed on are Penny McClain and Catherine "Canoe" Pickett. As a close friend, neighbor and occasional hiking companion, Canoe had a cheerful, adventurous spirit and beautiful smile that will stay with me forever. Thanks to Mary Darling for always being there with a positive word, suggestion, or offer of assistance. Much appreciation for John and Merci Rhodes, Homer Hansen and family. Yvonne Bourgeois deserves much credit for the earliest assistance on this project long before it manifested into its present form. Thanks to friend Lucretia Free for featuring my earliest desert fairy shrimp blurbs in the *Vail Voice*. Marilyn Martin also weighed in from time to time, as a positive, helpful presence.

And lastly, I heartily thank all of you, my readers, most of all.

In Memoriam

Cirsten Carle
March 7, 1958 - August 4, 2023

Who was a lover of animals, both wild and domestic ...

Who loved hiking and exploring southeastern Arizona wildlands ...

Who photographed award-winning sites for The Landscaping Artist (JB) ...

Who was an advocate of my monarch butterfly fieldwork and restoration projects ...

Whose sweet, twinkling smile and kind, generous soul will be remembered forever ...

About the Author

Photo by Mark Walker

JB—A lifelong, naturalist-at-large and twenty-first century cave man has extensively explored, studied, written about, and photographed the wildlands of southeastern Arizona, along with other areas of the west and Mexico. Whether on an all-day-long bushwhack hike and botanical expedition in the remotest corner of the Santa Catalina Mountains, rowing a primitive watercraft made from reeds out into the Sea of Cortez, fashioning stone spear points and primitive weaponry as a self-taught flintknapper, or stalking and tagging thousands of beautiful monarch butterflies as **MonarchQuestAZ**, he is equally at home in the outdoors, all year-round.

JB has tagged over 6,000 butterflies during six field seasons as **MonarchQuestAZ** while tracking down at least 100 tagged monarchs from all tagging programs along the California coast and from Mexican monarch preserves, including a dozen of his own tags. Prior to that, he excelled at designing and installing landscape projects singlehandedly as The Landscaping Artist, winning the first place-residential/professional award multiple times in the regional Xeriscape Contest. JB's award-winning projects have been featured in *Tucson HOME*, *Tucson Lifestyle/Home & Garden*, the *Arizona Daily Star*, and other publications.

JB lives in Vail, Arizona, and has remained true to his roots as a pure, "born naturalist" and never faltered from that path. He continues to direct long-acquired experience and knowledge gained from fieldwork, studies, and numerous expeditions into the current platform of writing/photography, wildlands restoration plantings, sustained-living projects, and native pollinator plant demo-gardens.

When not in the field or engaged in projects, JB can be found trail running in the nearby hills and washes, playing fingerstyle guitar, or absorbed in meditation crafting flaked stone points in his favorite flintknapping chair.

Literature Cited

Abbey, E. (1968). *Desert Solitaire*. Simon and Schuster.

Aburto-Oropeza, O., B. Erisman, V. Valdez-Ornelas, & G. Danemann. (2008). Commercially important serranid fishes from the gulf of california: Ecology, fisheries and conservation, *Ciencia y Conservación 1*, pp. 1–23.

Aitchison, S. (2010). *The Desert Islands of Mexico's Sea of Cortez*. University of Arizona Press.

Alcock, J. (1985). *Sonoran Desert Spring*. University of Chicago Press.

Alvarez-Borrego, Saúl. (1983). Gulf of California, in B.H. Ketchum, Ed., Estuaries and Enclosed Seas (Ecosystems of the World), Vol. 26. Elsevier Science Ltd.

Amann, A.W. Jr., J.V. Bezy, R. Ratkevich, & W.M. Witkind. (1998). *Ice Age Mammals of the San Pedro Valley: Southeastern Arizona*. Arizona Geological Survey.

Anderson, C.A., Durham, J.W., Shepard, F. P., Natland, M. L., & Revelle, R. (1950). *GSA Memoirs: 1940 EW Scripps Cruise to the Gulf of California 43*. Geological Society of America.

Baegert, J.J. (1979). *Observations in Lower California* (M.M. Brandenburg & C.L. Baumann, Trans.). University of California Press.

Bailowitz, R.A. & J.P. Brock. (1991). *Butterflies of Southeastern Arizona*. Sonoran Arthropod Studies, Inc.

Bailowitz, R.A. & H. Brodkin. (2007). *Finding Butterflies in Arizona: A Guide to the Best Sites*. Johnson Books.

Basora, J. (2011). Fum and Gebra. *Distraction: Cat and owl become friends,* [Video]. Youtube. https://www.youtube.com/watch?v=LK9KfeleYkA

Bell, W.H. & E.F. Castetter. (1937). *The utilization of mesquite and screwbean by the aborigines in the American Southwest*. University of New Mexico Press.

Bell, W.H. & E.F. Castetter. (1941). *The utilization of yucca, sotol, and beargrass in the American Southwest*. University of New Mexico Press.

Billings, Joe. (2016, August 21). A pointed quest: A 21st century caveman's attempt to make a fluted "paleo" spearpoint out of bottle glass—employing an aboriginal tool kit. *Sierra Vista Herald, p.* 5.

Billings, Joe. (2019). Opening a window on southwestern monarchs: Fall migrant monarch butterflies, *Danaus plexippus (L.)*, Tagged synchronously in southeastern Arizona migrate to overwintering regions in either Southern California or central Mexico. *Journal of the Lepidopterists' Society, 73*(4), pp. 257-267. DOI:10.18473/lepi.73i4.a1

Bird, G. (1985). The atl–atl or spear throwing stick. *The Artifact, 23* (3) 7–18. El Paso Archaeological Society.

Bowen, T. (1976). Seri Prehistory: The archaeology of the central coast of Sonora, Mexico. *Anthropological Papers of the University of Arizona, 27*. University of Arizona Press.

Bowen, Thomas. (2000). *Unknown Island: Seri Indians, Europeans, and San Esteban Island in the Gulf of California*. University of New Mexico Press.

Bowers, J.E. & S.P. McLaughlin. (1987). Flora and vegetation of the Rincon Mountains, Pima County, Arizona. *Desert Plants, 8* (2).

Brock, J.P. & K. Kaufman. (2003). *Kaufman Field Guide to Butterflies of North America*. Houghton Mifflin.

Browning, A. (1999). *Mountain Cowboy*. Sulphur Springs Valley Historical Society.

Brummermann, M. (2019, February 25). Pollination talk part 1: The dance of co-evolution https://arizonabeetlesbugsbirdsandmore.blogspot.com/2019/02/

Brusca, R.C. (1980). *Common Intertidal Invertebrates of the Gulf of California*. University of Arizona Press.

Brusca, R.C. (Ed.). (2010). *The Gulf of California: Biodiversity and Conservation*. Arizona Sonora Desert Museum Press and University of Arizona Press.

Buchmann, S.L. & G.P. Nabhan. (1997). *The Forgotten Pollinators*. Island Press.

Buchmann, S.L. (2015). *The Reason for Flowers: Their History, Culture, and Biology, and How They Change Our Lives*. Scribner-Simon and Schuster.

Callahan, E. (1979). The basics of biface knapping in the eastern fluted point tradition, a manual for flintknappers and lithic analysts. *Archaeology of Eastern North America. 7*, 1–180.

Cary, S.J. (2009). Butterfly landscapes of New Mexico. *New Mexico Magazine.*

Case, T.J, M.L. Cody & E. Ezcurra, Eds. (2002). *A New Island Biogeography in the Sea of Cortés*. Oxford University Press.

Castetter, E.F. & R.M. Underhill. (1935). The ethnobiology of the Papago Indians. *The University of New Mexico Bulletin: Ethnobiological Studies in the American Southwest. 4* (3).

Chambers, N. & T.O. Hawkins. (2002). *Invasive Plants of the Sonoran Desert: A Field Guide*. Sonoran Institute.

Cosgrove, C. B. (1947). Caves of the Upper Gila and Hueco areas in New Mexico and Texas. *Papers of the Peabody Museum of American Archaeology and Ethnology, 24* (2). Harvard University.

Cowgill, P. (1966, February 6). Retreat in Galiuros doesn't escape vandals. *Arizona Daily Star*, 7E.

Cowgill, P. (1975a, March 9). Old water tank in Galiuros tells story. *Arizona Daily Star*. 8B

Cowgill, P. (1975b, March 23). Road on Powers Hill lures 4WDs, trouble." *Arizona Daily Star*. 6B.

Cowgill, P. (1975c, March 23). On the trail. *Arizona Daily Star*. 6B.

Coyle, J. & N.C. Roberts. (1975). *Field Guide to the Common and Interesting Plants of Baja*. Natural History Publishing Co.

Dimmitt, M.A. (2000). Biomes and communities of the Sonoran Desert region. In S.J. Phillips & P.W.Comus, Eds., *Natural History of the Sonoran Desert*. Arizona Sonora Desert Museum Press.

Di Peso, C.C., Matson, D. S., & Gilg, A. (1965). The Seri Indians in 1692 as described by Adamo Gilg, S. J. *Arizona and the West*, 7(1), 33–56. http://www.jstor.org/stable/40167112.

Early-Capistrán, M.M. (2010, November). Shark fins and turtle leather: Historic marine animal exploitation on Mexico's southern Pacific coast. Oceans Past III Conference. Trinity College, Dublin, Ireland.

Early-Capistrán, M.M. (2014, October). Amazons, pirates, and turtles on the island of California, *The Appendix 2* (4).

Early-Capistrán, M.M., A. Sáenz-Arroyo, J.G. Cardoso-Mohedano, G. Garibay-Melo, H. Peckham, & V. Koch. (2017). Reconstructing 290 years of a data-poor fishery through ethnographic and archival research: The East Pacific green turtle (*Chelonia mydas*) in Baja California, Mexico. *Fish and Fisheries 19*(1) 57–77.

Eddy, F.W. & M.E. Cooley. (1983). Cultural and environmental history of Cienega Valley, Southeastern Arizona. *Anthropological Papers of the University of Arizona, (43)*1. University of Arizona Press.

Epple, A.O. & L.E. Epple. (1995). *A Field Guide to the Plants of Arizona*. A Falcon Guide, an Imprint of The Globe Pequot Press.

Eriksen, C.H. & D.Belk. (1999). *Fairy Shrimps of California's Puddles, Pools, and Playas.* Mad River Press.
Erisman, B. & O. Aburto-Oropeza. (2009). Gulf of California's deep-sea secrets. (Video Presentation). *Perspectives in Ocean Science series: Show # 16076.* University of California at San Diego Television (UC/SD/TV).
Eschmeyer, W.E., H.H. Hammann, & R.T. Peterson. (1983). *A Field Guide to the Pacific Coast Fishes.* Houghton Mifflin.
Felger, R.S. & M.B. Moser. (1985). *People of the Desert and Sea: Ethnobotany of the Seri Indians.* University of Arizona Press.
Fenenga, F. & J.B. Wheat. (1940). An atlatl from the Baylor Rock Shelter, Culberson County, Texas. *American Antiquity, 5*(3), 221–223.
Figueroa, A., J. Alvarado, F. Hernández, G. Rodriguez, & J. Robles. (1993). *The ecological recovery of sea turtles of Michoacán, Mexico: Special attention to the black turtle (Chelonia agassizi): Final Report.* World Wildlife Fund–U.S. Fish and Wildlife Service.
Fonseca, J. E. (2022) Vegetation change and floristic inventory of Cienega Creek Natural Preserve, Pima County, Arizona. *Canotia 18* (20), 89-169.
Forton, M. (2021). Documenting a lost B-24 in the Galiuro Mountains—the Galiuro firescape project. *The Society for Historical Archaeology Newsletter, (54)*3. 59–63.
Gillespie, W.B., M.M. Farrell, J.A. McDonald, P.M. Spoerl, & J.P. Wilson. (1995). Tearing up the ground with splendid results: Historic mining on the Coronado National Forest. *Heritage Resources: Management Report No. 15,* USDA Forest Service, Southwestern Region.
Gould, F.W. (1951). *Grasses of Southwestern United States.* University of Arizona Press.
Gould, R.A. (1970). *Spears and spear-throwers of the Western Desert aborigines of Australia.* American Museum of Natural History.
Griffith, J.S. & T.R. Tiersch. (1989, March). Ecology of fishes in Redfield Canyon, Arizona, with Emphasis on Gila *Robusta intermedia. The Southwestern Naturalist (34)*1, 131–134.
Guernsey, S.J. & A.V. Kidder. (1921). Basket-Maker caves of northeastern Arizona: Report on the explorations, 1916–17. *Papers of the Peabody Museum of Archaeology and Ethnology 8(*2).

Guernsey, S.J. (1931). Explorations in northeastern Arizona: Report on the Archaeological Fieldwork of 1920–1923. *Papers of the Peabody Museum of Archaeology and Ethnology, 11*(5).

Hall, Howard (Director). (1992). *Shadows of a Desert Sea* [Film], PBS-Nature/BBC.

Haynes, C. V. Jr., E.H. Lindsay, & J.J. Saunders. (2016). The Billings mastodon: A terminal Pleistocene locality in Santa Cruz County, Arizona. *PaleoAmerica, (2)*4, 362–367.

Heyerdahl, T. (1972). *The RA Expeditions*. Allen and Unwin.

Howell, D.J. (1974). Bats and pollen: Physiological aspects of the syndrome of chiropterophily. *Comparative Biochemistry and Physiology Part A: Physiology, (48)*2, 263–276.

Humphrey, Robert R. (1958). The desert grassland: a history of vegetational change and an analysis of causes. *The Botanical Review (24)*, 193–252.

Jaeger, Edmund C. (1961). *Desert Wildlife*. Stanford University Press.

Johnson, M.B. (2004). *Cacti, other succulents, and unusual xerophytes of Southern Arizona*. Boyce Thompson.

Jones, W.D. & C. Sacamano. (2000). *Landscape Plants for Dry Regions*. Fisher Books.

Kane, Charles W. (2006). *Herbal Medicine of The American Southwest: A Guide To the Identification, Collection, Preparation, and Use Of Medicinal and Edible Plants of the Southwestern United States*. Lincoln Town Press.

Kearney, T.H. & R.H. Peebles. (1951). *Arizona flora*. University of California.

Keen, Myra. (1971). *Sea Shells of Tropical West America: Marine Mollusks from Baja California to Peru*. Stanford University Press.

Kreutz, D. (2006, May 6). Power struggle. *The Arizona Daily Star*, 1E.

Krutch, J.W. (1961). *The Forgotten Peninsula: A Naturalist in Baja California*. University of Arizona Press.

Lamb, S.H. (1977). *Woody Plants of the Southwest: A Field Guide with Descriptive Text, Drawings, Range Maps and Photographs*. Sunstone Press.

Lowe, C.H. (1964). *Arizona's Natural Environment*. University of Arizona Press.

McGee, W.J. (1898). *The Seri Indians: Seventeenth Annual Report of the Bureau of American Ethnology, 1895-1896*. Government Printing Office.

Mielke, J. (1993). *Native plants for Southwestern Landscapes*. University of Texas Press.

Miller, R.R. (1974). Cortés and the first attempt to colonize California. *California Historical Quarterly 53*(1), 4–16.

Miller, M. (1984). California's first canoe. *Sea Frontiers, 30*(5).

Minch, J. & J. Minch. (2017). *Roadside Geology and Biology of Baja California*. John Minch Publishing.
Murie, O.J. (1974). *A Field Guide to Animal Tracks. A Peterson Field Guide*. Houghton Mifflin.
Myrick, D.F. (1975). *Railroads of Arizona, Volume 1: The Southern Roads*. Howell-North Books.
Negri, S. (2001, January). A cliff house in Southern Arizona's Redfield Canyon. *Arizona Highways*. Arizona Department of Transportation.
Nolan, B. (1936). Cool Water (song). *Wikipedia*. https://en.wikipedia.org/wiki/Cool Water (song).
Osselaer, H.J. (2018). *Arizona's Deadliest Gunfight*. University of Oklahoma Press.
Power, T. & J. Whitlatch. (1981). *Shoot-Out at Dawn: An Arizona Tragedy*. Phoenix Books.
Quirke, T. (1952). *Canoes the World Over*. University of Illinois Press.
Raymond, A. (1986). Experiments in the function and performance of the weighted atlatl. *World Archaeology, 18*(2), 153-77.
Rea, A.M. (1997). *At the Desert's Green Edge: An Ethnobotany of the Gila River Pima*. University of Arizona Press.
Rebman, J.P. & N.C. Roberts. (2012). *Baja California Plant Field Guide*. San Diego Natural History Museum/Sunbelt Publications.
Rickett, H.W. (1970). *Wildflowers of the United States, Volume 4: Southwestern States*. New York Botanical Garden.
Rife, A.N., O. Aburto-Oropeza, P.A. Hastings, B. Erisman, F. Ballantyne, J. Wielgus, E. Sala & L. Gerber. (2013). Long-term effectiveness of a multi-use marine protected area on reef fish assemblages and fisheries landings. *Journal of Environmental Management, 117*, 276–283.
Rose, F.S. (2012). *Mountain Trees of Southern Arizona: A Field Guide*. Arizona Sonora Desert Museum Press.
Sassaman, C., M.A. Simovich, & M. Fugate. (1997). Reproductive isolation and genetic differentiation in North American species of Triops (Crustacea: Branchiopoda: Notostraca). *Hydrobiologia, 359*, 125–147. https://doi.org/10.1023/A:1003168416080.
SeaWatch, (2010, August 25). Howard Hall on Reef Destruction in the Sea of Cortez. [Video] YouTube. https://www.youtube.com/watch?v=scCpFPb1fKM.
Schreiber, E.A. & R.L. Norton. (2002). Brown booby (Sula leucogaster). In A. Poole, & G. Gill (Eds.), *The Birds of North America*. Cornell Laboratory of Ornithology, Ithaca.

Seminoff, J.A., A. Resendiz, & W.J. Nichols. (2002a). Diet of east Pacific green turtles (Chelonia mydas) in the central Gulf of California, Mexico. *Journal of Herpetology 36* (3), 447–453.
Seminoff, J.A., A. Resendiz & W.J. Nichols. (2002b). Home range of green turtles (Chelonia Mydas) at a coastal foraging area in the Gulf of California, Mexico. *Marine Ecology Progress Series 242,* 253–265 DOI 10.3354/meps242253.
Seminoff, J.A. (2010). Sea turtles in the Gulf of California: biology, culture and conservation. In R. Brusca (Ed.). *The Gulf of California. Biodiversity and Conservation.* University of Arizona Press.
Shreve, F. & I.L. Wiggins. (1964). *Vegetation and Flora of the Sonoran Desert.* Stanford University Press.
Simovich, M.A., C. Sassaman & A. Chovnick. (1991). Post-mating selection of hybrid toads (Scaphiopus multiplicatus and Scaphiopus bombifrons). *Proceedings of the San Diego Society of Natural History 5,* 1–6.
Simpson, K. & S.J. Wells. (1984). *Archaeological Survey in the Eastern Tucson Basin: Saguaro National Monument, Cactus Forest Area.* Arizona Archaeological Center.
Stabler, D.F. (1985). Increasing summer flow in small streams through management of riparian areas and adjacent vegetation—a synthesis. *USDA Forest Service Technical Report RM* (120), 206–210.
Stark, F. (2011). *Centennial History of Lemhi County, Idaho.* Committee in Salmon, Idaho.
Starr, G. (2009). *Cool Plants for Hot Gardens.* Rio Nuevo Publishers.
Steinbeck, J. & E. Ricketts. (1951). *The Log from the Sea of Cortez.* Viking Press.
Stewart, B., P. Brodkin & H. Brodkin. (2001). *Butterflies of Arizona: A Photographic Guide.* West Coast Lady Press.
Stirling, M.W. (1960). The Use of the Atlatl on Lake Patzcuaro, Michoacán. *Bureau of American Ethnology Bulletin, 173,* 265–268. Smithsonian Institution.
Stock, C. (1972) *Rancho La Brea: A Record of Pleistocene Life in California.* Los Angeles County Museum of Natural History. Science Series No. 10:11.
Tenney, P-A. (2020). *Too Far West! The Lyman and Alaire Tenney Story.* Sulphur Springs Valley Historical Society.
Tershey, B & D. Breese. (1997). The birds of San Pedro Mártir Island, Gulf of California, Mexico. *Western Birds, 28,* 96–107.
Thomson, D.A. & N. McKibbin. (1976). *Gulf of California Fishwatcher's Guide.* Golden Puffer Press.

Thomson, D.A., L.T. Findley & A.N. Kerstitch. (1979). *Reef Fishes of the Sea of Cortez—the Rocky-Shore fishes of the Gulf of California*. John Wiley and Sons.

Trejo, C. (Director). (2015.) *Power's War*. [Film] Cameron Trejo Films

Udvardy, M.D.F. (1977). *The Audubon Society Field Guide to North American Birds: Western Region*. Alfred A. Knopf.

Van Devender, T.R., R.S. Felger, A.L. Reina-Guerrero & J.J. Sánchez-Escalante. (2006). Non-native and invasive plants in Sonora, Mexico. In T.R. Van Devender, F.J. Espinosa-García, B.L. Harper-Lore, T. Hubbard, (Eds.) *Invasive Plants on the Move. Controlling them in North America*. University of Arizona Press.

Verrier, J.T. (2018, January). Annotated flora of the Santa Catalina Mountains, Pima and Pinal Counties, Southeastern Arizona. *Desert Plants 33*, 2. University of Arizona for Boyce Thompson Arboretum.

Wagner, H.R. (1924, December) California voyages, 1539-1541: The voyage of Francisco de Ulloa; The voyage of Hernando de Alarcon; The voyage of Francisco de Bolaños. *California Historical Society Quarterly, 3*(4), 307-397. https://doi.org/10.2307/25613647

Waldorf, D. C. (1984). *The Art of Flintknapping*. Mound Builder Arts and Trading Co.

Wilson, J.P. (1977). *Guns and Gold: History of the Galiuro Wilderness, Coronado National Forest*. United States Dept. of Agriculture, U. S. Forest Service, Southwestern Region.

Wilson, John P. (1995). *Islands in the Desert: A History of the Uplands of Southeastern Arizona*. University of New Mexico Press.

Appendix

The Sunset of the Gulf Grouper—the Plight of the Former "King of the Reef" in the Sea of Cortez

Joe Billings

During my third Baja expedition in July 1986 while encamped in Bahía Agua Verde—constructing a primitive reed balsa—I speared a species of grouper for the first time that I later resolved not to again once I learned about the current plight of this fish. [See page 151.] I had been venturing farther and farther from camp hiking a long distance towards *Punta San Marcial* to explore vast underwater realms where all my reference points were below the surface. I recognized the five-pound Gulf grouper (*Mycteroperca jordani*) when I encountered it in the same area of scattered patch reefs, in roughly 40-50 feet of water. According to Reef Fishes of the Sea of Cortez these groupers are usually found below 100 feet in deeper water during the summer (Thomson et al., 1979). Being a 'breath-hold' diver-hunter it's far more practical for me to stay well above that range, most of the time. Reviewing the scientific literature on this fish, it reveals that the most current fisheries statistics and data of recent origin are completely incompatible against extensively gathered historical sources of information (Sáenz-Arroyo, et al., 2005a, Aburto-Oropeza, et al., 2008). This is the largest of the four eastern Pacific grouper species in the Sea of Cortez, of the genus *Mycteroperca*, attaining a maximum length of six and a half feet and 200 pounds (Eschmeyer, et al., 1983). While this fish has not been intensively studied, its life span has been determined to be up to forty-eight years, though this may be underestimated (Aburto-Oropeza, et al., 2008).

Detailed information on catches along the eastern Baja coastline and islands were obtained through interviews with fishermen (hereafter as fishers) who were actively working in these areas during the era beginning in the early 1940's through the end of the 1960's (Sáenz-Arroyo et al., 2005a). The results of these interviews clearly indicated that relentless overharvesting had severely reduced the Gulf grouper population in the Sea of Cortez to a minute fraction (1%) of its original abundance, by the early 1970's. This large, predatory fish is currently listed as "endangered" on the International Union for Conservation of Nature (IUCN) Red List (Erisman & Craig, 2018).

All of this was brought to light by an innovative marine biologist and her research team back in 2002. Working up and down the central Gulf coastline of the Baja Peninsula, Andrea Sáenz-Arroyo came up with a simple, straight-forward questionnaire provided to 108 fishers of eleven communities, with balanced representation among three generations. Participants were first asked to estimate the size of the largest individual Gulf grouper ever caught along with the year, catch locality, and gear used. Many of these "largest" specimens were in the 150—200-pound category as described by fishers from the earlier 30-year period. Secondly, they were asked to provide the total number of groupers caught on their best day of fishing including month, year, and locality. A 72-year-old fisher from Loreto relates a personal testimonial from the vicinity of San Nicolas Village along the central Gulf coast, east of the extreme south end of *Bahía Concepción*:

> In the 1950s all the rocky shore north to San Nicolas was crowded with Gulf grouper. During the night, the needlefish spawned close to the coastal Sargassum. Loads! You could even hear the noise they were producing from the beach. Since Gulf groupers feed on needlefish, next morning, you could see hundreds of Gulf groupers with their dorsal spines out of the water, eating needlefish. (Sáenz-Arroyo et al., 2005a)

In the mid-1990s, Daniel Pauly, a British Colombian fisheries scientist, created a small-scale revolution that reverberated across the world of marine biology and fisheries research through his concept of shifting environmental baselines. "Shifting baseline syndrome" described a short-sighted generational paradigm: The systematic data and fisheries statistics gathered during a given time frame were adopted to fit a static temporal reality without the benefit of long-range comparisons of data from past eras (Pauly, 1995). In the case of the Gulf grouper, extensive firsthand historical observations and fishers' experiences presented a vastly different picture of abundance versus the more recently derived fisheries baseline data. The latter side of this equation not only provided highly inaccurate demographics for this species but much of official fisheries information and related data collection on the Gulf grouper was not established until 1986, or later. So, what becomes currently acceptable as baseline information that influences catch recommendations is not only inherently distorted but can further disable a vulnerable species such as the Gulf grouper from ever returning to levels of even modest abundance. (Sáenz-Arroyo, et al. 2005b, Aburto-Oropeza, et al., 2008)

In another of Sáenz-Arroyo's testimonials, a 56-year-old diver from *Santa Rosalía* recounts this sighting:

> North to Santa Rosalia, in the 1970s we saw a big group of around 100 Gulf groupers. They used to swim in circles, going up and down. I have not seen that behaviour anymore or such an amount of Gulf groupers nowadays. (Sáenz-Arroyo et al., 2005a)

What the diver appears to be describing in this instance is a fish spawning aggregation (FSA). Gulf groupers are one of at least thirty or more fish species from seventeen families in the Gulf that engage in this activity in the process of completing their reproductive cycle (Erisman, et al., 2007, Erisman & Aburto-Oropeza, 2009). This phenomenon has only recently become the object of intensive study. Widely separated members of the same fish species population can travel long distances (100 km or more) to converge in massive gatherings over coastal reefs or offshore seamounts. They are comparable to a similar phenomenon occurring among seabirds such as the blue booby breeding colonies on *Isla San Pedro Martir*, or the sea turtles gathering on the beaches of *Michoacán*, or gray whales migrating south along the coastline of Baja. FSAs can take place over a period of a few days to several weeks and are often synchronized to lunar or tidal phases (Erisman, et al., 2018).

Imagine yourself surrounded by a spiraling vortex of hundreds, or even thousands of silvery, swirling shapes, ascending above you in the water column. Or being within range of a thick horizontal array of closely-aligned reddish-brown-spotted gray-green and white-mottled leopard groupers with perhaps several golden phase specimens mixed in? One percent of these robust, very pleasing-to-the-eye groupers make the transition to the golden color phase (Thomson, et al., 1979).

During the spawning aggregations of the Gulf grouper the males, which are larger than the females, set up territories adjoining each other over sandy bottom areas bordering the rocky reef where the actual spawning takes place (Rowell, et al., 2018). One Gulf grouper male and one female arise at opposite angles to meet in the upper water column in a pair-spawning system. During the day leading up to pair spawning both the Gulf grouper males and females exhibit seven distinct color phases based on specific substrate location (sand vs. rock) or activity (patrolling, resting, etc.). When a pair rises to engage in a spawning rush both display striking white color patches visible on the female's belly and the center of the male's back (Rowell, et al., 2018). Another discovery has revealed the sounds recorded by researchers exclusively made by the males at different sequences during spawning-related activity (Rowell, et al., 2018).

Fish spawning aggregations of Gulf groupers take place from March to June and within the period four days before the full moon until thirteen days after the full moon (Rowell, et al., 2018). Aggregation sites may become established where planktonic larvae (from fertilized eggs) can drift into the most favorable locations for juvenile growth and survival (Aburto-Oropeza, et al., 2008). Since aggregations tend to form at the same places at the same time every year, Gulf groupers are highly vulnerable to overfishing. Many of these well-known sites have been overharvested by fishers over a long history (Sáenz-Arroyo, et al., 2005a). With a high percentage of the regional population concentrated in one spot overharvesting results in the removal of this species from a much larger surrounding area. A preference for larger fish, predominantly males, during these harvests creates an imbalance in the sex ratio further impeding reproduction and sustainability of the fishery (Dennis, 2015). An organization with a key focus on FSAs was established earlier in 2000 dedicated to research, protection, and conservation of fish aggregations—Science and Conservation of Reef Fish Aggregations (SCRFA)—to mitigate the global decline of these critically imperiled populations and sites.

Spawning aggregations that took place at several sites which once teemed with abundance during the 1940s through the 1970s off the east-central Baja Peninsula have been extirpated (Sáenz-Arroyo, et al., 2005a). One well-known hub of activity was roughly six-to- eight miles offshore and halfway between San Nicolas Village and Loreto. As revealed in another firsthand anecdotal account by one of Sáenz-Arroyo's respondents, the San Bruno Seamount was the setting for a notorious incident of the most savage devastation and carnage through the use of dynamite:

> A 72-year-old fisher from San Nicholas remembered that in the 1950s the San Bruno Sea Mount [sic] "was crowded with Gulf grouper until one year a ship named La Avecita from Guaymas threw in dynamite and killed thousands of animals." He remembers that they could only carry away the boat's capacity of 70 tonnes from all

the animals killed. Two former captains and one of the former managers from El Club de Vuelos confirmed the story about this boat and its effect on the Gulf grouper population. Assuming that the average weight of a Gulf grouper caught in Punta Lobos during the El Club de Vuelos venture was 70 kg, then a catch of 70 tonnes taken by that one boat from one seamount in a single day equates to the removal of 1000 Gulf groupers. Once again, this catch far surpasses the entire Mexican yield in recent years. (Sáenz-Arroyo, et al., 2005a)

Several additional factors besides FSAs exacerbate Gulf groupers vulnerability: late onset of reproductive maturity (six-seven years) and a restricted geographical range (Sadovy de Mitcheson & Erisman, 2012). While listed in U.S. waters as "endangered" (Fed. Reg. 2016) it receives no such protection in Mexico and enforcement is virtually non-existent. Once the dominant apex predator and omnipresent "King of the Reef," it is now considered rare and even characterized as being at a high risk of extinction (Dennis, 2015).

For now at least, there's the semblance of a true spawning aggregational event that has been recently witnessed and recorded at the *Parque Nacional Cabo Pulmo* (*Cabo Pulmo* National Marine Park) (Rowell, et al., 2018). This unique preserve was initially established through the efforts of three generations of fishers of the Castro family who are indigenous residents of the community. Covering 7,111 hectares, *Cabo Pulmo* has become a landmark utopia of long-term natural resource and fisheries restoration as an inspiring example of what is possible (Erisman & Aburto-Oropeza, 2009).

Daniel Pauly's revolutionary "shifting environmental baselines" concept continues to make large ripples across the waters of marine science magnified through the beneficial impacts and depth of insights brought to the surface by devoted researchers as Andrea Sáenz-Arroyo and others (Pauly, 1995).

In April of 2010, Dr. Pauly gave a TED Talk in the Galapagos Islands on this topic. (Pauly 2012) Hopefully, the historical/anecdotal marine ecology he advocates can continue contributing more pragmatic research, presenting an accurate long-range picture of natural resources depletion and bringing about higher standards for fisheries sustainability. (Brusca, 2010) Maybe the Cabo Pulmo Preserve model can be followed elsewhere?

One thing that resonated from my own forty-five day Michoacán fieldwork mission under a CONANP (*Comisión Nacional de Áreas Naturales Protegidas*) permit in 2018 at the El

Rosario Monarch Butterfly Sanctuary was this: how committed those people were in taking ownership to set up the monarch sanctuary and preserve their heritage. (Billings, 2019)

If better hearts and minds can ultimately prevail over the long term in the Sea of Cortez it will be the stakeholders—the native artisanal fishers—that will truly take responsible "ownership" enough to cherish and preserve their precious heritage of Gulf grouper aggregations. This is what inspires hope, that someday the "King of the Reef" will return to occupy its former domain.

LITERATURE CITED

Aburto-Oropeza, O., B. Erisman, V. Valdez-Omelas, & G. Danemann. (2008). Commercially important Serranid fishes from the Gulf of California: Ecology, fisheries and conservation. *Ciencia Marina y Conservación 1*, 1-23.

Aburto-Oropeza, O. & Erisman, B. (2009, July 8). From Mangroves to the Deep: Connecting fisheries and ecosystems in the Gulf of California. In R. Wargo (Producer UCSDTV). *Gulf of California's Deep-Sea Secrets: Perspectives in Ocean Science*, # 16076. Center for Marine Biodiversity and Conservation, Scripps Institution of Oceanography.

Billings, J. (2019). Opening a window on Southwestern monarchs: Fall migrant monarch butterflies, *Danaus plexippus* (L.), tagged synchronously in southeastern Arizona migrate to overwintering regions in either southern California or central Mexico. *The Journal of the Lepidopterists' Society 73* (4), 257-267. https://doi.org/10.18473/lepi.73i4.a1.

Billings, J. [Forthcoming in 2024] Sea of Cortez expeditions: The reed boat project—Baja California Sur. *Journeys of a Pure Naturalist.*

Brusca, R. C. (ed.). 2010. *The Gulf of California: Biodiversity and Conservation*. Arizona-Sonora Desert Museum Press & University of Arizona Press.

Dennis, M. H. 2015. *Status Review of the Gulf Grouper* (*Mycteroperca jordani*). National Marine Fisheries Service—West Coast Division. Protected Resources Division, NOAA.

Erisman, B., & M. T. Craig. (2018). Gulf Grouper: *Mycteroperca jordani. The IUCN Red List of Threatened Species.* https://www.iucnredlist.org/species/14049/100466315.

Erisman, B., M.L. Buckhorn, & P.A. Hastings. (2007) Spawning patterns in the leopard grouper, Micteroperca rosacea, in comparison with other aggregating groupers. *Marine Biology, 151*, 1849-1861.

Erisman, B., W.D. Heyman, S. Fulton, & T. Rowell. (2018). *Fish Spawning Aggregations: A Focal Point Of Fisheries Management and Marine Conservation In Mexico*. Gulf of California Marine Program.

Eschmeyer, W.N., E.S. Herald, & H. Hammann. (1983). *A Field Guide to Pacific Coast Fishes of North America*. Houghton Mifflin.

Pauly, D. (1995). Anecdotes and the shifting baseline syndrome of fisheries. *Trends in Ecology & Evolution 10*, 430.

Pauly, D. (2012). *The Ocean's Shifting Baseline*, [Video]. Youtube. https://www.youtube.com/watch?v=Hui5YH-D6Go.

Rowell, T. J., Aburto-Oropeza, O., Cota-Nieto, J. J., Steele, M. A., & Erisman, B. E. (2018). Reproductive behaviour and concurrent sound production of Gulf grouper *Mycteroperca jordani* (*Epinephelidae*) at a spawning aggregation site. *Journal of fish Biology, 94*(2), 277–296. https://doi.org/10.1111/jfb.13888.

Sáenz-Arroyo, A., C.M. Roberts, J. Torre, & M. Cariño-Olvera. (2005a). Using fishers' anecdotes, naturalists' observations and grey literature to reassess marine species at risk: the case of the gulf grouper in the Gulf of California, Mexico. *Fish and Fisheries 6*, 121-133.

Sáenz-Arroyo, A., C.M Roberts, J. Torre, M. Cariño-Olvera, & R.R Enríquez-Andrade. (2005b). Rapidly shifting environmental baselines among fishers of the Gulf of California. *Proceedings of the Royal Society B, 272*, 1957–1962. https://doi.org/10.1098/rspb.2005.3175

Sadovy de Mitcheson, Y. & B. Erisman. (2012 January). Fishery and biological implications of fishing spawning aggregations, and the social and economic importance of aggregating fishes. In Sadovy de Mitcheson, Y. & P.L. Colin (Eds.) *Reef Fish Spawning Aggregations: Biology, Research and Management. 35*, 225-284.

Thomson, D.A., L.T. Findley, & A.N. Kerstitch. (1979). *Reef Fishes of the Sea of Cortez*. University of Arizona Press.

MonarchQuestAZ

Made in the USA
Monee, IL
19 February 2025

12371392R00159

Embark on a captivating journey into the heart of the natural world with JB, a season naturalist and self-proclaimed 21st century cave man in this extraordinary series of short storie A treat for enthusiasts of the great outdoors, JB's writing invites readers to traverse the untam landscapes of Southern Arizona, Mexico, and beyond. Discover the intricate botany of t Sonoran Desert, marvel at the pristine beauty of the Sea of Cortez, and accompany JB on vario expeditions through the lens of one of Arizona's up-and-coming outdoor writers. This collecti is testament to JB's deep knowledge and profound connection with the wilderness, making it essential read for anyone passionate about nature and eager to experience the world through t eyes of an expert explorer.

WWW.MONARCHQUESTAZ.COM

WHETHER IT'S SCRAMBLING UP CANYON WALLS OF THE GALIUROS, NAVIGATING THE SEA OF CORTEZ, OR BUSHWHACKING OVER TERRA INCOGNITA, JB IS ALWAYS ON A PURPOSEFUL JOURNEY OF DISCOVERY.

MonarchQuestAZ

9 798989 864904